AMC'S BEST DAY HIKES NEAR
BOSTON

Four-Season Guide to 60 of the Best Trails
in Eastern Massachusetts

THIRD EDITION

MICHAEL TOUGIAS • JOHN S. BURK • ALISON O'LEARY

Appalachian Mountain Club Books
Boston, Massachusetts

AMC is a nonprofit organization, and sales of AMC Books fund our mission of protecting the Northeast outdoors. If you appreciate our efforts and would like to become a member or make a donation to AMC, visit outdoors.org, call 800-372-1758, or contact us at Appalachian Mountain Club, 10 City Square, Boston, MA 02129.

outdoors.org/books-maps

Distributed by National Book Network.

Front cover photograph of Walden Pond © Ryan Smith
Back cover photographs, from left, of the Middlesex Fells © BU Outing Club, Creative Commons on Flickr, and of Plum Island © John S. Burk
Interior photographs © by John Burk unless noted otherwise
Maps by Ken Dumas © Appalachian Mountain Club
Book design by Abigail Coyle

Library of Congress Cataloging-in-Publication Data
Names: Tougias, Mike, 1955- author. | Burk, John S., author. | O'Leary,
   Alison, author. | Appalachian Mountain Club.
Title: AMC's best day hikes near Boston : four-season guide to 60 of the best
   trails in Eastern Massachusetts / Michael Tougias, John Burk, Alison O'Leary.
Description: Third Edition. | Boston, Massachusetts : Appalachian Mountain
   Club Books, [2017] | Includes index. | "Distributed by National Book Network"--T.p. verso.
Identifiers: LCCN 2016051244| ISBN 9781628420425 (paperback) | ISBN
   9781628420432 (ePub) | ISBN 9781628420449 (Mobi)
Subjects: LCSH: Hiking--Massachusetts--Guidebooks. |
   Trails--Massachusetts--Guidebooks. | Massachusetts--Guidebooks.
Classification: LCC GV199.42.M4 T68 2017 | DDC 917.4404/4--dc23 LC record available at https://lccn.
loc.gov/2016051244

Interior pages and cover are printed on responsibly harvested paper stock certified by The Forest Stewardship Council®, an independent auditor of responsible forestry practices.
Printed in the United States of America, using vegetable-based inks.

5 4 3 2   21 22

MIX
Paper from
responsible sources
FSC
www.fsc.org   FSC® C005010

LOCATOR MAP

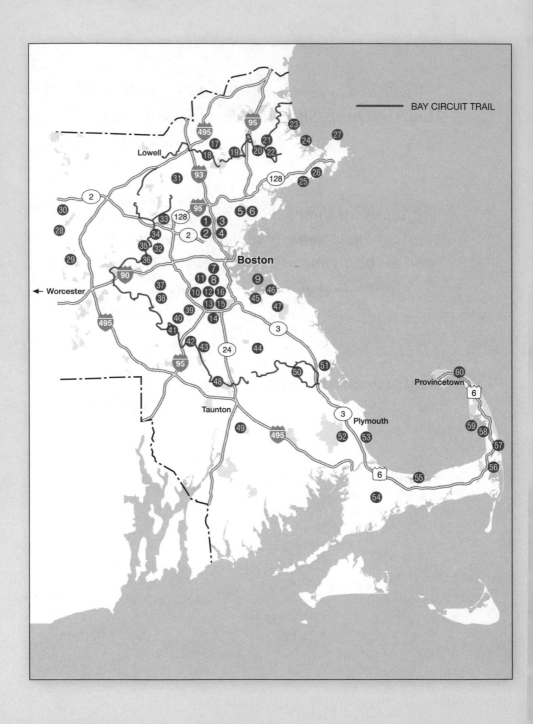

BAY CIRCUIT TRAIL

Lowell

Boston

Worcester

Taunton

Plymouth

Provincetown

CONTENTS

NATURE AND HISTORY ESSAYS

APPENDICES

AT-A-GLANCE TRIP PLANNER

TRIP NUMBER	TRIP NAME	LOCATION	DIFFICULTY	DISTANCE	ELEVATION GAIN
BOSTON/INSIDE ROUTES 95 AND 128					
1	Middlesex Fells: Skyline Trail	Stoneham, Medford, and Winchester, MA	Strenuous	6.8 mi	1,400 ft
2	Middlesex Fells: Reservoir Trail	Stoneham, Medford, and Winchester, MA	Moderate	5.2 mi	1,000 ft
3	Middlesex Fells: Rock Circuit Trail	Medford, Melrose, and Malden, MA	Strenuous	4 mi	875 ft
4	Middlesex Fells: Cross Fells Trail	Stoneham, Medford, Melrose, and Malden MA	Moderate-Strenuous	4.3 mi	865 ft
5	Breakheart Reservation	Saugus, MA	Moderate	2.7 mi	410 ft
6	Lynn Woods	Lynn, MA	Easy-Moderate	3.7 mi	450 ft
7	Jamaica Pond	Boston, MA	Easy	1.5 mi	Minimal
8	Arnold Arboretum	Boston, MA	Easy-Moderate	4.1 mi	230 ft
9	Spectacle Island	Boston, MA	Easy	3 mi	150 ft
10	Wilson Mountain Reservation	Dedham, MA	Easy-Moderate	2 mi	160 ft
11	Stony Brook Reservation	Boston, MA	Easy	2.6 mi	Minimal
12	Blue Hills Reservation: Observation Tower Loop	Canton and Milton, MA	Moderate	2 mi	400 ft
13	Blue Hills Reservation: Great Blue Hill Green Loop	Canton and Milton, MA	Easy-Moderate	2.8 mi	200 ft
14	Blue Hills Reservation: Ponkapoag Pond	Canton, MA	Easy	4 mi	Minimal
15	Blue Hills Reservation: Houghton's Pond Yellow Dot Loop	Milton, MA	Easy	1 mi	Minimal
16	Blue Hills Reservation: Skyline Trail	Canton, Milton, and Quincy, MA	Strenuous	9 mi; 2.4 mi	700 ft (cumulati
NORTH OF BOSTON					
17	Weir Hill Reservation	North Andover, MA	Moderate	2.3 mi	170 ft
18	Ward Reservation	Andover, MA	Easy-Moderate	0.6 mi; 4 mi	290 ft (cumulati
19	Bald Hill Reservation	Boxford, MA	Easy-Moderate	1.75 mi	150 ft
20	Ipswich River Wildlife Sanctuary	Topsfield, MA	Easy-Moderate	4 mi	50 ft

TIME	TRIP HIGHLIGHTS	FEE	GOOD FOR KIDS	DOG-FRIENDLY	PUBLIC TRANSPORT	X-C SKIING	SNOWSHOEING
5 hrs	Long-distance circuit, vistas			🐕	🚌		🅂
3 hrs	Views of three reservoirs		👪	🐕	🚌	🎿	🅂
3.5 hrs	Views, rugged hills, waterfall			🐕	🚌		🅂
5 hrs	Rocky hills, diverse forests			🐕	🚌	🎿	🅂
2 hrs	Saugus River, rocky outcroppings			🐕	🚌	🎿	🅂
2 hrs	Hilltop views, rock caves, pond		👪	🐕	🚌	🎿	🅂
45 mins	Historic pond, views, easy recreational path		👪	🐕	🚌	🎿	🅂
3 hrs	Scenic paths, botanical gardens		👪	🐕	🚌		🅂
1.25 hrs	Boston views, beaches		👪		🚌	🎿	🅂
1.5 hrs	Hilltop vista, swamp, rocky outcroppings		👪	🐕			🅂
1.5 hrs	Peaceful forest trails, wetlands		👪	🐕	🚌	🎿	🅂
1.5 hrs	Observation tower, Trailside Museum		👪	🐕	🚌		🅂
1.5 hrs	Wetlands, forest, Trailside Museum		👪	🐕	🚌	🎿	🅂
2 hrs	Large scenic pond, bog, views of Blue Hills		👪	🐕	🚌	🎿	🅂
30 mins	Easy loop, ideal for families		👪	🐕	🚌	🎿	🅂
6 hrs; 1.75 hrs	Long-distance trail, hilltop vistas			🐕	🚌		🅂
1.5 hrs	Hilltop view, trail along pond shore		👪	🐕		🎿	🅂
30 mins; 2 hrs	Bog, wetlands, Solstice Stones		👪	🐕		🎿	🅂
2 hrs	Hilltop meadow, historic farm site, wetlands		👪	🐕		🎿	🅂
2 hrs	Boardwalks, ponds, small island, Rockery	$	👪				🅂

TRIP NUMBER	TRIP NAME	LOCATION	DIFFICULTY	DISTANCE	ELEVATION GAIN
21	Bradley Palmer State Park	Hamilton and Topsfield, MA	Easy	3.3 mi	255 ft
22	Appleton Farms Grass Rides	Hamilton, MA	Easy–Moderate	2.7 mi	80 ft
23	Parker River National Wildlife Refuge at Plum Island	Newburyport, MA	Easy	1.4 mi	40 ft
24	Crane Beach Loop	Ipswich, MA	Moderate	3 mi	270 ft
25	Coolidge Reservation	Manchester-by-the-Sea, MA	Easy	3 mi	150 ft
26	Ravenswood Park	Gloucester, MA	Easy–Moderate	2.5 mi	Minimal
27	Halibut Point State Park and Reservation	Rockport, MA	Easy	1.5 mi	Minimal
WEST OF BOSTON					
28	Wachusett Reservoir and Reservation	West Boylston, MA	Easy	4.2 mi	225 ft
29	Mount Pisgah Conservation Area	Northborough, MA	Easy	1.75 mi	115 ft
30	Oxbow National Wildlife Refuge	Harvard, MA	Easy	1.9 mi	Minimal
31	Great Brook Farm State Park	Carlisle, MA	Easy	2.25 mi; 3 mi	Minimal
32	Great Meadows National Wildlife Refuge	Concord, MA	Easy	1.7 mi	Minimal
33	Minute Man National Historical Park: Battle Road Trail	Concord, Lincoln, and Lexington, MA	Moderate	5 mi	Minimal
34	Walden Pond	Concord, MA	Easy	3 mi	100 ft
35	Lincoln Conservation Land	Lincoln, MA	Moderate	3 mi	50 ft
36	Nobscot Hill and Tippling Rock	Sudbury and Framingham, MA	Moderate	4 mi	515 ft
37	Broadmoor Wildlife Sanctuary	Natick, MA	Moderate	3 mi	50 ft
38	Rocky Narrows Reservation and Sherborn Town Forest	Sherborn, MA	Moderate	2.7 mi	165 ft
39	Noanet Woodlands	Dover, MA	Moderate	3.5 mi	230 ft
40	Rocky Woods Reservation	Medfield, MA	Easy–Moderate	3.5 mi; 3.1 mi	180 ft (southern); 360 ft (northern)
41	Noon Hill Reservation	Medfield, MA	Moderate	2 mi	280 ft

TIME	TRIP HIGHLIGHTS	FEE	GOOD FOR KIDS	DOG-FRIENDLY	PUBLIC TRANSPORT	X-C SKIING	SNOWSHOEING
2 hrs	Former estate, well-maintained trails	$	✓	✓		✓	✓
1.75 hrs	Meadow overlook, farm site, forest	$		✓	✓	✓	✓
1 hr	Barrier beach, renowned for birding	$	✓				✓
2.5 hrs	Dunes, white-sand beach, Castle Neck estuary	$		✓	✓	✓	
2 hrs	Hilltop vista, pond, beach, historic Ocean Lawn		✓	✓		✓	✓
2 hrs	Rare magnolia swamp, boardwalk			✓		✓	✓
1 hr	Rocky shoreline, historic quarry, views to Maine	$	✓	✓	✓		✓
2.25 hrs	Shore views, excellent birding and wildlife		✓				✓
1.5 hrs	Scenic vistas, streams, good for kids		✓	✓		✓	✓
1.25 hrs	Nashua River and associated wetlands		✓	✓		✓	✓
1.5 hrs	Scenic pond, historic mill and mill site	$	✓	✓		✓	✓
1 hr	Concord River floodplain, abundant wildlife		✓		✓	✓	✓
3 hrs	Historic sites; farm, field, and wetland views		✓	✓	✓	✓	✓
1.5 hrs	Pond views, Thoreau cabin site	$	✓		✓	✓	✓
1.5 hrs	Forested hill, Sudbury River floodplain		✓	✓	✓	✓	✓
2.25 hrs	Highest point on Bay Circuit Trail, outstanding views		✓	✓			✓
1.5-2 hrs	Boardwalks along wetlands, glacial drumlins	$	✓				✓
1.5 hrs	Rugged hillsides, highlight of Charles River Valley		✓	✓		✓	✓
1.75 hrs	Historic millponds, hilltop vista		✓	✓		✓	✓
1.5 hrs; 1.75 hrs	Scenic vistas, ponds, rock canyon	$	✓	✓		✓	✓
1.0 hr	Scenic vista, millpond		✓	✓		✓	✓

TRIP NUMBER	TRIP NAME	LOCATION	DIFFICULTY	DISTANCE	ELEVATION GAIN
SOUTH OF BOSTON/CAPE COD					
42	Moose Hill Wildlife Sanctuary	Sharon, MA	Moderate	2.5 mi; 1.75 mi	130 ft (The Bluffs), 50 ft (Ovenbird/ Kettle trails)
43	Borderland State Park	North Easton, MA	Moderate	3.5 mi	50 ft
44	Ames Nowell State Park	Abington, MA	Easy	2 mi	Minimal
45	Great Esker Park	Weymouth, MA	Easy	1.5 mi	285 ft
46	World's End	Hingham, MA	Moderate	4.5 mi	300 ft
47	Whitney and Thayer Woods	Hingham and Cohasset, MA	Easy	3 mi	200 ft
48	Wheaton Farm Conservation Area	Easton, MA	Easy	2.75 mi	Minimal
49	Massasoit State Park	Taunton, MA	Moderate	4 mi	Minimal
50	Burrage Pond	Hanson and Halifax, MA	Easy	3 mi	90 ft
51	North Hill Marsh Wildlife Sanctuary	Duxbury, MA	Moderate	3.3 mi	110 ft
52	Myles Standish State Forest	Plymouth and Carver, MA	Moderate-Strenuous	3 mi; 4.5 mi; 7.5 mi	50 ft
53	Ellisville Harbor State Park	Plymouth, MA	Easy	3 mi	40 ft
54	Lowell Holly Reservation	Mashpee and Sandwich, MA	Moderate	2.7 mi	100 ft
55	Sandy Neck Circuit	Barnstable, MA	Moderate	1.6 mi; 4.7 mi; 9 mi; 13 mi	Minimal
56	Nickerson State Park	Brewster, MA	Easy-Moderate	3.25 mi	50 ft
57	Fort Hill	Eastham, MA	Easy	2 mi	50 ft
58	Wellfleet Bay Wildlife Sanctuary	South Wellfleet, MA	Easy	2 mi	50 ft
59	Great Island	Wellfleet, MA	Moderate	4 mi	120 ft
60	Cape Cod National Seashore: Pilgrim Heights	Truro, MA	Easy	1.3 mi	115 ft

1.5–2 hrs	Hilltop overlook, meadows, wildlife	$	✓		✓		✓
1.75 hrs	Close-up views of ponds, meadows	$	✓	✓		✓	✓
1 hr	Variety of wildlife and terrain		✓				✓
1 hr	Unique geologic ridge; river and marsh views		✓	✓	✓		✓
3 hrs	Scenic views, coastal peninsula	$	✓	✓	✓	✓	✓
1.75 hrs	Rhododendron and laurel groves, glacial boulders		✓	✓		✓	✓
1.5 hrs	Pond views, pine woods		✓	✓		✓	✓
2.5 hrs	Glacial topography, waterfowl, historic sites		✓				✓
2 hrs	Views of open cranberry bog		✓				✓
2 hrs	Large pond and marshes, cranberry bog		✓	✓		✓	✓
2–4 hrs	Pitch-pine and scrub-oak woods, kettle ponds		✓	✓		✓	✓
1.5 hrs	Rocky beach, harbor seal colony, salt marsh		✓	✓			
1.5 hrs	Beech and American holly groves, ponds		✓	✓		✓	✓
2–3 hrs	Barrier beach, dunes, large salt marsh			✓		✓	✓
1.75 hrs	Large kettle pond, beaches, vista		✓	✓		✓	✓
1 hr	Scenic coastal views, meadows, red maple swamp		✓		✓	✓	✓
1.5 hrs	Tidal flats, salt marsh, wildlife, family trails	$	✓				✓
2.5 hrs	Tall dunes, pine woods, marsh, historic site				✓	✓	✓
1 hr	Overlooks, historic sites, great for families		✓		✓	✓	✓

PREFACE

As a longtime admirer of the natural areas and wildlife of northern and western New England, I was pleased to have the opportunity while working on this book to experience the natural diversity of eastern Massachusetts. Despite high population density and development, the region offers the opportunity to explore tidal flats and salt marshes bordering scenic ocean beaches; to enjoy challenging, full-day hikes in the rugged Middlesex Fells and Blue Hills; and to stroll through deep woods and around lakes and ponds visited by moose, black bears, fishers, and common loons. Many of the preserves lie inside the Interstate 95/Route 128 corridor, including several within Boston's city limits, while others offer solitude in less-traveled locales.

For this third edition, we have added five new hikes: Bradley Palmer State Park, Nobscot Hill and Tippling Rock, Ames Nowell State Park, Massasoit State Park, and Burrage Pond. We have also revisited and updated 55 hikes from the previous edition. Complementing the hike descriptions are essays on the region's natural and human history, and appendices with updated information on the Bay Circuit Trail and cross-country skiing opportunities. Sixteen of the hikes fall along the Bay Circuit Trail, a 231-mile trail that links nearly 60 communities in eastern Massachusetts. The near completion of the trail is an exciting development for the region, as the route offers countless recreational opportunities and serves as a conservation corridor.

While exploring these trails, I've been fortunate to enjoy many memorable moments and sightings, including snowy owls and other rare birds in the marshes and dunes of Plum Island, colorful spring blooms at the Arnold Arboretum, fall foliage from hilltop vistas on the Bay Circuit Trail, and a spectacular sunset over the tidal flats of Wellfleet Bay Wildlife Sanctuary. It is my hope that readers will enjoy similar scenes from this diverse group of natural areas.

—John S. Burk, 2016

Hiking and visiting natural places can "wash your spirit clean," according to naturalist John Muir. I believe it's true and have been fortunate to arrange my work life around spending time outdoors. New England's beauty is on my doorstep every day, and I strive to cherish it every time I enter.

Writing a guidebook about these places is a different exercise than experiencing and enjoying the places we describe. In working on this edition of *Best Day Hikes,* I sought to inspire folks to get out and explore while making it as easy as possible to do so with updated information on trail routes, descriptions, and driving directions. It would be too easy to fill the book with praise for the places and descriptions of their beauty but fall short on the basic information necessary to determine if a particular trip is feasible or desirable.

Along with fresh descriptions of the bird and animal species you may encounter, I sought to add historical tidbits where possible to heighten a visitor's appreciation of the people who shaped the land, either by helping to create trails or by their work. Two examples that come to mind are the bridges, buildings, and stone tower in the Blue Hills that were created by the Civilian Conservation Corps in the 1930s and the cranberry bogs found in some parks south of Boston.

Improving on the last version of the book, I sought to add new hikes from a less-represented area of the state, the interior South Shore, specifically Burrage Pond in Hanson/Halifax and Massasoit State Park in Taunton. Both are good representatives of the area's coastal forest rooted in sandy soil with kettle ponds interspersed among low drumlins. While humans have made changes to the natural topography, creating cranberry bogs and damming the natural flow of rivers here, the wildlife has adapted and, where sufficient habitat remains, has flourished.

It's particularly heartwarming to meet local residents and speak to caretakers of the properties we highlight in this book because they tend to be fiercely protective and proud of these parks, pitching in to clean up after storms and volunteering to show newcomers around. We hope the readers of this book will embrace our natural areas and treat them with care.

—Alison O'Leary, 2016

ACKNOWLEDGMENTS

The three of us have been exploring special outdoor places in Massachusetts for many years. Though it is easy to take the region's numerous conserved lands for granted, we would like to acknowledge the many people past and present who have made efforts to protect open space for future generations. Today more and more people are realizing the benefits of protecting wild places, and the work goes on.

A great number of individuals and organizations were helpful in preparing the material for this and the previous editions. Thanks to the Appalachian Mountain Club, Arnold Arboretum of Harvard University, Barnstable Marine and Environmental Affairs Division, Bay Circuit Alliance, Boston Harbor Islands National Recreation Area, Cape Cod National Seashore, Town of Easton, Essex County Greenbelt Association, Town of Lincoln, Lynn Woods Reservation, Mass Audubon, Massachusetts Department of Conservation and Recreation, Minute Man National Historical Park, Sherborn Forest and Trail Association, Sudbury Valley Trustees, The Nature Conservancy, The Trustees of Reservations, and the U.S. Fish and Wildlife Service. Special thanks to Michael Arnott, Patti Austin, Holly Berube, Kevin Block, Maggi Brown, Nina Coleman, Mike Francis, Beth Gula, David McKinnon, Stacy Miller, Sue Moynihan, Mike Nelson, Leslie Obleschuck, Matt Poole, Mary-Ellen Schloss, and Julie Warsowe for providing feedback and updates about specific places.

Michael Tougias would like to thank Tom Foster and Wayne Mitton, regional supervisors for The Trustees of Reservations, for sharing their knowledge of the land and its wildlife. This guidebook grew out of two books in AMC Books' earlier Nature Walk series: *Nature Walks in Eastern Massachusetts* and *More Nature Walks in Eastern Massachusetts*. A special thanks to Carol Tyler, who drew the original maps, and to then-editor Gordon Hardy, whose knowledge and enthusiasm made them better books.

John S. Burk and Alison O'Leary would like to thank editors Shannon Smith and Dan Eisner; AMC's production manager, Abigail Coyle; and former AMC publisher, Leti Taft-Pearman. Kevin Breunig, Beth Gula, and Kristen Sykes provided valuable feedback on the hike sites. Additional thanks go to the members of the AMC Books staff who worked on the first two editions of this book.

INTRODUCTION

While eastern Massachusetts is home to the large urban area of Boston and its suburbs, there are pockets of wilderness near the city where you can walk in solitude. Many of the locations described here are not well known and can give you the feeling of being in a remote area. Others are more popular but have hidden trails where few visitors go. The reservations range in size from 30 acres to well over 1,000. All are surprisingly rich in wildlife.

For me, hiking combines the physical joy of walking with the thrill of seeing wildlife. A special day in the woods can make your spirits soar. Maybe it's a walk on a colorful autumn day, a winter's trek just after a heavy snow, or a stroll on the first warm day of spring, when all the earth seems to be awakening.

Of course, seeing a fox, a coyote, or a deer at close range can make any walk a special one. I've included some of my more memorable wildlife encounters in the book, such as the goshawk I saw at Bald Hill Reservation and the ruffed grouse that tried to draw me away from its chicks at Rocky Narrows. Just about every wild species seen in the state can be found at the reservations detailed here.

I'm fond of quoting Thoreau because he spent much of his life exploring eastern Massachusetts, and he liked nothing better than a long tramp through the woods or a paddle up a river. He viewed walking as a way to lose oneself: "What business have I in the woods, if I am thinking of something out of the woods?" He walked often and far afield: "I think that I cannot preserve my health and spirits, unless I spend four hours a day at least—and it is commonly more than that—sauntering through the woods and over the hills and fields, absolutely free from all worldly engagements." And if Thoreau saw wildlife, all the better. It was not unusual for him to sit and wait patiently for some creature to appear or to stop his walk to watch wildlife for the rest of the day. I've found my own hikes to be vastly more enjoyable if I follow Thoreau's example.

My lifelong passion has been to explore Massachusetts, looking for off-the-beaten-path places. At first glance, it would appear that this book and my prior books are giving away my secrets and bringing more people to these secluded spots. But I've learned that people protect the things they love. I am pleased to share some of my special places with you and hope that by raising appreciation for nature we can protect more wild places before they are forever lost to development.

—Michael Tougias

HOW TO USE THIS BOOK

With 60 hikes to choose from, you may wonder how to decide where to go. The locator map at the front of this book will help you narrow down the trips by location, and the At-a-Glance Trip Planner that follows the table of contents will provide more information to guide you toward a decision.

Once you settle on a destination and turn to a trip in this guide, you will find a series of icons that indicate whether the hike is a good place for kids, whether dogs are permitted, whether snowshoeing or cross-country skiing is recommended, whether the location is accessible via public transportation, and whether fees are charged.

Information on the basics follows: location, rating, distance, elevation gain, estimated time, and maps. The ratings are based on the authors' perception and are estimates of what the average hiker will experience. You may find the hikes to be easier or more difficult than stated. The estimated time is also based on the authors' perception. Consider your own pace when planning a trip.

The elevation gain is calculated using measurements and information from USGS topographic maps, landowner maps, and Google Earth. Information is included about the relevant USGS maps, as well as where you can find trail maps. The bold-faced summary provides a basic overview of what you will see on your hike.

The directions explain how to reach the trailhead by car and, for some trips, by public transportation. GPS coordinates for parking lots are also included. When you enter the coordinates into your device, it will provide driving directions. Whether or not you own a GPS device, it is wise to consult an atlas before leaving your home.

Under "Trail Description," you will find instructions on where to hike, the trails on which to hike, and where to turn. You will also learn about the natural and human history along your hike, as well as information about flora, fauna, and any landmarks and objects you may encounter.

The trail maps that accompany each trip will help guide you along your hike, but it would be wise to take an official trail map with you. They are often—but not always—available online, at the trailhead, or at the visitor center.

Each trip ends with a section titled "More Information," providing details about the locations of bathrooms, access times and fees, a property's rules and regulations, and contact information for the place where you will be hiking. "Nearby" includes information about where restaurants or shops that can be found near the trailhead.

TRIP PLANNING AND SAFETY

Although elevations in and around Boston are relatively low compared with other regions of New England and the hikes detailed in this guide aren't particularly dangerous, you'll still want to be prepared. Some of the walks traverse moderately rugged terrain along rocky hills, while others lead to sandy beaches, ponds, and fields where you'll have extended periods of exposure to sun and to areas where walking is slow in soft sand. Many reservations in eastern Massachusetts have complex trail networks based on old cart and carriage roads, some of which are unmarked. Allow extra time in case you get lost.

You will be more likely to have an enjoyable, safe hike if you plan ahead and take proper precautions. Before heading out for your hike, consider the following:

- Select a hike that everyone in your group is comfortable taking. Match the hike to the abilities of the least capable person in the group. If anyone is uncomfortable with the weather or is tired, turn around and complete the hike another day.
- Plan to be back at the trailhead before dark. Before beginning your hike, determine a turnaround time even if you have not reached your intended destination.
- Check the weather. If you are planning a ridge or a summit hike, start early so that you will be off the exposed area before the afternoon hours, when thunderstorms most often strike, especially in summer. An average of twenty thunderstorms occur in the region annually. The weather in eastern Massachusetts is highly variable. Hikers at coastal locations should be prepared for wind year-round, especially during winter, when windchill is a concern. Compared with inland locations, the climate is generally cooler along the immediate coast during warm months and milder in winter. Significant storms—including heavy winter snowfalls, spring rainstorms, and tropical storms in late summer and fall—may cause flooding, potentially dangerous ocean tides, and other hazards. When exploring beaches or other areas along the coast, be sure to check tide tables in advance and to keep an eye on the water at all times.

- Bring a pack with the following items:
  - ✓ Water: Two quarts per person is usually adequate, depending on the weather and the length of the trip
  - ✓ Food: Even if you are planning a one-hour hike, bring some high-energy snacks, such as nuts, dried fruit, or snack bars; pack a lunch for longer trips
  - ✓ Map and compass: Be sure you know how to use them; a handheld GPS device may also be helpful, but it is not always reliable
  - ✓ Headlamp or flashlight, with spare batteries
  - ✓ Extra clothing: Rain gear, wool sweater or fleece, hat, and mittens
  - ✓ Sunscreen
  - ✓ First-aid kit, including adhesive bandages, gauze, nonprescription pain-killers, and moleskin
  - ✓ Pocketknife or multitool
  - ✓ Waterproof matches and a lighter
  - ✓ Trash bag
  - ✓ Toilet paper
  - ✓ Whistle
  - ✓ Insect repellent
  - ✓ Sunglasses
  - ✓ Cell phone: Be aware that cell phone service is unreliable in rural areas; if you are receiving a signal, use the phone only for emergencies to avoid disturbing the backcountry experience for other hikers
  - ✓ Binoculars (optional)
  - ✓ Camera (optional)
- Wear appropriate footwear and clothing. Wool or synthetic hiking socks will keep your feet dry and help prevent blisters. Comfortable, waterproof hiking boots will provide ankle support and good traction. Avoid wearing cotton clothing, which absorbs sweat and rain, and contributes to an unpleasant hiking experience. Polypropylene, fleece, silk, and wool all wick moisture away from your body and keep you warm in wet or cold conditions. To help avoid bug bites, you may want to wear pants and a long-sleeve shirt.
- When you are ahead of the rest of your hiking group, wait at all trail junctions until the others catch up. This avoids confusion and keeps people from getting separated or lost.
- If you see downed wood that appears to be purposely covering a trail, it probably means the trail is closed due to overuse or hazardous conditions.
- If a trail is muddy, walk through the mud or on rocks, never on tree roots or plants. Waterproof boots will keep your feet comfortable. Staying in the center of the trail will keep it from eroding into a wide hiking highway.

- Leave your itinerary and the time you expect to return with someone you trust. If you see a logbook at a trailhead, be sure to sign in when you arrive and to sign out when you finish your hike.
- After you complete your hike, check for deer ticks, which can carry dangerous Lyme disease.
- Poison ivy is always a threat when hiking. To identify the plant, look for clusters of three leaves that shine in the sun but are dull in the shade. If you do come into contact with poison ivy, wash the affected area with soap as soon as possible.
- Wear blaze-orange items in hunting season. In Massachusetts, the peak hunting season for deer and game birds generally runs from mid-October to the end of December, with shotguns permitted from late November to early or mid-December. Yearly schedules are available at mass.gov and in fliers and brochures available at town halls and other public areas.

Biting insects are present during warm months, particularly in the vicinity of wetlands. They can be a minor or a significant nuisance, depending on seasonal and daily conditions. One serious concern is the eastern equine encephalitis virus (commonly referred to as EEE), a rare but potentially fatal disease that can be transmitted to humans by infected mosquitoes. Southeastern Massachusetts' many swamps provide ideal mosquito habitats; the threat is generally greatest in the evening hours, when mosquitoes are most active.

There are a variety of options for dealing with bugs, ranging from sprays that include the active ingredient diethyl meta toluamide (commonly known as DEET) to more skin-friendly products. Head nets, which often can be purchased more cheaply than a can of repellent, are useful during especially buggy conditions.

Remember, hiking should be fun. If you are uncomfortable with the weather or are tired, turn back and make the complete hike another day. Don't create a situation where you risk yourself or your companions. And, try not to walk alone. Be sure someone knows your intended route and expected return time. Always sign in at a trailhead register if one is available. The unexpected can occur. Weather can change, trail markings can become obscured, you can fall, and you can get lost. But you are more likely to avoid real danger if you have anticipated the unexpected.

LEAVE NO TRACE

The Appalachian Mountain Club is a national educational partner of Leave No Trace, a nonprofit organization dedicated to promoting and inspiring responsible outdoor recreation through education, research, and partner-  ships. The Leave No Trace program seeks to develop wildland ethics—ways in which people think and act in the outdoors to minimize their impact on the areas they visit and to protect our natural resources for future enjoyment. Leave No Trace unites four federal land management agencies— the U.S. Forest Service, the National Park Service, the Bureau of Land Management, and the U.S. Fish and Wildlife Service—with manufacturers, outdoor retailers, user groups, educators, organizations such as AMC, and individuals.

The Leave No Trace ethic is guided by these seven principles:

1. *Plan Ahead and Prepare.* Know the terrain and any regulations applicable to the area you're planning to visit, and be prepared for extreme weather or other emergencies. This will enhance your enjoyment and ensure that you've chosen an appropriate destination. Small groups have less impact on resources and the experiences of other backcountry visitors.

2. *Travel and Camp on Durable Surfaces.* Travel and camp on established trails and campsites, rock, gravel, dry grasses, or snow. Good campsites are found, not made. Camp at least 200 feet from lakes and streams, and focus activities on areas where vegetation is absent. In pristine areas, disperse use to prevent the creation of campsites and trails.

3. *Dispose of Waste Properly.* Pack it in, pack it out. Inspect your camp for trash or food scraps. Deposit solid human waste in cat holes dug 6 to 8 inches deep, at least 200 feet from water, camps, and trails. Pack out toilet paper and hygiene products. To wash yourself or your dishes, carry water 200 feet from streams or lakes and use small amounts of biodegradable soap. Scatter strained dishwater.

4. *Leave What You Find.* Cultural or historic artifacts, as well as natural objects such as plants and rocks, should be left as found.

5. *Minimize Campfire Impacts.* Cook on a stove. Use established fire rings, fire pans, or mound fires. If you build a campfire, keep it small and use dead sticks found on the ground.

6. *Respect Wildlife.* Observe wildlife from a distance. Feeding animals alters their natural behavior. Protect wildlife from your food by storing rations and trash securely.

7. *Be Considerate of Other Visitors.* Be courteous, respect the quality of other visitors' backcountry experiences, and let nature's sounds prevail.

AMC is a national provider of the Leave No Trace Master Educator course. AMC offers this five-day course, designed especially for outdoor professionals and land managers, as well as an introductory two-day Leave No Trace Trainer course, at locations throughout the Northeast.

For Leave No Trace information and materials, contact the Leave No Trace Center for Outdoor Ethics, P.O. Box 997, Boulder, CO 80306. Phone: 800-332-4100 or 303-442-8222; fax: 303-442-8217; web: lnt.org. For information on the AMC Leave No Trace Master Educator training course schedule, see outdoors.org/education/lnt.

BOSTON/INSIDE ROUTES 95 AND 128

Boston and its inner suburbs might seem unlikely places to find nature preserves and hiking trails. Yet amid the development of New England's largest metropolitan area, a surprising array of diverse areas offers recreational opportunities and provides crucial habitat for flora and fauna.

Boston's landscape has changed substantially over the past 400 years. The first European settlers arrived in 1623, and by the 1630s, Boston Harbor was regarded as an ideal location for ships that brought goods to and from England. To accommodate rapid population growth during the nineteenth century, many of the city's largest hills were excavated and used to fill coves and marshy areas.

In response to the increasing urbanization, metropolitan planners, including the renowned landscape architect Frederick Law Olmsted, designed a chain of parks collectively known as the Emerald Necklace because they form a strand of green "gems" that extends from Boston Common west and south to Franklin Park. These urban sanctuaries are home to roughly 50 distinct historical sites. One of the highlights is the Arnold Arboretum in Jamaica Plain, where beautifully designed paths wind past extensive botanical collections from around the world and lead to hilltop vistas. East of the Arboretum is Jamaica Pond, the largest pond in Boston and home to a popular recreational trail.

A short distance southwest of downtown Boston is the quieter and wilder Stony Brook Reservation, which encompasses a rocky, forested valley and wetlands between the Roxbury and Hyde Park neighborhoods.

Just outside of Boston, expansive preserves offer chances for hiking over terrain that ranges from gentle to rugged. The largest is the popular 7,000-acre Blue Hills Reservation. A chain of 22 forested low hills includes the 635-foot Great Blue Hill, home to a historical stone tower with long views in all directions and to the nation's oldest continuous weather observatory. Several ponds and wetlands lie within the reservation, including Ponkapoag Pond, where a side trail leads into a bog.

Facing page: The Boston skyline
as seen from Spectacle Island, the
highest point in Boston Harbor.

To the north, the Middlesex Fells, Lynn Woods, and Breakheart reservations combine to protect roughly 6,000 acres along the corridors of Routes 95 and 128. Numerous low hills, rocky outcroppings, ponds, and wetlands characterize all three reservations. At the Middlesex Fells, a cluster of hills composed of igneous and sedimentary rock offers scenic views, uncommon botanical communities, and hiking trails ranging from easy to challenging.

The Boston Harbor Islands are a short distance offshore from the city's waterfront. These islands have a long and diverse history, as they were used by American Indians in pre-Colonial times and were later home to coastal defense forts, factories, hospitals, and other municipal buildings. Thirty-four of the islands are now protected from development as part of a partnership between national and state parks. A number of these islands are open to the public for recreation, including Spectacle Island, which was a barren landfill until the late 1990s. Now revegetated with a variety of carefully selected trees and shrubs and home to scenic swimming beaches, picnic areas, and walking trails, the island boasts striking views as the highest point in the harbor.

1

MIDDLESEX FELLS: SKYLINE TRAIL

This hike, which loops the western side of the Fells, includes steep ascents and offers a great view of Boston from the Wright's Tower area.

DIRECTIONS

From I-93, take Exit 33 to MA 28, travel around Roosevelt Circle to South Border Road, and proceed to the Bellevue Pond parking area on the right. *GPS coordinates: 42° 25.854′ N, 71° 06.469′ W.*

By public transportation, take the MBTA Orange Line to Wellington Station then the #100 bus to Roosevelt Circle Rotary. From there, walk south to the rotary and follow South Border Road (on the right) less than 0.25 mile to Bellevue Pond.

TRAIL DESCRIPTION

This popular loop trail is located in the western section of the Middlesex Fells Reservation. Marked with white blazes, it makes a long circuit that mostly follows the low hills ringing the three Winchester reservoirs. In places, it joins several of the reservation's other popular trails, including Cross Fells Trail and Reservoir Trail. Although Skyline Trail is rated as a strenuous outing due to the distance and rolling terrain, the steep sections are fairly brief. For an easier walk that also loops around the reservoirs, see Trip 2.

This loop is a counterclockwise circuit that begins at Bellevue Pond, the parking area for which is off South Border Road in Medford. It may also be reached at other areas, including the Sheepfold entrance. From the Bellevue Pond parking area, follow the dirt Quarry Road north along the eastern shores of the pond. At the pond's northern tip, the white-blazed Skyline Trail bears right off Quarry Road to ascend Pine Hill.

LOCATION
Stoneham, Medford, and Winchester, MA

RATING
Strenuous

DISTANCE
6.8 miles

ELEVATION GAIN
1,400 feet

ESTIMATED TIME
5 hours

MAPS
USGS Boston North; online: mass.gov/eea/docs/dcr/parks/trails/fells.pdf

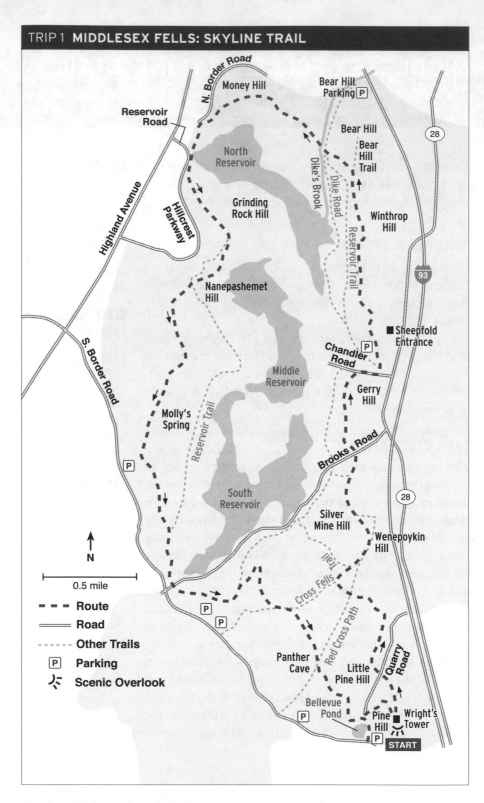

N. Border Road

Money Hill

Bear Hill Parking P

Reservoir Road

Bear Hill

28

North Reservoir

Bear Hill Trail

Dike's Brook

Dike Road

Grinding Rock Hill

Winthrop Hill

Highland Avenue

Hillcrest Parkway

Reservoir Trail

Nanepashemet Hill

93

Sheepfold Entrance

Chandler Road

Middle Reservoir

Gerry Hill

S. Border Road

Reservoir Trail

Molly's Spring

Brooks Road

28

South Reservoir

Silver Mine Hill

Wenepoykin Hill

P

N

Cross Fells Trail

0.5 mile

- - - **Route**
═══ **Road**
----- **Other Trails**
P **Parking**
⅄ **Scenic Overlook**

P

P

Panther Cave

Red Cross Path

Little Pine Hill

Quarry Road

Bellevue Pond

P

Pine Hill

Wright's Tower

P

START

At the top of Pine Hill, there are commanding views of Boston, its harbor, the Blue Hills, and busy Interstate 93 below. Atop the hill is Wright's Tower, which was built during the 1930s in memory of Elizur Wright, a businessman who worked hard to preserve the Middlesex Fells in the late nineteenth century. The tower is open weekends May through November, staff and weather dependent. From the tower, the trail continues north along a rocky ridge before turning west to drop into the valley between Pine and Little Pine hills, where it again crosses Quarry Road. Follow the path as it winds over the top of 211-foot-high Little Pine Hill then climbs over another hill, turns sharply left (west), and crosses Red Cross Path.

Near the summit of Wenepoykin Hill, Skyline Trail turns to the right (north) and joins the blue-blazed Cross Fells Trail for a short distance to the summit. Continue to follow Skyline Trail to the north as it traverses several hills, including Silver Mine Hill. Skyline Trail then rejoins Cross Fells Trail for a short distance as it descends to cross the dirt Brooks Road. Skyline Trail continues north over Gerry Hill and then descends to Chandler Road (dirt) along the Winchester Reservoir fence, where it briefly follows the orange-blazed Reservoir Trail. In spring, listen for the calls of migratory songbirds, such as American redstarts and scarlet tanagers, and check the trail edge for the tracks of white-tailed deer and raccoons. Turn right here and follow both trails east toward the reservation's Sheepfold entrance.

After a few hundred feet, Reservoir Trail cuts across the access road and through the lower lot then goes up a small hill where it turns right then left, adjacent to the old soapbox derby track. There is a slight reroute at the southern base of Winthrop Hill, so you have to go right and then left up the 291-foot-high hill, where there is a fine view of the Winchester North Reservoir. From here, the trail continues north along a ridge toward Bear Hill. After walking about 0.2 mile from the summit of Winthrop Hill, you'll reach a junction where Skyline Trail turns sharply to the left and continues down the slope of the hill. You have the option here of detouring straight ahead onto short Bear Hill Trail, which makes a quick climb to Bear Hill's 317-foot summit.

At the base of the descent, Skyline Trail crosses Dike Road (dirt) through an overgrown meadow and a pine grove then continues over the fairly level, wooded Money Hill. On the western slope of Money Hill, the two trails meet again and descend, crossing North Border Road (dirt) into a ravine north of the Winchester North Reservoir dam.

Walk across a small wood bridge that crosses a brook formed by outflow from the reservoir then follow Reservoir and Skyline trails, which wind up on the western slope of the ravine. A short distance to the south is the old municipal firehouse, near the Winchester–Stoneham town line. (Access to the reservoirs and shoreline is restricted.) The trail passes close by residences near Reservoir Road along the reservation's northwest boundary then reaches the paved Hillcrest Parkway, a town road where there is parking and trail access.

A hiker takes in the view from Middlesex Fells' Skyline Trail. Landmarks like the Prudential Tower and gold dome of the Massachusetts State House can be seen from this vantage point. Photo by Christina Xu, Creative Commons on Flickr.

Walk along the left-hand side of the road for a short distance then follow the trails back into the woods on the left. After crossing a dirt service road, the trails diverge at a junction where Reservoir Trail exits to the right. Stay straight here and follow Skyline Trail over a pair of low hills. Skyline Trail then crosses Reservoir Trail and climbs steeply to the top of 295-foot-high Nanepashemet Hill, where there are limited views.

From Nanepashemet Hill, continue to follow Skyline Trail, which leads south over rolling terrain, crossing a series of hills and dirt roads near the reservation's western boundary. As the trail approaches the southern tip of South Reservoir, it once again merges with Reservoir Trail, which comes in from the left. Follow the combined paths as they bend south then east around the corner of the reservoir near South Border Road, where there is parking and access to the trails. The trails wind up a hill then split again. Bear right and follow the white-blazed Skyline Trail, which ascends another hill and ridge, then drops down to cross the dirt Middle Road.

After walking a short distance from Middle Road, you'll reach a junction where Skyline Trail briefly follows the blue-blazed Cross Fells Trail. Cross Fells Trail is a one-way path that connects many of the Middlesex Fells Reservation's trails; it is described in Trip 4. At the next junction, Skyline Trail turns right and heads toward a rocky outcropping known as Panther Cave. Although panthers, more commonly known as mountain lions, are now officially considered extirpated from the Northeast, they and eastern timber wolves were once the region's top predators. Frequent rumors fuel lively debates, but the last confirmed sighting of a mountain lion in Massachusetts was in 1858, in the western part of the state; since then, there has been one confirmed report of scat in 1997 and another of tracks in 2011.

The trail passes close by the cave then descends to cross Red Cross Path and Straight Gully Brook. You have one last climb to make, as the trail winds up the southwestern slopes of Little Pine Hill, then closes the loop at the northern tip of Bellevue Pond. Turn right and walk back to the parking area.

DID YOU KNOW?

A herd of more than 25 sheep once grazed the Sheepfold. The Fells' popularity increased greatly with the opening of a trolley line that ran through the Fells from 1910 to the 1950s.

MORE INFORMATION

The reservation is open year-round, dawn to dusk; there is no fee. Dogs are allowed but must be leashed outside of the 5.5-acre Sheepfold off-leash area. For more information, contact DCR at 617-727-1199 or 617-727-5380, or visit mass .gov/dcr. Trail maps are available in boxes at parking areas; at the DCR North Region Headquarters at 4 Woodland Road, Stoneham, MA, 02180; through the Friends of the Middlesex Fells, fells.org; and at AMC's Boston office.

NEARBY

Historical sites in Medford include the Amelia Earhart residence at 76 Brooks Street, the Jonathan Wade House, and the site of Fannie Farmer's home at the intersection of Paris and Salem streets. There are numerous places to eat in Medford Square.

2

MIDDLESEX FELLS: RESERVOIR TRAIL

This pleasant circuit around the three Winchester reservoirs offers an easier alternative to the reservation's more rugged trails.

DIRECTIONS

From I-93, take Exit 33 to MA 28 north and follow it 2.2 miles until you reach the Sheepfold entrance. Turn left and continue to the parking lot. *GPS coordinates:* 42° 27.153' N, 71° 06.349' W.

By public transportation, from Wellington Station on the MBTA Orange Line, take the #100 bus to Fellsway West, opposite Elm Street. From there, walk 1.2 miles to the Sheepfold entrance.

TRAIL DESCRIPTION

Reservoir Trail makes a long but mostly easy circuit around the Winchester reservoirs, which were created from 1874 to 1880 by the impoundment of brooks and other water sources in the watershed. Reservoir Trail can be reached from several locations. It is described here starting from the reservation's Sheepfold entrance on the east side of the reservoirs. Public access to the reservoirs is restricted, and violators are subject to a fine.

From the entrance, follow the orange-blazed trail along the fence near the southern and western edges of the Sheepfold picnic/off-leash dog area. The trail soon leaves the fence then crosses an old paved soapbox derby track and enters the woods on an old bridle path. It leaves the path and follows the valley below the slopes of Winthrop Hill, crossing the white-blazed Skyline Trail before merging with the green-blazed Mountain Bike Trail just below the crest of Bear Hill then descending to meet the dirt Dike Road at its intersection with North Border Road.

LOCATION
Stoneham, Medford, and Winchester, MA

RATING
Moderate

DISTANCE
5.2 miles

ELEVATION GAIN
1,000 feet

ESTIMATED TIME
3 hours

MAPS
USGS Boston North; online: mass.gov/eea/docs/dcr/parks/trails/fells.pdf

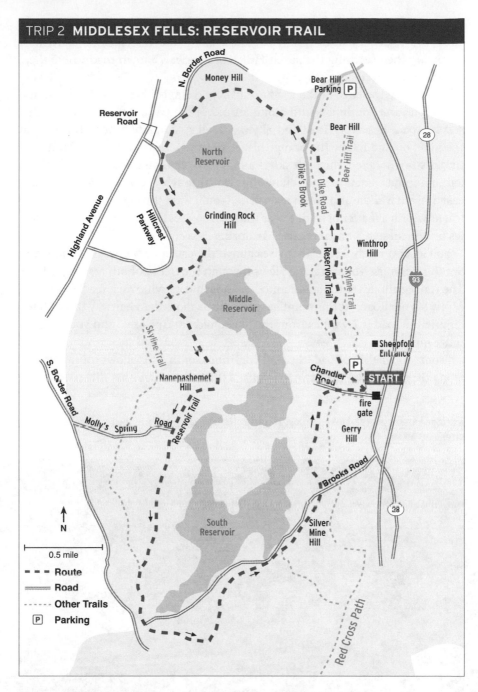

North Border Road
Money Hill
Bear Hill Parking P
Reservoir Road
Bear Hill
28
North Reservoir
Dike's Brook
Bear Hill Trail
Highland Avenue
Hillcrest Parkway
Grinding Rock Hill
Dike Road
Winthrop Hill
Reservoir Trail
Skyline Trail
93
Middle Reservoir
Skyline Trail
Sheepfold Entrance
Nanepashemet Hill
P
Chandler Road
START
S. Border Road
Molly's Spring Road
Reservoir Trail
fire gate
Gerry Hill
N
Brooks Road
28
0.5 mile
South Reservoir
Silver Mine Hill
- - - Route
Road
Other Trails
P Parking
Red Cross Path

Continue to follow the orange blazes along North Border Road until the trail leaves the road before Gate 19 to follow the shoreline of North Reservoir. In this area you'll pass through an old meadow that is now overgrown and has reverted to forest. Like many areas of New England, much of the Middlesex Fells area was cleared for agriculture during Colonial times. Near Gate 18, the Reservoir,

Skyline, and Mountain Bike trails converge and follow the same route, going close by residences near Reservoir Road along the reservation's northwest boundary then reaching the paved Hillcrest Parkway, a town road where there is parking and trail access.

Walk along the edge of the road for a short distance then bear left back into the woods and continue south along an old bridle path. After crossing a dirt service road, Reservoir Trail and Skyline Trail split again; bear to the right at the junction and follow the orange blazes to the southwest. (Skyline Trail continues straight here.) The path skirts a marshy area then crosses a brook. Turn left at another junction and follow the trail through the woods to the southeast, toward Middle and South reservoirs. You'll walk through portions of three towns within a matter of minutes, as the path crosses the corner at the boundaries of Winchester, Stoneham, and Medford.

You'll soon reach a bluff that rises above the causeway between Middle and South reservoirs. There are fine views through the trees of both reservoirs here. The trail continues to the south and descends into a ravine then reaches the dirt Molly Spring Road. At this point, you are a little more than halfway through the circuit; the road is 2.9 miles from the Sheepfold parking area, and you have 2.3 more miles to go.

From Molly Spring Road, the trail continues south and follows rolling terrain along the eastern slopes of two low hills. After crossing another dirt road, you'll

A bridge crosses peaceful Dike's Brook. This trip offers an alternative to the Fells' more strenuous hikes.

reach another junction with Skyline Trail, which comes in from the right near the South Reservoir standpipe. The combined Reservoir, Mountain Bike, and Skyline trails then turn to the left (east) to curve around the southern arm of South Reservoir and West Dam. The trails almost reach South Border Road at Gate 12, where there is parking and access to the trails, before going over a hill to a bridle path. The trails go straight then bend left (north) off one bridle path and onto another, where they separate. Skyline Trail turns to the right (east) up a hill, while Reservoir Trail continues straight ahead to the north.

As Reservoir Trail winds through the woods along the shore of South Reservoir, it leaves the road and heads northeast, parallel to nearby East Dam Road (dirt). Follow the path as it descends into a ravine adjacent to small East Dam then ascends the other side and continues to parallel the municipal road. After going north over the west shoulder of Silver Mine Hill, the trail passes close to the sealed shaft of a silver mine. Watch for concrete posts marking an old fence that once circled the mine shaft. The trail continues north then reaches Chandler Road (dirt). Turn right here and follow Chandler Road to the east. Skyline Trail soon comes in from the right. Follow both trails left at the next junction then walk back to your car.

DID YOU KNOW?

The Friends of the Fells is a stewardship and advocacy organization that shares knowledge and enjoyment of the parks through a variety of programs, including hikes for various ages, educational programs on botany, and scavenger hunts. To learn more, visit fells.org.

MORE INFORMATION

The reservation is open year-round, dawn to dusk; there is no fee. Dogs must be leashed except at the designated area at Sheepfold. For more information, contact DCR at 617-727-1199 or 617-727-5380, or visit mass.gov/dcr. Trail maps are available in boxes at many parking areas or at the DCR North Region Headquarters at 4 Woodland Road, Stoneham, MA, 02180; through the Friends of the Middlesex Fells, fells.org; and at AMC's Boston office.

NEARBY

The Griffin Museum of Photography at 67 Shore Road in Winchester features exhibits and holds lectures and programs related to photography. Restaurants in Winchester are along and off of Main Street (MA 38).

3

MIDDLESEX FELLS: ROCK CIRCUIT TRAIL

This rugged and rocky trail offers some of the best views in the reservation, including those from Boojum Rock, MIT Observatory site, White Rock, and Melrose Rock.

DIRECTIONS

From I-93, take Exit 33 to MA 28 north, which is also Fellsway West. At the first traffic circle, take the first exit to stay on MA 28/Fellsway West. At Elm Street, turn right and drive 0.6 mile to a rotary. At the rotary, take the second exit for Woodland Road and, 0.1 mile later, turn left onto Woodland Path. Turn left into the skating rink parking area. *GPS coordinates: 42° 26.668′ N, 71° 05.678′ W.*

By public transportation, take the MBTA Orange Line to Wellington Station then take the #99 bus to the skating rink parking area.

TRAIL DESCRIPTION

Rock Circuit Trail is a moderately challenging trail that leads to some of the best views in the Middlesex Fells. It passes a number of low, rocky ridges and hilltops that offer fine views of Boston and the neighborhoods surrounding the reservation. Living up to its name, it is very rocky and offers rewarding but rugged hiking over rolling terrain, although the last segment follows a series of old paths and roads over much easier terrain. You may meet other hikers completing this loop as preparation for long-distance outings in the White and Green mountains. It is not well suited to families with young children. While the route is well marked with white blazes, there are many junctions with other trails. If you don't see white blazes for a few minutes, backtrack to the trail.

LOCATION
Medford, Melrose, and Malden, MA

RATING
Strenuous

DISTANCE
4 miles

ELEVATION GAIN
875 feet

ESTIMATED TIME
3.5 hours

MAPS
USGS Boston North; online: mass.gov/eea/docs/dcr/parks/trails/fells.pdf

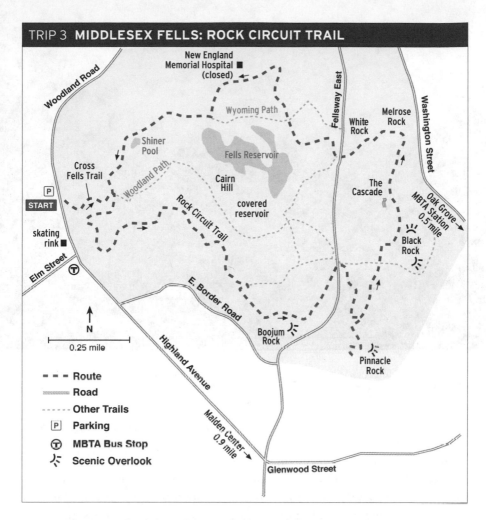

From the ice rink parking lot, carefully cross Woodland Road and follow the combined Woodland Path and Cross Fells Trail into the woods to a junction where the Rock Circuit Trail loop begins. Turn right here, off of Cross Fells Trail, and follow the white blazes up the hill to a ridge, where there are views across the reservation's forests to sections of Medford. This is the first of many hills and ridges you will ascend during this outing. None of these is especially high or steep, but the terrain is rugged in places. The trail then descends from this ridge and drops into a valley between the hills.

Follow the trail past a small seasonal brook then left across a bridle path. The trail climbs southeast up a ridge, soon turning to the right (south) and dropping into another valley. At this point, you'll begin a long, gentle climb up to 275-foot-high Boojum Rock, which rises out of the reservation's southeast corner. Along this stretch, where the Massachusetts Institute of Technology sited an observatory in 1899, there are several open rock ledges with fine views of the

Rock Circuit Trail offers some great views of Boston and the surrounding towns. A strenuous outing, this trip can be used as training for tackling hikes in the White and Green mountains.

Greater Boston area. Bring binoculars or a telephoto camera lens for close-up views of the various landmarks.

From the low vegetation atop these ridges, you may hear a mockingbird imitating other birds. Mockingbirds often repeat each call three times before moving on to the next item in their repertoires. The imitations aren't limited to bird calls, as mockingbirds also mimic car alarms and ringing telephones. In spring, you'll see colorful migratory songbirds, such as scarlet tanagers and a variety of woodland warblers.

After the last view from Boojum Rock, the trail drops sharply and heads east to cross a bridle path then reaches the paved Fellsway East. Carefully cross this town road then follow the white-blazed trail as it winds to 250-foot Pinnacle Rock, from which there are excellent views. From Pinnacle Rock, backtrack a short distance to the East Path trail junction, then follow Rock Circuit Trail north. This portion of the route follows a rough ridge along the reservation's east boundary. You'll soon reach Black Rock, where there are fine views to the east and north across the neighborhoods adjacent to the reservation. This open, rocky hilltop is a good spot to stop for lunch.

From Black Rock, continue to follow the trail north, along the crest of the ridge. You'll pass the Cascade, a seasonal waterfall where Shilly Shally Brook tumbles to the valley below, and then you'll reach Melrose Rock, where there are more views. The trail turns to the west and crosses 256-foot-high White Rock, which is the last of the overlooks along the route.

From White Rock, carefully follow the white blazes across an old cart path then left through the woods back toward Fellsway East. Cross the road, then continue to follow Rock Circuit Trail west through the woods, near the north and east shores of the Fells Reservoir. (There are no views of the water.) Here the walking becomes easier and faster, a welcome break for your feet after the extended stretches along the narrow, rocky ridges. The trail crosses Wyoming Path and leads through the forest to a low ridge east of the now-closed New England Memorial Hospital, where it meets the southern terminus of Virginia Woods Trail.

Bear left here and follow Rock Circuit Trail, which leaves the ridge and heads west through a shady pine grove then crosses a series of cart paths. Although there are many junctions here, the route is well marked and easy to follow. After passing the northwest corner of a small pond called Shiner Pool, you'll complete the Rock Circuit loop at the junction with Cross Fells Trail. Backtrack the short distance to Woodland Road and the parking area.

DID YOU KNOW?

Spot Pond, the largest body of water in the Fells, is just west of I 93 and the North, Middle, and South Reservoirs (see Trip 4 map for further detail). The area near Spot Pond Brook (east of the boating center on Spot Pond) was the site of a mill and manufacturing center called Haywardville from the mid-1700s to the late 1800s. Rubber items were the primary products during the latter phase of manufacturing here, but the surrounding towns took away rights to water access, causing the plants to close. The state took over Haywardville in 1894 when the parkland was planned.

MORE INFORMATION

The reservation is open year-round, dawn to dusk; there is no fee. Dogs are allowed on-leash (an off-leash area is at Sheepfold, off Chandler Road, west of I-93). For more information, contact DCR at 617-727-1199 or 617-727-5380, or visit mass.gov/dcr. Trail maps are available in boxes at parking areas and at the DCR North Region Headquarters at 4 Woodland Road, Stoneham, MA, 02180; through the Friends of the Middlesex Fells, fells.org; and at AMC's Boston office.

NEARBY

Boating in Boston at Spot Pond rents a variety of watercraft and offers lessons for beginners; see boatinginboston.com for information. The Flynn Ice Rink, operated by Friends of the Flynn Rink for the DCR, is open from mid- or late September to mid- or late March. For more information, call 781-395-8492. There are many restaurants in Malden and Melrose.

4

MIDDLESEX FELLS: CROSS FELLS TRAIL

The blue-blazed Cross Fells Trail serves as a handy connector between the eastern and western sections of the reservation, touching every major trail.

DIRECTIONS

From I-93, take Exit 33 to MA 28/Fellsway West, following it for 0.5 mile, and turn right onto Elm Street. At the rotary, take the second exit onto Woodland Road and travel 1.2 miles. Turn right onto Pond Street and take the next right onto Fellsway East. In 0.3 mile, stay left for Washington Street. After 0.8 mile take a right onto Goodyear Avenue and follow it up the hill to a small turnout at the end. Parking is limited; this area is best reached on foot. *GPS coordinates:* 42° 26.614′ N, 71° 04.439′ W.

By public transportation, take the MBTA Orange Line to Oak Grove Station and walk 0.5 mile down Washington Street until you reach Goodyear Avenue. Turn left and take it until you reach the trailhead at the end of the road.

TRAIL DESCRIPTION

Cross Fells Trail is a 4.3-mile, one-way connecting path that crosses the heart of Middlesex Fells Reservation. It passes many junctions with the reservation's other trails, including Skyline Trail, and is often used by hikers to create long circuits. Along the way, there are views of diverse forest communities, including uncommon pitch-pine groves along the rocky hilltops. A variety of birds, mammals, reptiles, and amphibians live within the various habitats. You can also make a short detour off the route to explore hilltops, such as Boojum Rock. Cross Fells Trail is well marked throughout with dark blue blazes, and it is easy to follow despite the numerous intersections.

LOCATION
Stoneham, Medford, Melrose, and Malden, MA

RATING
Moderate to Strenuous

DISTANCE
4.3 miles

ELEVATION GAIN
865 feet

ESTIMATED TIME
5 hours

MAPS
USGS Boston North; online: mass.gov/eea/docs/dcr/parks/trails/fells.pdf

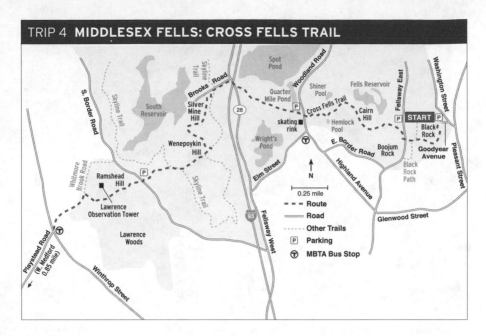

Although we describe here the full-length, one-way traverse of the trail from Goodyear Avenue to Winthrop Street in Medford, you have the option of walking portions of it in segments or combining it with other trails. You can backtrack from your endpoint to the parking areas, use two cars, or arrange for transportation where the trail crosses public roads, which are detailed below. The route follows rolling, periodically rocky terrain with a number of short climbs and descents over the reservation's hills.

From the small parking area at the end of Goodyear Avenue, follow the trail as it bears left to follow East Path (Rock Circuit Trail leaves to the right just beyond the entrance) then turn right onto Fells Path. The trail rises and crosses Rock Circuit Trail then follows more cart paths for a short distance before reaching Fellsway East, a paved town road.

Carefully cross this active road then follow the blue blazes to the right at a junction where Rock Circuit Trail diverges to go left, up the hill to Boojum Rock. (There are excellent views south and east across the reservation's woodlands to Boston and the surrounding area from Boojum Rock, and hikers have the option of making a short detour there.) Cross Fells Trail then bends to the left and winds up a hill adjacent to Boojum Rock. At this point, you are 1 mile from Woodland Road and the ice rink parking area. Follow the trail across a partially open hilltop, through a grove of pitch pines, along a wire fence south of the Fells Reservoir, and across the next hilltop.

Pitch pines are hardy trees that thrive in marginal growing conditions most other species can't tolerate. In addition to rocky hilltops, such as those in the Middlesex Fells, they are found in areas with sandy, acidic soils, such as Cape Cod and other parts of southeastern Massachusetts. Pitch pines are distinguished

Portions of Middlesex Fells Reservation are great for families. Use a topographic trail map to plan any outings for small children, as the elevation can rise steeply in a short distance. Photo by Matthew Grymek.

from other pine trees by their ball-shaped needle bundles and thick, plated bark. Pitch pines can grow as high as 55 feet, although on these windy hilltops they generally have a lower, more twisted profile.

At a four-way junction at Hemlock Pool, continue straight and follow the trail along the pool's north edge then merge onto Woodland Path. After turning right on a cart road, the trail again meets Rock Circuit Trail just west of Woodland Road. Follow the blue blazes for a short distance to the road then cross it (watch for traffic) and continue to the ice rink parking area.

From the back edge of the parking area, the trail passes the southern end of Quarter Mile Pond and heads west over the hills. After walking 0.3 mile past the ice rink, you'll reach a junction where another trail exits left and continues south to Wright's Pond. Continue to follow Cross Fells Trail west as it winds through the woods and descends to Fellsway West (MA 28). When the trail reaches the road, turn right and walk under the I-93 underpass, picking up the trail again on the other side.

From Fellsway West, Cross Fells Trail follows the dirt Brooks Road to a junction with the green-blazed Mountain Bike Trail and the white-blazed Skyline Trail, a popular long-distance circuit detailed in Trip 1. Turn left here and follow the combined Cross Fells and Skyline trails left (south) up a low hill. Soon Cross Fells Trail leaves to the right (west) to follow a ridge above Brooks Road.

Continue to follow the orange-blazed Cross Fells Trail, which bends to the left (south) and picks up a series of bridle paths before turning left (east) into the woods to rejoin Skyline Trail on the summit of Wenepoykin Hill, where there's a partial view of Boston. You may spot a white-tailed deer in this fairly quiet section of the reservation, even this close to Boston.

From Wenepoykin Hill, Cross Fells Trail crosses the dirt East Dam Road then continues south downhill to a brook and goes on to rejoin another section of Skyline Trail. The two trails continue west until Cross Fells Trail turns to the left (southwest) to pick up a group of bridle paths and then reaches the paved South Border Road.

Carefully cross the road then reenter the woods and begin a short, easy climb up Ramshead Hill. The remains of the former Lawrence Observation Tower are visible at the summit. Descend the hill then follow a series of old bridle paths to the reservation's Whitmore Brook entrance on Winthrop Street in Medford, across from Playstead Road (the end of the MBTA Sullivan Square–West Medford bus line). The entrance is 4.3 miles from the Goodyear Avenue trailhead and the endpoint of this one-way traverse. If you're backtracking to the Goodyear Avenue trailhead, retrace your steps, making sure to follow the blue blazes at the intersections.

DID YOU KNOW?

The English word "fell" comes from the Old Norse word *fjall*, meaning hilly, rocky terrain. Both sedimentary and igneous rock can be found at the Fells.

MORE INFORMATION

The reservation is open year-round, dawn to dusk; there is no fee. For more information, contact DCR at 617-727-1199 or 617-727-5380, or visit mass.gov /dcr. Trail maps are available in boxes at parking areas; at the DCR North Region Headquarters at 4 Woodland Road, Stoneham, MA, 02180; through the Friends of the Middlesex Fells, fells.org; and at AMC's Boston office.

NEARBY

The 26-acre Stone Zoo, located at 149 Pond Street in Stoneham, includes species from a wide variety of locales, such as the Canadian north woods, the southwestern United States, Africa, and the Himalaya highlands. There are numerous restaurants in Stoneham on Main Street (MA 28).

5
BREAKHEART RESERVATION

This walk leads to a variety of features, including the Saugus River and its associated wetlands, an outcropping, rocky hills, and ponds.

DIRECTIONS

From I-95, take Exit 44 for US 1 south. After you pass Salem Street, drive 2.4 miles and take the Lynn Fells Parkway exit. Turn right onto Forest Street and continue to the parking areas adjacent to the visitor center and the Kasabuski Rink. *GPS coordinates:* 42° 29.008′ N, 71° 01.664′ W.

By public transportation, take the MBTA #429 bus to Saugus Plaza; Forest Street, where the hike begins, is 0.7 mile south.

TRAIL DESCRIPTION

Breakheart Reservation encompasses more than 700 acres of forests, wetlands, and rocky hills along the south banks of the Saugus River. It offers recreational opportunities, wildlife habitats, and travel corridors in the midst of a heavily developed area. In Colonial times, the reservation was common land used by residents of the present-day towns of Saugus and Wakefield, and farms and mills were established throughout the area. In the late nineteenth century, two local residents purchased the land, made it a private game preserve, and created Pearce and Silver lakes. In 1935, the state purchased the property and established Breakheart Reservation.

This hike explores a variety of features in the eastern and central portions of the reservation. Because it follows rolling terrain and several rocky stretches, it is rated as a walk of moderate difficulty, although none of the climbs is especially long or steep.

LOCATION
Saugus, MA

RATING
Moderate

DISTANCE
2.7 miles

ELEVATION GAIN
410 feet

ESTIMATED TIME
2 hours

MAPS
USGS Boston North, USGS Lynn; online: saugus.org/FOBR

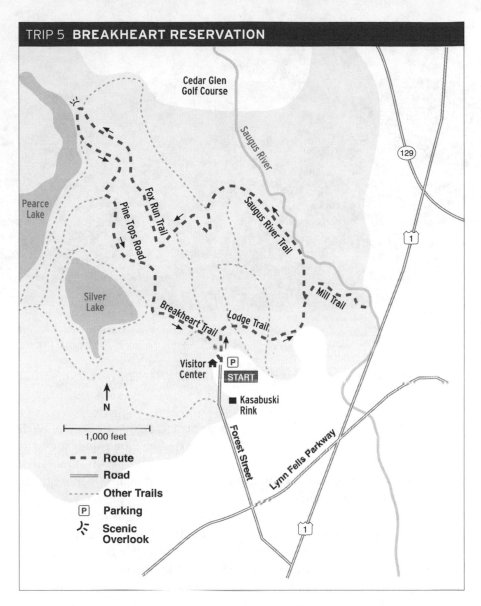

Cedar Glen
Golf Course

Saugus River

129

1

Pearce
Lake

Fox Run Trail

Pine Tops Road

Saugus River Trail

Mill Trail

Silver
Lake

Breakheart Trail

Lodge Trail

Visitor
Center

P

START

Kasabuski
Rink

N

Forest Street

Lynn Fells Parkway

1

1,000 feet

- - - **Route**
──── **Road**
.... **Other Trails**
P **Parking**
⅄ **Scenic Overlook**

From the parking area and visitor center, walk around the gate onto the paved Pine Tops Road then quickly turn left at a marked junction onto Saugus River Trail. This dirt path, which is marked with yellow blazes, leads east toward the river, crossing the red-blazed Lodge Trail. The rocky path narrows through a young hardwood forest then passes an apartment building on the right and curves left through mature woodlands.

You'll reach a junction where the blue-blazed Mill Trail forks to the right. This short side trail curves to the right then bears left as it approaches a viewpoint at an old mill site along the riverbank. Several tall pines grow out of a layer of thin soil atop the mill's large stone wall. Walk quietly here while you

From the Breakheart visitor center, follow Pine Tops Road to Saugus River Trail.

approach the river, as a variety of wildlife is present. One wading bird to watch for is the black-crowned night heron, which is most often found along the coast but occasionally nests in marshy inland areas near woodlots. Its two most distinctive traits are its black head patch and its activity at night, when it quietly stalks wetlands while hunting.

Return to the junction and continue to the right on Saugus River Trail. The path leads northwest along the edge of the wetlands that border the river, which is part of Lynn's water supply. The trail then passes through a field of rocks and boulders, with a large rock ledge visible on the hillside to the left. Here the walking briefly becomes slower; children should use caution in this area. In summer, a variety of wildflowers bloom in the sunlit openings along the river. The bright red cardinal flower is found along rivers and streams in late July and August. More widespread and visible but less welcome is purple loosestrife, an exotic species that has spread throughout wetlands in Massachusetts, where it crowds out native vegetation. Tiny bluet and jewelwing damselflies perch on the ferns and shrubs bordering the trail. Check muddy areas for tracks and signs of raccoons, mink, river otters, and white-tailed deer.

Beyond the rocky area, the trail continues over easy ground through low vegetation and a pine grove along the riverbank. After passing Link Trail on the left, it continues through a pine grove to a junction at a wood bridge. Before following Saugus River Trail away from the river to the left, step onto the bridge for a view of the water and its surrounding vegetation. From the bridge, Saugus River Trail follows an old cart road past stone walls and more rock ledges. It turns to the right at a marked junction then climbs a small hill and follows rolling terrain along the reservation boundary before rejoining Pine Tops Road, roughly 45 to 50 minutes into the hike.

Turn left here and follow the paved path south past a picnic area. After a few minutes, you'll arrive at a small clearing opposite a view into a ravine on the left. Turn right and follow Saugus River Trail, marked with light-yellow blazes, up the hill. The trail soon ends at the junction with the red-blazed Fox Run Trail. Turn right and follow Fox Run Trail to the base of a giant rock ledge that children will enjoy exploring. The path goes to the left, skirting the base of the rock face, then climbs to its top, where there are limited views through the trees.

The trail descends through a large hemlock grove, where many trees have been infested and killed by hemlock woolly adelgid. The trail then makes a quick, moderately steep climb to an open hilltop, where there's a neat view to Eagle Rock and Pearce Lake across the valley below. The path steeply descends the rock—use caution here, as pine needles can be slippery—and ends at Pine Tops Road, at the swimming beach on the northeast shores of Pearce Lake, approximately 1.6 miles from the trailhead. Swimming is allowed at the lake when lifeguards are present from Memorial Day to Labor Day. Pearce and Silver lakes and their associated marshes are home to bass, pickerel, painted and snapping turtles, double-crested cormorants, and osprey.

From Pearce Lake, follow Pine Tops Road south. The paved path, popular with dog walkers and joggers, follows gently rolling terrain through the center of the reservation. After walking fifteen minutes from the lake, you'll reach a four-way intersection at Silver Lake. This hike continues to the left here, on Breakheart Trail, although you can detour right and take the short path to the lakeshores.

Breakheart Trail makes a quick climb up Breakheart Hill, one of seven rocky hills within the reservation that exceed 200 feet. A short path on the right leads to the summit. The trail then descends to join the lower portion of Fox Run Trail near the reservation entrance. Bear right and make the short walk to the visitor center and parking area.

DID YOU KNOW?

The reservation's paved trails—Forest Street, Pine Tops Road, Elm Road, and Hemlock Road—were built during the 1930s and were added to the National Register of Historic Places in 2003.

MORE INFORMATION

Trails are open dawn to dusk. Swimming is allowed at Pearce Lake from Memorial Day to Labor Day. For more information, visit mass.gov/dcr or the Friends of Breakheart Reservation at saugus.org/FOBR.

NEARBY

Saugus Iron Works National Historic Site at 244 Central Street offers guided tours of the seventeenth-century Iron Works House and industrial site. Restaurants are on US 1 (Newburyport Turnpike).

6

LYNN WOODS

Easy fire road trails lead to overlooks atop low, rolling hills and to the famous Dungeon Rock.

DIRECTIONS

Take I-95 to Exit 44 for MA 129 east in Lynn. Follow it through the rotary to a well-marked right onto Great Woods Road. Continue 0.3 mile to the park entrance and large parking area at the road's end, at a baseball field. *GPS coordinates:* 42° 29.588′ N, 70° 58.639′ W.

By public transportation, take the #436 bus from the Central Square–Lynn station on the MBTA Commuter Rail to the Great Woods Road stop.

TRAIL DESCRIPTION

At 2,200 acres, Lynn Woods Reservation is one of the largest municipal forest parks in the United States. Located northwest of Lynn Center, near the city's boundary with Saugus and Lynnfield, it is home to a variety of features. Low rolling hills with views to Boston rise above a series of swamps and wetlands, such as the narrow Walden Pond (not to be confused with the famous Walden Pond in Concord, see Trip 34), which bisects the reservation.

This hike begins at the reservation's east entrance on Great Woods Road and makes a loop that visits overlooks atop Mount Gilead and Burrill Hill, Dungeon and Union rocks, and the shores of Walden Pond. The main fire roads are orange-blazed, while other trails are blue- or green-blazed.

From the back side of the parking lot, walk around the green gate to the left (at a sign for the stone tower) onto Great Woods Road, which is an unpaved extension of the entrance road. On your right are short side paths that quickly lead to the southwest corner of Walden Pond. This

LOCATION
Lynn, MA

RATING
Easy to Moderate

DISTANCE
3.7 miles

ELEVATION GAIN
450 feet

ESTIMATED TIME
2 hours

MAPS
USGS Boston North, USGS Lynn; online: lynnwoods.org

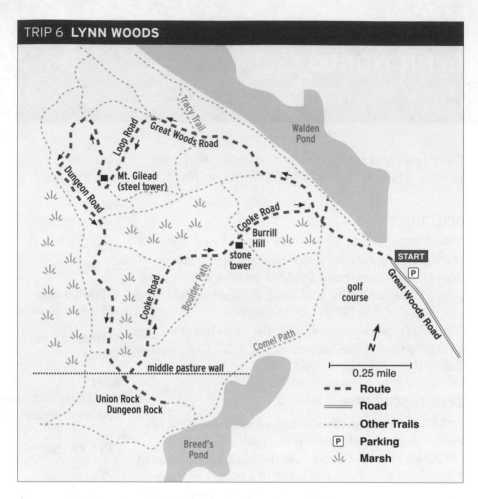

Tracy Trail
Loop Road
Great Woods Road
Walden Pond
Dungeon Road
Mt. Gilead (steel tower)
Cooke Road
Burrill Hill
stone tower
Boulder Path
Cooke Road
START
P
Great Woods Road
golf course
Comet Path
N
middle pasture wall
0.25 mile
Union Rock
Dungeon Rock
Breed's Pond

- - - Route
═══ Road
········· Other Trails
P Parking
Marsh

narrow, "L"-shaped pond offers nice views along its shores. You can visit the pond at either the start or the finish of the walk, as the hike returns via this section of the trail.

Great Woods Road continues to the northwest, rising gently past a rocky brook before leveling at a cluster of glacial boulders. In late spring or early summer, listen for the distinctive *pee-a-wee* call of the eastern wood peewee, one of many migratory songbirds that call this forest home. Another familiar sound is the flutelike call of the hermit thrush. More than 100 other species of birds have been documented here, and according to Ranger Dan Small, large pileated woodpeckers are among the more recent arrivals. You may hear their loud hammering on dead trees from a long distance away.

You'll soon arrive at a "Y" junction where Cooke Road—the return leg of this hike—branches to the left. Continue straight here on Great Woods Road. Walden Pond will be visible through the trees to the right. Tall oaks line the trail, along with clusters of eastern hemlocks, many of which are infested with the deadly hemlock woolly adelgid, visible as white spots underneath branches where the needles meet the wood.

At 0.8 mile from the trailhead, Great Woods Road passes a marked junction with Tracy Trail on the right then reaches another "Y" junction at the site of an old foundation. Bear left here onto Loop Road, following signs to the summit of Mount Gilead. After an easy 0.3-mile climb, you'll reach the 272-foot summit, where an old steel fire tower rises high above a small clearing. Although the tower is inaccessible, rock ledges a short distance beyond it offer a fine view south across the reservation's forests to the Boston skyline and the ocean. This sunlit, open area is an ideal spot for a picnic or a rest break. In summer, watch for crickets hopping in the grass and dragonflies, such as lancet clubtails, circling on hunting rounds.

From the summit, Loop Road winds past more rock ledges. Note the lower vegetation here, even at the hilltop's relatively modest elevation. After a few minutes of easy walking, the trail reaches a four-way junction with a fire road, where you should go left. (A blue-blazed trail goes straight.) The road briefly follows a contour below the summit then descends to meet Dungeon Road at Junction C5-3.

Turn left here onto Dungeon Road, which leads south along the east side of Mount Gilead, passing rocky outcroppings and two junctions with other trails on the left. A grove of hemlocks partially shades the sunlit road, which rises easily along rolling terrain. An opening in the woods on the left behind a rest bench indicates Long Swamp, one of several swamps and wetlands that lie within the bounds of the reservation. It's a potential location for sighting some of the park's elusive residents, including mink, fisher cats, and beavers. Barred owls may be heard calling during quiet times, especially dawn and dusk.

Stone Tower, a 48-foot-tall fieldstone structure atop Lynn Woods' Burrill Hill, was created as a fire tower in 1936 under the Works Progress Administration.

Shortly after Dungeon Road curves to the left and passes more trail junctions on the right, it meets Cooke Road (also known as Burrill Hill Road) at Junction C7-1. Although this hike continues left on Cooke Road, you can make a short detour straight on Dungeon Road to visit the nearby Dungeon and Union rocks. Side paths on the right lead to both of these unique geological features. Dungeon Rock is an especially colorful part of Lynn Woods' history, as pirates are believed to have stashed treasure in the vicinity. During the mid-seventeenth century, an earthquake closed the rock cave. In subsequent years, a treasure hunter spent a considerable amount of effort reopening the cave in an unsuccessful attempt to locate the loot. Within the rock is a 135-foot-deep tunnel open to tours during certain hours; contact the park for more information.

After exploring the rocks, backtrack to the junction and turn right onto Cooke Road. This pleasant path leads north through the woods above the east side of Long Swamp. After passing a junction with a side trail that descends into the valley on the left, the road curves to the right and gradually rises to the large stone tower atop 285-foot Burrill Hill. You can climb a portion of the tower for more views south toward Boston.

Complete the circuit by following Cooke Road as it descends at a moderate grade to its end at the junction with Great Woods Road, next to Walden Pond. Turn right and make the short walk back to the reservation entrance.

DID YOU KNOW?

The Penny Bridge on the northwest side of Tomlin's Swamp got its name from the stone bridge built there for early settlers. Each paid a penny to use the bridge until the cost of construction was repaid.

MORE INFORMATION

The reservation is open to blackberry and blueberry picking, mushroom hunting, hiking, mountain biking, and horseback riding; bikes are allowed only on official, blazed trails, and horses are allowed only on fire roads. Dogs must be leashed. Camping, fishing, and motorized vehicles are prohibited. Picnics are allowed, but grills, stoves, and fires are not permitted. Maps are available at the Lynn City Hall and the Friends of Lynn Woods website, lynnwoods.org. Contact the park at lynnwoodsranger@aol.com or 781-477-7123.

NEARBY

Lynn Museum and Historical Society at 590 Washington Street features exhibits dedicated to the town's seafaring, manufacturing, and commercial histories. There are restaurants nearby in Wyoma Square at the intersection of Parkland Avenue and Lynnfield Street.

7

JAMAICA POND

An easy recreational trail offers a popular and pleasant circuit around historical Jamaica Pond.

DIRECTIONS

Take Jamaicaway to Kelly Circle then bear north on Parkman Drive at the rotary. Turn right onto Perkins Street and look for parking areas on the right, along the edge of the pond and recreational path. If no parking spot is available, try the side roads that branch off Jamaicaway, opposite the pond's south shore. *GPS coordinates:* 42° 19.213′ N, 71° 07.331′ W.

By public transportation, take the MBTA Orange Line to the Green Street station; the pond is about one mile west of the station.

TRAIL DESCRIPTION

Jamaica Pond is a modestly sized, 68-acre pond in Boston's densely populated Jamaica Plain neighborhood. Located along Arborway, one mile east of the Arnold Arboretum, it is a highlight of Boston's Emerald Necklace chain of parks. Like many other ponds in eastern Massachusetts, it is a kettle pond, formed by the melting of a large ice block as glaciers retreated from the Northeast more than 10,000 years ago. Fed by springs, it is the largest natural water body in the lower Charles River watershed and is the largest and cleanest pond within Boston's city limits. It served as a drinking-water reservoir until 1848, before pollution and the region's growth necessitated the use of larger sources to the west. In more recent times, it was a popular ice-skating area, although skating is now prohibited.

Due to its location and easy access, this is a very popular area, and you'll likely encounter a constant stream of people, including dog walkers and joggers, on nice days. The

LOCATION
Boston, MA (Jamaica Plain)

RATING
Easy

DISTANCE
1.5 miles

ELEVATION GAIN
Minimal

ESTIMATED TIME
45 minutes

MAPS
USGS Boston South; online: emeraldnecklace.org

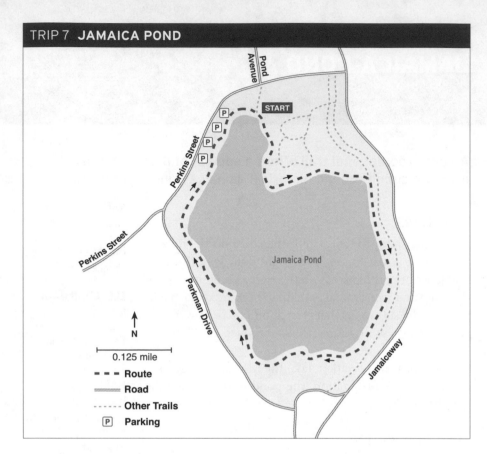

trail offers an easy, level walk with continuous views across the water, making it a fine choice for families with young children who will enjoy close-up views of ducks and geese. You'll likely see many anglers, as the pond is stocked by the state in season and is home to trout, bass, perch, pickerel, and hornpout.

This hike follows a clockwise direction from Perkins Street. From the parking areas, follow the recreational path left along the pond's northwest shores, passing right along the water's edge. Watch for a tiny island across the water, which marks a promontory between two of the pond's glacial bowls. It was expanded into a permanent island by the parks department in the early twentieth century. It was once planted with a group of willow trees, the last of which was blown over by Hurricane Bob in 1991.

The trail soon curves to the right, away from the road, then makes its only left turn as it winds along Pinebank Promontory. This is a fine spot for young children to watch for some of the birds in this urban sanctuary, including mallard ducks, double-crested cormorants, and Canada geese. Mallards, easily distinguished by the male's bright green head, are New England's most familiar and commonly viewed duck; they are regularly seen both in wilderness areas and urban parks. You may be treated to a view of ducklings learning to swim

A very popular recreation area with locals, Jamaica Pond is the largest natural body of water in the lower Charles River watershed.

or wandering along portions of the path. In winter, the pond has been visited by a variety of waterfowl, including common loons; pie-billed, red-necked, and horned grebes; American wigeons; and ring-necked ducks.

The path curves back to the right and follows the pond's south shores on a contour below the busy Jamaicaway. Hard as it may be to imagine today, Jamaica Pond was once part of a rural area outside of downtown Boston, and wealthy residents built homes around it to escape the crowded city during the eighteenth and early nineteenth centuries. The homes were removed when the city of Boston acquired the land and established Jamaica Pond Reservation in 1891. During high-water periods, the trees that line the water's edge may be partially flooded.

After walking half a mile from Perkins Street, you'll reach the boathouse, which is administered by the Courageous Sailing Center. Rowboats, sailboats, and kayaks are available for rent from April to October (call 617-522-5061 for more information; private boats are not permitted on the pond). The boathouse and the bandstand adjacent to the pond were built in 1911 and 1912, and 6,000 people attended the first concert on the grounds. Next to the boathouse is the Boston Park Rangers' Nature Center at Jamaica Pond, home to a natural history collection that includes displays, wildlife mountings, and American Indian and geological artifacts. Programs are held at the center during warm months.

The pond was also a historically active place during winter, home to ice-cutting operations and figure skating from the mid-nineteenth century onward.

From the boathouse, the trail continues along Jamaicaway for a short distance then turns right near the traffic circle and heads north along the western shores below Parkman Drive for 0.3 mile, with views across the water of the boathouse to the south. If you're here early in the morning, you may witness a beautiful sunrise across the water. In autumn, the narrow ring of deciduous oaks, maples, and birches adds a photogenic splash of color to the pond's edges. During spring and summer, check the treetops for colorful migratory songbirds, such as northern parulas, magnolia and blackpoll warblers, and northern orioles.

At a huge tree near the junction of Parkman Drive and Perkins Street, the trail turns right one final time and follows the northwest shores of the pond paralleling Perkins Street. If you parked on Perkins Street, your car will be on the left.

DID YOU KNOW?

The Emerald Necklace, designed by Frederick Law Olmsted, encompasses 1,100 acres of urban parks in Boston and Brookline that are connected by parkways and waterways.

MORE INFORMATION

Biking, swimming, wading, and private boating are prohibited. Contact the Boston Parks and Recreation Department at 617-635-4505 or visit cityofboston.gov/parks.

NEARBY

The pond's natural and human histories are well documented, with several journals and diaries at the Jamaica Plain Historical Society (jphs.org) and online detailing skating and other activities at the pond. Restaurants and shops are located on Centre Street, South Street, and Hyde Park Avenue and in nearby Roslindale Square. Arnold Arboretum (see Trip 8) is a short distance south of the pond.

8

ARNOLD ARBORETUM

Paved roads and footpaths pass botanical collections, leading to scenic hilltops with long views of downtown Boston and the Blue Hills.

DIRECTIONS

The Arboretum is located at 125 Arborway (MA 203), near Centre Street and Murray Circle. From I-95 (reached by I-90), take Exit 20 and follow MA 9 (East Worcester Street) east toward Brookline–Boston. After 2.9 miles, bear slightly right at Florence Street. Turn right onto Hammond Pond Parkway and continue to the rotary then take the third exit onto Newton Street. Follow Newton Street to Pond Street then turn right onto Arborway. At the rotary, continue to follow Arborway to the Arboretum on the right. This hike begins at the main entrance at the Arborway gate; on-street parking is available at most of the other entrance gates along Arborway and along Bussey Street. *GPS coordinates:* 42° 18.461′ N, 71° 07.203′ W.

By public transportation, take the MBTA Orange Line to Forest Hills Station and exit through the Arnold Arboretum door. Continue west on Arborway (toward MA 1) to the gate. Or take the #39 bus to Custer Street in Jamaica Plain and walk down Custer three blocks to the Arboretum.

TRAIL DESCRIPTION

Renowned for its beautifully landscaped grounds and historical botanical collections, Arnold Arboretum is a highlight of the Emerald Necklace, a 5-mile-long chain of urban parks totaling more than 1,000 acres that extends from Boston Common west and south through the city to Franklin Park.

LOCATION
Boston, MA (Jamaica Plain)

RATING
Easy to Moderate

DISTANCE
4.1 miles

ELEVATION GAIN
230 feet, including both hills

ESTIMATED TIME
3 hours

MAPS
USGS Boston South; online: arboretum.harvard.edu/wp-content/uploads/basic-map-b+w.pdf (the website offers other specific landscape maps as well as an interactive map; see arboretum.harvard.edu for more information)

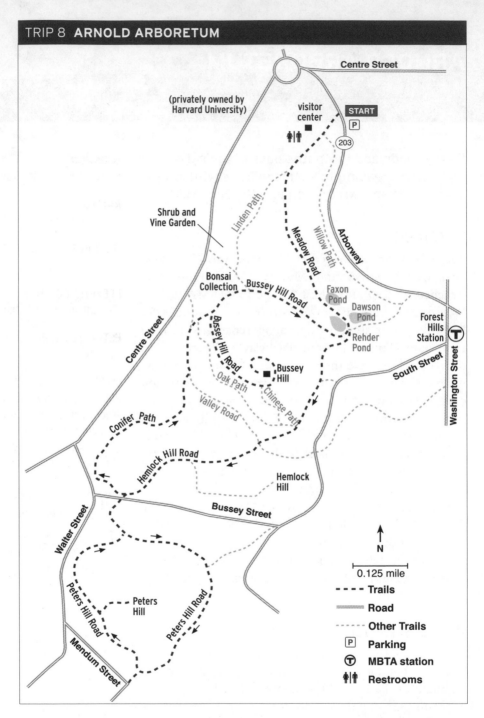

Spread throughout the Arboretum's 265 acres are more than 15,000 trees, shrubs, and vines representing some 4,500 species from around the world. The Arboretum was founded in 1872 and named for James Arnold, who donated funds to begin the project. Since 1882 it has been run under a cooperative agreement between Harvard University, which manages the grounds and directs education and research, and the city of Boston, which is responsible for security and infrastructure. An arboretum is a living museum—a place where trees and other woody plants are grown and cultivated for scientific research, education, and aesthetics.

This route, which combines paved roads and two gravel paths, passes most of the Arboretum's diverse botanical collections and leads to a pair of sweeping vistas atop 240-foot Peters Hill and 200-foot Bussey Hill. The walking is easy, and detailed maps are posted at major junctions. In addition to the paths described in this hike, there are self-guided trails that allow visitors to explore and enjoy the collections. The Arboretum's website and printed maps include information about the species present and the best times to see them.

The walk begins at the main gate on Arborway. On your right is the Hunnewell Building, where the Arboretum's visitor center and a large diorama of the grounds are located. Research scientists based here travel around the world to study trees and plants. From the building, head south on the wide, paved Meadow Road.

On the left are shadbushes, blueberries, and azaleas, with dogwoods, golden rain trees, and redbuds to your right. The grounds were designed by the legendary landscape architect Frederick Law Olmsted and by the Arboretum's first director, Charles Sprague Sargent, to highlight both scenic and scientific aspects. Along the way, you'll see tags hanging from the plantings, with information about the species, its original location, and the year it was planted.

After an easy half-mile of walking, you'll arrive at a junction near three small ponds and the Bradley Rosaceous Collection. Here the main road bears to the right and continues toward Bussey Hill and the lilac collection. (It is the return leg of the loop described here; those looking for a shorter outing can follow it to the Bussey Hill overlook.) This hike continues straight on Beech Path, a quarter-mile-long, narrow gravel trail that leads through the forsythia collection along the base of the hill.

Shortly after passing a giant beech tree on the right, the path ends at the junction of the paved Valley Road and Hemlock Hill Road; at this point, you've walked 0.75 mile. Continue straight on Hemlock Hill Road, passing groves of rhododendrons and mountain laurel. This is one of the Arboretum's better wildlife-viewing areas, as it is home to Bussey Brook and clearings adjacent to the planted trees that offer habitat diversity. A familiar resident of the grounds is the eastern cottontail rabbit, the most common rabbit throughout North America. This is due to its prolific reproductive rate. Under ideal circumstances, a single pair can produce as many as 350,000 offspring within five years. Cottontails are an important source of food for predators, such as coyotes and foxes.

As you walk along the road, up the slope to your left are the evergreen groves that Hemlock Hill is named for. The eastern hemlock trees sadly have been

The Arnold Arboretum is a highlight of Boston's Emerald Necklace. With 15,000 trees, shrubs, and vines in 265 acres, the arboretum is a must-see for any botanical garden enthusiast.

devastated by the spread of hemlock woolly adelgid (HWA) in recent decades, and the dead trees are being replaced by pioneer species, such as black birch, as well as experimental plantings of Asian hemlocks. The Arboretum is especially susceptible to HWA infestation due to its mild climate and its location along the coastal Atlantic flyway; transient birds are largely responsible for the spread of HWA, typically a forest pest. The hill has been used for research yielding data on how to protect individual trees.

After walking for roughly a quarter-mile along Hemlock Hill Road, you'll arrive at the Bussey Street gate. Carefully cross the street and continue straight into the Peters Hill area. The road soon forks into a loop of slightly less than a mile. Bear to the left and follow the curving path as it rises gently past colorful crabapples, hawthorns, and a grove of cypresses planted in a wet area. After turning right near the Mendum Street gate, you'll soon reach a short side path on the right that leads to the 240-foot summit of Peters Hill. Here are long views across the grounds to the Boston skyline. Amid the tall buildings, look carefully for the low gold dome of the State House, to the right of the Prudential tower. This scenic clearing presents opportunities for bird-watchers; look for tree swallows and bluebirds using the nesting boxes.

After enjoying the view, return to the main road and follow it right as it descends to complete the loop then backtrack to Bussey Street. After recrossing the street, bear left away from Hemlock Hill then quickly right onto the narrow Conifer Path, which begins near the Walter Street gate and offers a pleasant, shady stroll beneath a variety of pines, spruces, larches, junipers, and other evergreens. At the end of the path, go left on paved Valley Road and follow it for a short distance to the junction with Bussey Hill Road. Turn right here and follow the road as it curves uphill at an easy grade to the partially open top of Bussey Hill, where there is a view south to the Blue Hills Reservation.

From the overlook, backtrack along Bussey Hill Road and continue to follow it as it curves right and descends to the lilac collection. This area is especially scenic and popular in early and mid-May, when the lilacs are in peak bloom; the Arboretum hosts a well-known festival annually in early May. Shortly beyond the lilacs, the road returns to the junction with Meadow Road at the three ponds. Turn left and retrace your steps to the visitor center.

DID YOU KNOW?

Arnold Arboretum is North America's oldest arboretum that has been open to the public since its inception; others are older but started as private estates or cemeteries.

MORE INFORMATION

The grounds are open sunrise to sunset year-round. The Hunnewell Visitor Center is open weekdays from 10 A.M. to 5 P.M.; closed Wednesdays. Contact the Arboretum at 617-524-1718 or visit arboretum.harvard.edu.

NEARBY

Restaurants and shops are located on Centre Street, South Street, and Hyde Park Avenue and in nearby Roslindale Square. A detailed map of restaurants is available at the visitor center in the Hunnewell Building. Jamaica Pond is a short distance north of the Arboretum.

INTRODUCED PESTS: A THREAT TO OUR EASTERN FORESTS

While walking along the trails through hemlock groves at this and other reservations in Massachusetts, you may notice that many of the trees are dead or dying. This is due to infestation by hemlock woolly adelgid (HWA), a tiny, aphid-like insect that poses a substantial threat to eastern hemlock trees throughout the forests of eastern North America.

HWA, which is native to Asia, was introduced to North America during the 1950s in Virginia and has gradually spread through the forests of the Northeast and South. The insects are carried by wind and by animals, such as deer, squirrels, and birds. HWA became established in southern New England during the 1980s. It has caused extensive eastern hemlock mortality in coastal areas and river valleys in Connecticut, Massachusetts, and Rhode Island but has been slower to affect cooler, higher elevations.

Although the adelgids themselves are less than one-sixteenth of an inch in size, evidence of infestation is easy to observe, as their puffy white egg masses are often obvious at the base of hemlock needles. Adelgids kill their hosts by feeding on tissues and starches that are essential to the trees' survival. Once infested, a tree can die in four to ten years or even faster in milder southern regions such as the Great Smoky Mountains.

Because eastern hemlock is a "climax" forest species that takes a long time to recover once disturbed (as opposed to a "pioneer" species, such as the white pine or black birch, which respond well to disruption), HWA is of considerable concern. Research into control measures is ongoing. Options for treating individual trees include injecting chemicals into the roots and spraying entire trees with repellent oils. In larger forest groves, adelgid predators, such as ladybugs, have been introduced.

HWA is just one of many pests that have affected North America's forests. The American chestnut, which was once one of the Northeast's most significant species from both ecological and economic perspectives, was all but eliminated by a blight in the early twentieth century. Since 2008, an outbreak of Asian long-horned beetles in the Greater Worcester area has resulted in the removal of 35,000 trees and the establishment of a 110-square-mile quarantine zone. This insect poses a serious threat to many important hardwood species, including maples, birches, and poplars. A smaller outbreak near the Arnold Arboretum is believed to have been contained. In recent years, the emerald ash borer, which causes rapid mortality to ash trees, has also begun to spread across Massachusetts. Researchers are working to document and contain these and other threats to New England's forests.

9

SPECTACLE ISLAND

Once a landfill, Spectacle Island offers amazing views of Boston and the coast from the highest point in Boston Harbor.

DIRECTIONS

The main ferry departure point is Long Wharf in Boston; another ferry leaves from Hingham Shipyard but does not go directly to Spectacle Island. It is best to take public transit to Long Wharf, but if driving from the north, take I-93 south to Exit 24A (Government Center). Take the right fork then stay left. At the traffic light, turn onto Atlantic Avenue. From the south, take I-93 north to Exit 20 (South Station). Follow Atlantic Avenue for five blocks. There are parking facilities at the Harbor Garage, near the New England Aquarium, and the Boston Harbor Hotel, both on the right. Ferry service is provided by Boston Harbor Cruises, which is located on Long Wharf. *GPS coordinates: 42° 21.598′ N, 71° 02.977′ W.*

By public transportation, take the MBTA Blue Line to Aquarium Station.

TRAIL DESCRIPTION

The Boston Harbor Islands are a group of 34 islands rich in history, natural resources, and scenic views. From the American Revolution through World War II, Boston Harbor was an important coastal defense site, and old forts and gun batteries are still visible today on some of the islands. The islands have been the sites of a wide variety of other institutions, including factories, hospitals, and fishing villages. Today, they are protected by a partnership that includes the National Park Service and the Massachusetts Department of Conservation and Recreation.

LOCATION
Boston, MA

RATING
Easy

DISTANCE
3 miles

ELEVATION GAIN
150 feet

ESTIMATED TIME
1.25 hours

MAPS
USGS Boston North; online: bostonharborislands.org/ spectacle-island

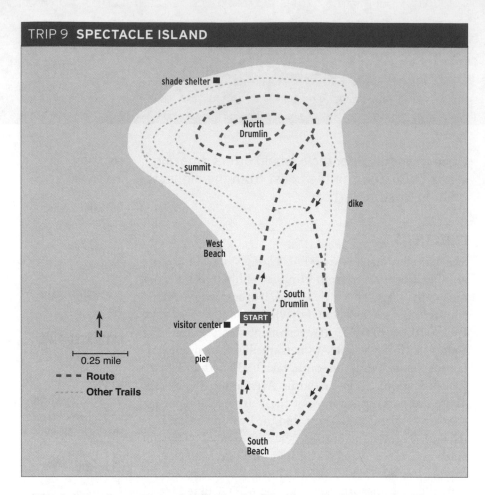

shade shelter ■

North
Drumlin

summit

dike

West
Beach

South
Drumlin

↑
N

0.25 mile

visitor center ■ START

- - - **Route**
- - - - **Other Trails**

pier

South
Beach

This hike explores Spectacle Island, which has been revitalized after serving as a landfill for many years. The island comprises two glacial drumlins (low rolling hills), the northernmost of which is the highest point in the harbor at 155 feet. This route climbs North Drumlin then follows a portion of the island's perimeter trail (which is 1.8 miles long and ADA accessible) as it loops back to the pier. The walking is easy along well-maintained gravel paths, with a gradual, gentle climb to the top of North Drumlin. Interpretive signs along the route detail the island's natural and cultural history, and a brochure is available.

As you depart the ferry at the island's boat dock, the visitor center will be at the end of the pier to your right. Be sure to stop by to check out the exhibits and photographs. Rangers are available to answer questions about trails, history, flora and fauna, and planning your visit. The trail begins to the left of the visitor center, adjacent to West Beach and the perimeter trail. It leads uphill at a gradual grade, with views of Boston across the harbor to the left and of the mostly open hillside on the right. You'll soon reach a marked junction for the trails to North and South drumlins. Continue straight on the main path, following signs for

North Drumlin. You'll pass a crossover path at the next intersection that leads right toward a gazebo.

As the trail rises up North Drumlin, you'll gain a good perspective of the island's vegetation. The picturesque grasslands, trees, and shrubs visible today are a marked contrast from the past: The island served as a landfill for the city of Boston until 1959. During the 1990s, earth from the Big Dig project was brought over to cover the landfill, and it was then replanted with nearly 30,000 varieties of trees, shrubs, and grasses, creating the present parklike setting.

Thanks to its varied habitats and open areas, the island is an interesting bird-watching destination. Species such as bobolinks, savannah sparrows, fish crows, and swallows all may be seen here. Bird variety is greatest during spring and fall, when shorebirds, hawks, and songbirds are migrating along the coast. Raccoons, coyotes, turkeys, and deer are present here as well. Some of the wildflowers that grow in the openings and along the trail edges include Queen Anne's lace and bird's-foot trefoil, which is identified by its yellow, pea-shaped flowers. The flowers' nectar nourishes a variety of butterflies, including red admirals, monarchs, pearl crescents, cabbage whites, and yellow mustards.

The path curves to the left as it winds up North Drumlin. The Boston skyline and waterfront come back into view, and you'll see a continuous stream of planes taking off from nearby Logan Airport, which lies across the harbor on a peninsula to the right. At a fork where another gravel path descends to the right,

Spectacle Island, one of the 34 Boston Harbor Islands, features two glacial drumlins (low rolling hills) with beautiful ocean views.

continue to follow the main trail uphill. Just below the summit, the trail forks into a short loop.

The 155-foot summit of North Drumlin is the highest point in Boston Harbor, and the panoramic views are striking. Most visitors are drawn to the buildings of downtown Boston, which is just 4.5 miles west of the island, but be sure to scan the surrounding areas for views of the Blue Hills, Dorchester Bay, the other islands, and the open ocean.

After enjoying the overlooks, retrace your steps downhill, back to the interpretive sign that details the revegetation project. At the next junction, bear left and follow the path to the gazebo. From the gazebo, the interpretive trail continues south above the island's east shores. (The perimeter trail will be visible below, on your left.) At a marked junction, a trail offers the option of a short detour to South Drumlin. Though the views are not quite as sweeping as those from North, this overlook is worth a visit if you have time.

From this junction, the interpretive trail descends to join the perimeter trail. Bear to the right where the paths meet and continue on a pleasant and easy walk along the base of South Drumlin, with planted evergreens and shrubs along the hill on the right. As the path approaches South Beach at the island's southern tip, it curves right, and Boston comes back into view across the water. You'll soon see the visitor center and pier in the distance to the right. Complete the loop by following the path along the fence back to the visitor center and picnic tables.

DID YOU KNOW?

On nearby Little Brewster Island is the 89-foot-tall Boston Harbor Light. Built on the rocky island in 1716, it's the oldest working lighthouse in the country. It was automated in 1996.

MORE INFORMATION

The island is open year-round, although the ferry operates only from mid-May to Columbus Day. Visitor centers and concessions with snacks and light meals are located at Spectacle and Georges islands. There is a carry-in, carry-out policy on all islands. Short, ranger-led kayak trainings are available near the pier in summer; contact the DCR for the weekly schedule. The ferry fee is $17 for adults for round-trip service to and from the islands, including use of the interisland ferries, and $10 for children; toddlers are free. See bostonharborislands.org for a seasonal ferry schedule and information on departure locations.

NEARBY

Visitors to Spectacle Island easily can combine their trip with a stop at Georges Island, where you can tour historic Fort Warren, or at one of the other islands. Ferry schedules and maps are available at the terminals. There are waterside cafes on Spectacle and Georges islands.

10

WILSON MOUNTAIN RESERVATION

Enjoy a short stroll to a hilltop overlook and explore trails adjacent to wetlands and rocky outcroppings.

DIRECTIONS

From I-95, take Exit 17 to MA 135 east and go 0.6 mile into Dedham. Park at the second small lot on the right side of the street (just before a ball field), where a sign welcomes you to the reservation. *GPS coordinates:* 42° 15.549' N, 71° 11.835' W.

TRAIL DESCRIPTION

Thanks are due to the people who saved Wilson Mountain from development in 1994 and kept it natural. Just 10 miles from Boston, these 200 wooded acres could have become the site of a mall or housing lots. Instead, with funds made available through the Open Space Bond Bill, it is now managed by the Department of Conservation and Recreation (DCR) and is open to all.

This walk combines several of the reservation's trails to form a loop that includes a summit vista and a short boardwalk through wetlands. The perimeter trail is blazed in blue, and the summit trail has red blazes. Begin your walk by following the main trail that starts behind the iron gate. Beware of poison ivy in the area, identifiable by its three green leaves with pointed tips that shine in the sun. Just 30 feet down the path is a side trail going off to your right into lowlands, but you should stay straight on the main trail.

About 50 feet farther, the main trail splits at a granite marker; bear right, following the trail that leads uphill into a white-pine grove. Rhododendron bushes grow in the shade on your right along the steep hillside. At the next fork in the trail, bear to the right. The pines here

LOCATION
Dedham, MA

RATING
Easy to Moderate

DISTANCE
2 miles

ELEVATION GAIN
160 feet

ESTIMATED TIME
1.5 hours

MAPS
USGS Medfield; online: mass.gov/eea/docs/dcr/ parks/trails/wilson.pdf

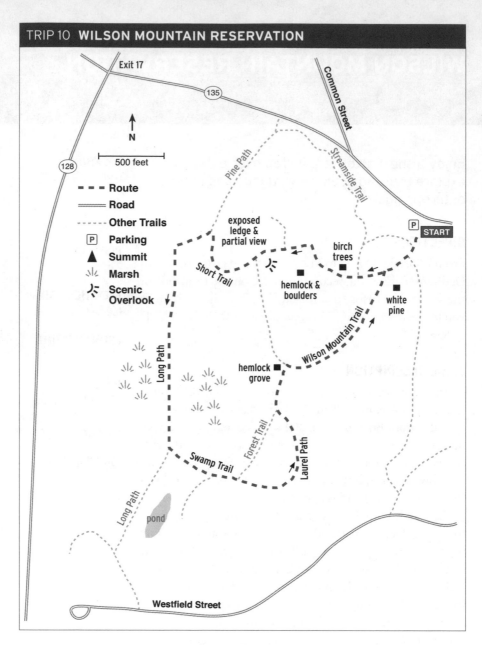

Exit 17

135

N

128

500 feet

- - - Route
——— Road
----- Other Trails
P **Parking**
▲ **Summit**
🌾 **Marsh**
🌿 **Scenic Overlook**

Common Street

Pine Path

Streamside Trail

exposed ledge & partial view

birch trees

Short Trail

hemlock & boulders

white pine

Wilson Mountain Trail

Long Path

hemlock grove

Forest Trail

Laurel Path

Swamp Trail

Long Path

pond

P START

Westfield Street

are crowded together and consequently grow tall and thin, with most of the branches near the upper parts of the trees, where they receive some sunlight. If a pine is growing in an open field, it will fill out more evenly, with branches at lower levels thanks to unobstructed sunshine.

Farther down the trail, a side path comes in on the right by some birch trees. Stay straight, following the main trail uphill. On the right, where the hill slopes downward, a few mountain laurel bushes grow in the understory.

This trip features a short boardwalk through wetlands, as well as a summit vista.

Some of the forest birds you are likely to see include tufted titmice (small gray birds with tufted caps at the backs of their heads), chickadees (black-and-white coloring), and nuthatches (usually on tree trunks looking for insects). Another common bird is the flicker, about the size of a blue jay with a brown back and a black crested breast, most easily identified by its white rump, seen in flight. While nuthatches usually work their way down a tree, flickers go up the trunk. They make their nests in tree cavities, one reason why dead standing timber is so important to birds.

As you continue on the trail, the pines give way to mixed woodlands of ash, maple, oak, hemlock, and birch. These trees, some quite large, provide hikers with almost total shade during periods of summer heat. In the understory grows mountain laurel, the leaves of which are 3 to 4 inches long, dark green and glossy on the top and yellow-green underneath. Mature leaves are thick and leathery. The saucer-shaped flowers, which bloom at the end of June, can vary from pink to white and other shades in between. Mountain laurel can reach heights of 20 feet in southern Connecticut, but that height is rare in northern New England.

Huge boulders, called glacial erratics because they were haphazardly deposited by glaciers, litter the forest floor. In spring, look for delicate pink lady's slippers growing beneath the trees, identified by their drooping, slipper-shaped flowers. Lady's slippers are protected by law and should never be picked.

The trail soon makes a 90-degree turn to the left, roughly three-quarters of a mile after the start of the walk, and now ascends more steeply up Wilson Mountain. About 50 feet up the trail, it splits; bear left on the path that climbs to the exposed granite ledge. Children will love climbing on the rocks here. After a few minutes traversing rocky terrain, you will arrive at the partially open summit, a sunny spot to enjoy the warming rays and a view north to the Boston skyline. The total walk to the summit from the parking lot is an easy twenty minutes. (At this point, if you are hiking with younger children, you may want to retrace your steps back to the parking lot.)

To continue this loop from the overlook, bear right at Junction 23 (the trail that forks to the left leads to more ledges with no open views) and follow the unmarked Short Trail. Oaks and maples dominate the woods, with sassafras growing in the understory. Identified by its mitten-shaped leaves, the sassafras tree rarely grows taller than 30 feet. Short Trail is fairly level for its first quarter-mile then descends to a junction. Turn left here on the blue-blazed path, known as Long Path, which leads south on an easy walk past rocky outcroppings. After approximately half a mile, bear left at Junction 15, where Long Path leaves to the right. Swamp Trail soon curves to the left as it follows the edge of a wetland then crosses it on a short boardwalk.

After crossing another stream and passing a small pool on the right, follow the trail to the left at Junction 16. Watch for bright green six-spotted tiger beetles hopping around the trail's narrow sunlit openings. The path curves north and follows a contour along the hillside then winds to rejoin Wilson Mountain Trail, which comes down from the summit ridge at Junction 24. From here it's a short walk downhill to the parking area.

DID YOU KNOW?

The northern face of Wilson Mountain may remind people of forest more typical of northern New England than Massachusetts. Because this section does not receive the summer sun, it is cooler and moister than the mountain's other slopes. Yellow birches, white birches, and hemlocks thrive here.

MORE INFORMATION

The reservation is open year-round, seven days a week; there is no fee. There are no restrooms. Dogs are allowed on-leash; mountain biking is prohibited. For more information, call 617-698-1802 or visit mass.gov/dcr.

NEARBY

The historical area of Dedham Square is surrounded by majestic homes that date to the 1700s with lovely gardens and towering trees, perfect for a stroll. The square offers restaurants, cafes, and necessities.

11

STONY BROOK RESERVATION

This easy walk explores forests, rocky outcroppings, wetlands, and a scenic pond within Boston's city limits.

DIRECTIONS

From I-95, take Exit 17 for MA 135 toward Needham/Natick. At the exit, turn right on West Street toward Dedham. The road becomes Common Street then, in the center of Dedham, becomes High Street (still going straight, under a highway overpass). Take a slight right after the overpass to stay on High Street. After crossing Milton Street, High Street becomes Sawmill Lane as it crosses a bridge then becomes Dedham Boulevard, then Dedham Parkway. At its intersection with Turtle Pond Parkway and Enneking Parkway, go left onto Enneking and proceed 0.5 mile to the parking lot, which might be difficult to see. *GPS coordinates:* 42° 15.512′ N, 71° 08.154′ W.

By public transportation, take the MBTA Commuter Rail to Hyde Park Station. Walk 0.3 mile northwest on Gordon Avenue, turn left onto Enneking Parkway, and walk 0.4 mile until you reach the parking lot. You also can take the MBTA #40 bus from Forest Hills Station to the intersection of Turtle Pond Parkway and Enneking Parkway. From there, walk 0.2 mile east until you reach the parking lot.

TRAIL DESCRIPTION

Stony Brook Reservation is a 613-acre oasis of forests, wetlands, rocky outcroppings, and glacial drumlins nestled between Boston's West Roxbury and Hyde Park neighborhoods, constituting the largest open space within city limits. In spite of the reservation's location in Boston, you may enjoy a surprising degree of solitude. This hike makes a hairpin-shaped loop through the area on the east side

LOCATION
Boston, MA (near West Roxbury and Hyde Park)

RATING
Easy

DISTANCE
2.6 miles

ELEVATION GAIN
Minimal

ESTIMATED TIME
1.5 hours

MAPS
USGS Boston South; online: mass.gov/eea/docs/dcr/parks/trails/stonybrook.pdf

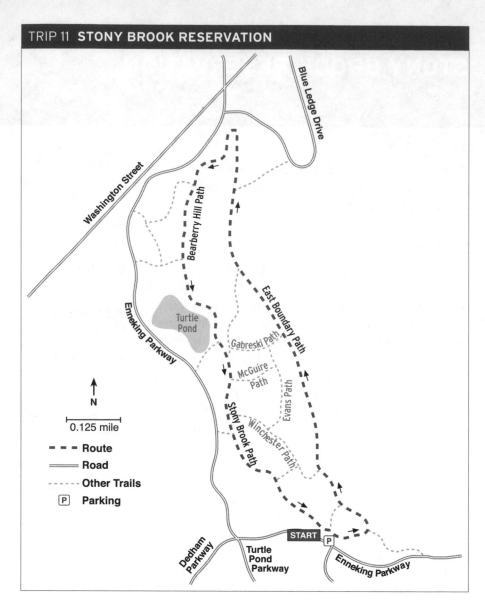

Turtle
Pond

Bearberry Hill Path

Washington Street

Blue Ledge Drive

East Boundary Path

Enneking Parkway

Gabreski Path

McGuire
Path

Evans Path

Stony Brook Path

Winchester Path

N

0.125 mile

- - - Route
—— Road
----- Other Trails
P Parking

START P

Dedham
Parkway

Turtle
Pond
Parkway

Enneking Parkway

of the Enneking Parkway, combining two of the paved recreational paths with footpaths and old cart roads.

From the parking area, walk past the light green gate and turn right on the paved recreation path. This blue-blazed trail soon passes through a field of boulders as it skirts a rocky outcropping known as Bold Knob. (An unmarked path here leads right to the reservation boundary.) The trail continues to the north, passing a wetland in the woods to the right. At a junction at marker 210, Winchester Path leaves left and connects to a series of short woodland trails. This walk, on East Boundary Path, continues along the recreational trail, which crosses a rocky

Stony Brook Reservation boasts 613 acres of forest, the largest open space within Boston's city limits.

seasonal brook then follows a fence along the edge of the George Wright Golf Course.

Areas where different habitats meet, such as the border of the forest and the golf course clearings, are beneficial for wildlife, as the "edge effect" allows opportunities both for foraging and protection, and you should scan these openings carefully for glimpses of coyotes, foxes, white-tailed deer, eastern cottontail rabbits, and wild turkeys. All of these species thrive in mixed habitats, and their populations have increased rapidly throughout New England as the region has become reforested and fewer of the animals are hunted.

The reservation is also home to a variety of birdlife. Recent surveys and bird counts by local groups indicate that at least 70 species are present at various times of the year. These expansive woodlands in the heart of a heavily developed area offer crucial habitat for migratory songbirds, which are most visible in midspring and early summer. Three of the most conspicuous are black-throated green warblers, red-eyed vireos, and ovenbirds.

At marker 240, the paved Stony Brook Path comes in from the left. This hike continues straight, along East Boundary Path, which passes through a large wetland. Here the animals you might encounter include minks and raccoons, both of which frequent the reservation's water bodies. Raccoons are much more tolerant of humans and are also often found in urban and suburban neighborhoods. Great blue and green herons; black, mallard, and wood ducks; and double-crested cormorants also live in the wetlands here.

East Boundary Path soon reaches its end at the reservation's boundary, near Enneking Parkway and Blue Ledge Drive. Just before the trail reaches gate 29, turn left on a narrow footpath at marker 250. At this point, you are 1.2 miles from the trailhead. The path winds beneath tall pines and oaks; crosses a rocky, partially open area; and slopes downhill to bear left again, near Enneking Parkway. From here, Bearberry Hill Path follows a wide, old cart road along the base of Bearberry Hill, a 246-foot drumlin that rises to your left. The hill is one of the higher points of the reservation, which features topography ranging from 15 feet above sea level to 338-foot Bellevue Hill. Bearberry is an evergreen shrub with tiny, white, bell-shaped flowers that bloom in May and June. It thrives in sandy and exposed rocky habitats.

Continue to follow the path straight through the next junction then bear left at marker 238 on a short side path that arcs to the north shore of Turtle Pond. Here a wooden fishing platform offers nice views and is an ideal spot for a break. Sunfish and perch are among the fish present in the pond.

From the pond, begin the last leg of the hike by following the trail past large rocky outcroppings, staying straight at junction 232 then going left at junction 230. When the trail ends at the next junction, turn right onto the paved, blue-blazed Stony Brook Path and follow it south toward the entrance. You'll pass junctions with several of the short forest trails and more rocky outcroppings.

Stony Brook Path continues to the southeast. After about 20 to 30 minutes of easy walking from Turtle Pond, you'll reach post 202, adjacent to the parking area. The green gate and your car will be on your right.

DID YOU KNOW?

At 338 feet, Bellevue Hill is the highest point in the city of Boston.

MORE INFORMATION

The reservation is open year-round from dawn to dusk. Dogs must be leashed. For further details, call 617-333-7404 or visit mass.gov/dcr for trail maps.

NEARBY

The southern tip of Stony Brook Reservation is home to a recreational area that includes tennis courts, baseball and soccer fields, picnic areas, an ice rink, and a swimming pool. There are restaurants on Hyde Park Avenue and on River Street in Cleary Square.

12

BLUE HILLS RESERVATION: OBSERVATION TOWER LOOP

A hike to Blue Hills' observation tower takes you through a variety of woodland terrain, with an outstanding view at the top.

DIRECTIONS

From I-93, take Exit 2B and follow MA 138 north 1 mile to the parking lot on the right, adjacent to the Trailside Museum. *GPS coordinates:* 42° 13.016′ N, 71° 07.165′ W.

By public transportation, take the MBTA Red Line to Ashmont Station then take the high-speed trolley line to Mattapan. From there, take the #716 bus to the Trailside Museum.

TRAIL DESCRIPTION

The 635-foot summit of Great Blue Hill is the highest point in the Blue Hills chain. From the observation tower at the top of the hill, there are sweeping views to Boston and beyond. Great Blue Hill lies at the western end of the Blue Hills Reservation. At its base is the Blue Hills Trailside Museum, operated by Mass Audubon. The trails here are popular on weekends, so plan accordingly. If you are hiking with young children, you might want to go only partway up the hill or reverse the walk and go up the gentler incline first. Another option is to walk up the paved Summit Road, which is closed to public vehicles (see trail map).

Begin your hike from the trailhead that starts at the parking lot just to the right of the Trailside Museum (as you face it from the street). There is a signboard, with red dots on trees marking the trail. This is the most direct route to the summit, and it rises steeply in some places. On your right are the open slopes of the Blue Hills Ski Area.

About fifteen minutes into the hike, you will cross a narrow trail and then the paved Summit Road. Proceed

LOCATION
Canton and Milton, MA

RATING
Moderate

DISTANCE
2 miles

ELEVATION GAIN
400 feet

ESTIMATED TIME
1.5 hours

MAPS
USGS Norwood; online: mass.gov/eea/docs/dcr/parks/trails/blue-hills-trail-map-2016.pdf

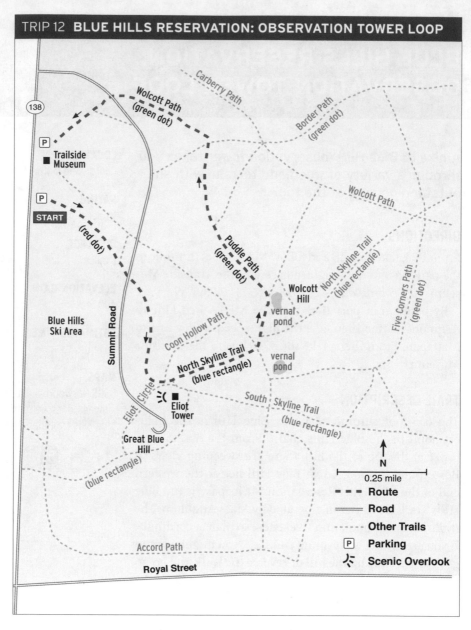

Carberry Path

Border Path
(green dot)

138

Wolcott Path
(green dot)

Wolcott Path

P

Trailside
Museum

P

START

(red dot)

Puddle Path
(green dot)

Wolcott
Hill

North Skyline Trail
(blue rectangle)

Five Corners Path
(green dot)

Blue Hills
Ski Area

Summit Road

Coon Hollow Path

vernal
pond

North Skyline Trail
(blue rectangle)

vernal
pond

Eliot Circle

Eliot
Tower

South Skyline Trail
(blue rectangle)

Great Blue
Hill

(blue rectangle)

N

0.25 mile

- - - Route
—— Road
---- Other Trails
P Parking
𐅂 Scenic Overlook

Accord Path

Royal Street

through an area of red pines. You can distinguish them from the more common white pines because their needles are thicker and a bit longer, and their bark is lighter, with a rusty hue. This portion of the trail has exposed granite ledges, and children will love the challenge of "mountain climbing." This is a great place to introduce kids to mountainous hikes without taxing their endurance. Be sure to stop every now and then after the first ten minutes of climbing, both to catch your breath and to admire the view of the Boston skyline over your shoulder. The birch growing in this rocky soil are mostly of the gray variety, which are among

The Eliot Tower provides sweeping views of Boston and the ocean beyond.

the first trees to colonize an area of poor soil or land where a fire has destroyed a more mature forest.

Continue to follow the red dots. After walking 0.6 mile from the trailhead, you will arrive at the summit's stone observation tower. The Eliot Tower is named for Charles Eliot, a famed landscape architect and lover of open spaces. There are two picnic benches beneath the shelter of the tower structure. Low-bush blueberries grow in sunny spots. In autumn, their scarlet leaves contrast nicely with the gray bedrock.

The summit of Great Blue Hill offers sweeping vistas of Boston and the ocean beyond, but the trees and hilltops in the foreground may capture your attention. From this vantage point you can see interesting patterns of tree species, particularly in fall, when the rust-colored oaks dominate, with patches of hemlock and white pine scattered about the hills.

The summit also provides a good spot for watching hawks during their spring and fall migrations. Early September is usually the best time for a successful hawk watch. Go on days when the wind is out of the north or west, as this helps propel the hawks (mostly broadwings) on their southerly journeys.

Although the most direct route back to the parking area is via another section of the red dot trail, called Coon Hollow Path, you may want a more gradual descent in a northwesterly direction. Follow North Skyline Trail (marked on a granite post), which begins near the back of the tower. The trail is marked by blue rectangles, but be aware that South Skyline Trail is also marked by blue rectangles. As you descend North Skyline Trail, you will have partial views of the surrounding hills, which will give you an appreciation for just how large the reservation is. The footing can be a bit tricky due to many small rocks and the trail's steepness.

Near the base of the hill, you will reach an intersection. Take the second left onto Puddle Path, which is marked by both blue rectangles and green dots. (Do not take the first hard left on the unmarked trail going uphill.) In 30 feet, the blue rectangle trail goes to the right, but you will stay straight on Puddle Path, following the green dots. In a couple of minutes, you will come to a fork in the trail. Go left, continuing to follow the green dots.

Puddle Path is a wide trail passing through an area of handsome beech trees. Even in the dead of winter, the lower branches are covered with paper-thin tan leaves, which do not fall off until new growth begins in spring. Follow the main trail straight past an unmarked trail on the right. Turn left here onto the wide Wolcott Path, ignoring the narrow trail on the left just before the "T" intersection. The trail then crosses the northern end of Summit Road and soon arrives at the north parking lot and the museum. Walk through the museum to return to your starting point at the south lot.

Outside the Trailside Museum is a water-filled pool and pen, which is home to a river otter. Spend some time here, as the otter puts on quite a show, diving beneath the water and rolling on the surface. Next to the otter pen are other areas for injured wildlife, such as deer, turkey, hawks, and owls. Inside the Trailside Museum, you'll find interpretive exhibits, such as a wigwam, and live animals, including a timber rattlesnake, a copperhead, and a snapping turtle.

Plan future visits to travel the trails to the east of Great Blue Hill. You might want to consider making an all-day hike with a friend, leaving one car at the opposite end of the reservation. Skyline Trail is approximately 9 miles long, and some hikers use this as a training ground to get in shape before climbing the White Mountains of New Hampshire.

DID YOU KNOW?

Founded in 1885, Blue Hill Meteorological Observatory is the source of the longest continuously recorded weather data in North America. Many pioneering weather discoveries have been made here, and it is an important resource in ongoing studies of climate change.

MORE INFORMATION

The Blue Hills are open year-round, dawn to dusk. There is no fee; dogs are allowed on-leash. For more information, contact DCR Blue Hills at 617-698-1802 or visit mass.gov/dcr. The Trailside Museum is open Friday to Sunday, 10 A.M. to 5 P.M.; there is an admission fee. Call 617-333-0690 or visit massaudubon.org. The museum schedule is subject to change.

NEARBY

The Neponset River Reservation protects a large natural estuary with extensive tidal marshes at its mouth and a complex of freshwater wetlands. Over the past century the state has acquired 750 acres of this watershed. There are several access points to the reservation, including Pope John Paul II Park on Gallivan Boulevard. A second entrance is located on Hallett Street.

AN URBAN OASIS

Blue Hills Reservation is a large oasis of forested land just a few miles from downtown Boston. There are 22 hills within the chain, the highest of which is 635-foot Great Blue Hill, followed by 517-foot Chickatawbut Hill, in the northern section of the reservation. In addition to the low wooded hills, the reservation encompasses a stretch of the Neponset River, the adjoining wetlands of Fowl Meadow, Ponkapoag and Houghton's ponds and several smaller ponds, and the Quincy Quarries Historic Site, now a popular rock-climbing destination.

For more than 10,000 years before Europeans arrived, the Massachusetts tribe of American Indians lived by the Blue Hills. The word "Massachusetts" means "people of the great hill." The area was ideally situated for the tribe due to its close proximity to the ocean and to the Neponset River, as well as its high vantage points and the presence of quarry materials (brown volcanic rock, or hornfels) used to make tools and weapons.

The Blue Hills received their present name from European explorers, who described the hills as having a bluish tint when observed from boats on the ocean. The colonists who subsequently settled in the area cleared much of the land for agriculture, built houses and barns, and cut the forests on the hills. In 1825, a large-scale quarry was established that produced granite for buildings, monuments, and fortifications across the nation. Today, sixteen individual sites within the reservation are listed on the National Register of Historic Places.

The windswept summit of Great Blue Hill is home to the Blue Hill Observatory, founded in 1885 by the meteorologist Abbott Lawrence Rotch as a private scientific center for weather-related experiments. The observatory is the oldest continuously operated weather station in the country and retains long-term data especially important to climate-change studies.

In 1893, the Metropolitan Parks Commission purchased the Blue Hills land to establish one of the first state parks in Massachusetts. Today the extensive woodlands offer habitat and travel corridors for large animals, such as white-tailed deer, red foxes, eastern coyotes, and raccoons. It is also home to many smaller creatures we sometimes overlook, including butterflies, dragonflies, salamanders, and both migratory and year-round birds.

13

BLUE HILLS RESERVATION: GREAT BLUE HILL GREEN LOOP

This loop meanders through the Great Blue Hill section of the reservation, following the cols between the hills without ascending any summits.

DIRECTIONS

From I-93, take Exit 2B and follow MA 138 north 1 mile to the parking lot on the right, adjacent to the Trailside Museum. *GPS coordinates:* 42° 13.016′ N, 71° 07.165′ W.

By public transportation, take the MBTA Red Line to Ashmont then take the high-speed trolley line to Mattapan. From there, take the #716 bus to the Trailside Museum.

TRAIL DESCRIPTION

The Green Loop offers a pleasant, fairly easy walk for hikers who wish to explore the western portion of the Blue Hills Reservation without climbing any of the hills. The route begins at the north parking lot next to the Blue Hills Trailside Museum, at the base of Great Blue Hill, and follows a series of trails that wind through the reservation's extensive forests and past wetlands and rocky outcroppings. From the trailhead at the parking lot, follow the green blazes northeast. The trail crosses the paved access road that leads to Great Blue Hill's summit then joins Wolcott Path and continues beneath white pine, oak, and maple trees. A field is visible through the trees to the left.

At junction 1085, the loop proper begins. Here Puddle Path, the return route, comes in from the right. Continue straight on Wolcott Path for a few hundred feet to marker 1100 then turn left onto Border Path. Smooth, easy Border Path leads northeast through the woods and crosses Balster Brook at the outlet of a wetland. Stay straight at

LOCATION
Canton and Milton, MA

RATING
Easy to Moderate

DISTANCE
2.8 miles

ELEVATION GAIN
200 feet

ESTIMATED TIME
1.5 hours

MAPS
USGS Norwood; online: mass
.gov/eea/docs/dcr/parks/trails/
blue-hills-trail-map-2016.pdf

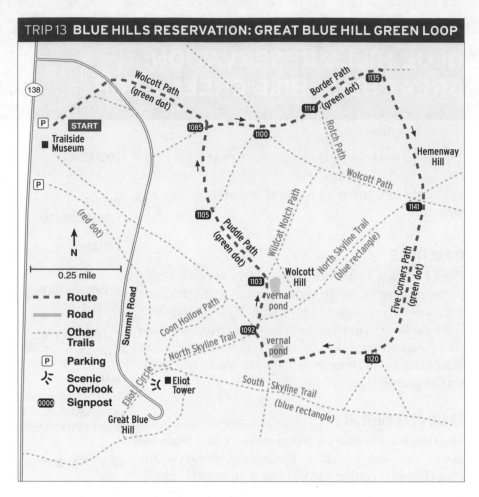

a fork at marker 1114 when Rotch Path branches to the right. The trail slopes downhill to another stream crossing.

This is a relatively quiet corner of the reservation and a good place to watch for a variety of wildlife. The Blue Hills wetlands are home to seven species of turtles. The most common are painted turtles, which are often observed basking on logs, rocks, and aquatic vegetation during warm months. Also present are much larger snapping turtles, which have a powerful bite. Less common species include spotted, box, musk, Blanding's, and wood turtles. Visit in the early morning or evening, and you may glimpse a white-tailed deer or a red fox.

You'll soon arrive at a four-way junction (marker 1135). Turn right here off of Border Path and follow the green-blazed trail, which continues southwest through the col between Wolcott Hill, rising to your right, and Hemenway Hill, on the left. After walking 0.4 mile from Border Path, you'll reach a six-way junction of the reservation's trails, including North Skyline Trail (which leads to the summits of nearby Great Blue Hill and Wolcott Hill to the west, Hancock Hill to the east), at marker 1141. A map is posted at this intersection. The Green

Loop continues straight here on Five Corners Path and leads south for 0.3 mile along the base of Wolcott Hill, which rises to the west.

At marker 1120, turn right and begin an easy climb past a series of glacial boulders on the south slopes of Wolcott Hill. These rocks were deposited by melting glaciers at the end of the most recent ice age, more than 10,000 years ago. The antenna atop Great Blue Hill comes into view a short distance west of Wolcott Hill.

The trail bears right at a junction near a small wetland then right again at nearby marker 1092. You're now heading north on Wildcat Notch Path, which leads through the narrow valley between the eastern slopes of Great Blue Hill and the west side of Wolcott Hill. After passing another small pond, where you may see birds such as robins, blue jays, and tufted titmice drinking or bathing, bear left at marker 1103 onto Puddle Path. Puddle Path continues straight (left) at marker 1105 and slopes gently downhill to close the loop where it meets Wolcott Path. Turn left here and retrace your steps to the Trailside Museum parking area, following the green blazes.

DID YOU KNOW

Six of our native species of turtle are threatened or endangered, including the box turtle, the bog turtle, and the red-bellied cooter. They've lost habitat to development and are often struck by cars when trying to cross roads.

An otter grooms in the outdoor exhibit at the Blue Hills Trailside Museum. River otters' thick fur traps a layer of air next to the skin—insulation that allows the otter to swim in winter.

MORE INFORMATION

Blue Hills Reservation is open year-round from dawn until dusk. For more information, visit mass.gov/dcr or call 617-698-1802. Trail information and maps ($3) are available at the Trailside Museum, as well as at the reservation headquarters at 695 Hillside Street in Milton, behind the state police station.

Mass Audubon operates two educational facilities within the reservation. The Trailside Museum is open to the public Friday to Sunday, 10 A.M. to 5 P.M.; there is an admission fee. Call 617-333-0690 or visit massaudubon.org. Chickatawbut Hill Education Center offers workshops and programs for organized groups by reservation only.

NEARBY

The Forbes House Museum on Adams Street in Milton preserves the home of Captain Robert Bennet Forbes, a member of one of the prominent families involved in maritime sailing and trading during the nineteenth century. It is open for tours on Sundays and Thursdays. Restaurants are located along Adams Street in Milton and Hancock Street in the center of Quincy.

14

BLUE HILLS RESERVATION: PONKAPOAG POND

A short hike to a quaking bog via Maple Avenue gives you a chance to see rare plant species, while the pond loop offers a longer outing.

DIRECTIONS

From I-93 take Exit 2A for Washington Street in Canton. Turn left just before the first set of lights into the golf course parking lot. Signs lead you directly to the reservation. *GPS coordinates:* 42° 11.514′ N, 71° 06.997′ W.

By public transportation, take the MBTA Red Line to Ashmont then take the high speed trolley line to Mattapan. From there, take the #716 bus to the Ponkapoag Golf Course.

TRAIL DESCRIPTION

Due to its location near I-93, Ponkapoag Pond is a popular hiking and cross-country skiing destination. If you come on a weekday, however, the reservation is usually free of people, even after work hours. The main trail loops 200-acre Ponkapoag Pond and a regionally uncommon Atlantic white cedar swamp located on the property's northwest side. The pond attracts all sorts of wildlife, including ospreys and great blue herons.

From the golf course parking lot on the right side of the buildings, look for a paved road that passes through the fairways (no cars allowed). It is easy to spot the entrance to this road thanks to the row of stately sugar maples lining it. Appropriately enough, the road is called Maple Avenue. Walk down this road, through the golf course, and to the edge of Ponkapoag Pond. The paved road ends here, and a wide, well-maintained dirt trail circles the pond. If you go left, you can reach the quaking bog in about 0.5 mile—a good ramble if you are with young

LOCATION
Canton, MA

RATING
Easy

DISTANCE
4 miles (around the pond)

ELEVATION GAIN
Minimal

ESTIMATED TIME
2 hours

MAPS
USGS Norwood; online: mass
.gov/eea/docs/dcr/parks/trails/
blue-hills-trail-map-2016.pdf

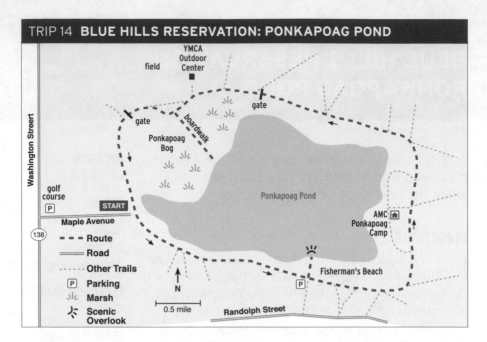

Map legend:
- - - - Route
——— Road
- - - - - Other Trails
P Parking
⚜ Marsh
⚟ Scenic Overlook

children. The floating boardwalk leading into the bog begins opposite a field and some cabins operated by the YMCA.

The following directions take you completely around the pond. At the end of Maple Avenue, go right onto the dirt road. The trail hugs the edge of the pond, offering plenty of spots to reach the shoreline. A little more than 0.5 mile down the trail is an open area with a nice view of the Blue Hills across the water. The road opposite the beach leads to Randolph Street. This entrance is known as Fisherman's Beach. Cartop boats can be carried down the path and launched here. (The entrance off Randolph Street is right next to Temple Beth David, across the street from Westdale Road.)

The first mile of the pond trail has rich, moist soil. Trees commonly associated with more northern forests—yellow birch, hemlock, maple, beech—grow above the ferns. Although the trees are quite large, most of them are probably less than 100 years old. As in much of Massachusetts, settlers here cleared the forests for pastures and farmland, using the wood for lumber and fuel.

Along the trail, look for skunk cabbage, one of the first harbingers of spring. It has large, cabbagelike leaves and sometimes grows right through late-season snow. It has an odor quite similar to a skunk's. During the summer months, the aroma of skunk cabbage along the trail is replaced by the pleasant fragrance of sweet pepperbush. You can identify this plant by the clusters of tiny white flowers growing in dense, slender spikes at the ends of its branches. The plant can reach a height of 10 feet and has narrow green leaves.

Great blue herons frequent the pond, thanks to the abundance of warm-water fish. Both herons and anglers try their skill at catching largemouth bass and pickerel, but the heron tend to fish for those smaller than 5 inches.

Shore-bound anglers have the best chance of catching fish in spring, when the fish are seeking warm, shallow water for spawning and feeding. Osprey occasionally stop at the pond, so if you're visiting during their spring or fall migration, be sure to bring binoculars. The sight of an osprey diving from the sky to snatch a fish with its talons is one you will never forget. Red-winged blackbirds also descend upon the pond, and in springtime, you can see the red-shouldered males arrive first in huge flocks. They explore the entire shore-line as they wait for female birds. Mosquitoes also inhabit the reservation, so come prepared.

As the trail passes around the back of the pond, green-dot markers attached to trees help guide you. You'll pass a group of cottages on the left managed by the Appalachian Mountain Club; to stay on the trail, keep to the right at all junctions leading toward the cabins. (Feel free to take a detour for a closer look. AMC's Ponkapoag Camp features twenty cabins and a limited number of seasonal tentsites available for those who wish to extend their hike to an overnight. Visit outdoors.org for more information and to request a reservation.) At the third trail junction, go down a small hill where a map is posted. Soon the trail intersects with another; go left, following the green markers. Finally, turn left again when you come to a gate. You are now at the north side of the pond. The YMCA Outdoor Center is located a little farther down the trail. The boardwalk to the bog is opposite the field.

The bog has been designated a National Environmental Study Area due to its uncommon ecosystem. A beautiful stand of Atlantic white cedar grows here along with the unusual pitcher plant. Because the nutrients in the bog soil are limited, pitcher plants and other carnivorous plants, such as the sun-dew, obtain their nourishment from insects. While many people are familiar with the Venus flytrap (indigenous to the southeastern United States), which captures its prey by snapping shut over them, the bog plants of the Northeast use a different method of entrapment. The pitcher plant attracts insects onto its leaves with its scent and colorful veins. Once the insect touches down, it has a hard time escaping. Tiny hairs in the plant point downward, trapping the insect and drowning it in the liquid at the bottom of the pitcher, after which the plant's enzymes digest the insect. To identify the plant, usually 1 to 2 feet tall, look for its pitcher-shaped, reddish-green leaves. In summer, it will have a large, solitary, purplish-red flower on a leafless stalk.

The boardwalk starts out in a dense jungle of swamp maples and other trees before it reaches the white cedars, finally penetrating the more open area of the bog, which is dominated by leather leaf. In summer, you will see the pink flowers (about a half-inch wide) of sheep laurel. The sheep laurel grows between 1 and 3 feet tall and looks similar to the more common mountain laurel. It thrives in bog areas and is expanding its range at Ponkapoag as the bog expands. Each year, the pond becomes shallower as vegetation closes its ring around the pond. There are no underground streams and few springs to

Ponkapoag Pond, a popular hiking destination in the Blue Hills, features a regionally uncommon Atlantic white cedar swamp. Photo by Jennifer Wehunt.

replenish and oxygenate the water. Sphagnum moss flourishes in the stagnant water of the bog, and as it dies, it fills the pond.

Once you are finished exploring the bog, retrace your steps along the boardwalk to the main path by the YMCA Outdoor Center and go left. It's only a short walk (about 0.5 mile) down the main trail to reach the golf course and then Maple Avenue, which will lead to the parking area.

DID YOU KNOW?

Ponkapoag Pond is not a natural pond; it was formed in 1940 by the construction of a 1,300-foot earthen gravity dam.

MORE INFORMATION

Blue Hills Reservation is open year-round, dawn to dusk; there is no fee. There are no restrooms. Dogs are allowed on-leash. For more information, contact DCR Blue Hills at 617-698-1802 or visit mass.gov/dcr.

AMC's Ponkapoag Camp, on the eastern shore of Ponkapoag Pond, rents cabins and tentsites for overnights. Reservations are required; contact AMC at 617-523-0655 or visit outdoors.org/lodging for more information.

NEARBY

Mass Audubon's Visual Arts Center, located at 963 Washington Street in Canton, houses collections of natural-history photography and art, and offers related programs and exhibitions. The grounds are also home to the Mildred Morse Allen Wildlife Sanctuary, where trails explore forests, a red maple swamp, and meadows. There are restaurants in Canton on Washington Street and along MA 27.

15

BLUE HILLS RESERVATION: HOUGHTON'S POND YELLOW DOT LOOP

This easy, 1-mile pond loop is a popular walk for families with small children.

DIRECTIONS

Take I-93 to Exit 3 (Houghton's Pond). At the end of Blue Hill River Road, turn right onto Hillside Street and follow it 0.3 mile until you reach the parking lot on your right. *GPS coordinates: 42° 12.579′ N, 71° 05.826′ W.*

By public transportation, take the MBTA Red Line to Ashmont and then take the high-speed trolley line to Mattapan. From there, take the #716 bus to the intersection of Washington Street and Royall Street. Walk 1.2 miles east on Blue Hill River Road, which will turn into Hillside Street along your walk.

TRAIL DESCRIPTION

One of the attractions of the Blue Hills Reservation is its wide variety of hiking trails, with options ranging from challenging, full-day traverses to pleasant, easy strolls through quiet woodlands and around scenic ponds. One of the reservation's most popular destinations is Houghton's Pond, a small pond nestled at the base of the southern slopes of the Blue Hills chain. It is a short distance east of Great Blue Hill and north of the much larger Ponkapoag Pond.

The easy loop trail encircling Houghton's Pond is especially good for families with young children. It is just long enough to feel like a real outing, and there are continuous views across the water to hold kids' attention. Although the trail intersects with a number of other footpaths and dirt roads (closed to vehicles), it is easy to follow, as it is well marked with yellow dots. The trail is 1 mile long and can be completed in half an hour or less.

LOCATION
Milton, MA

RATING
Easy

DISTANCE
1 mile

ELEVATION GAIN
Minimal

ESTIMATED TIME
30 minutes

MAPS
USGS Norwood, online: mass.gov/eea/docs/dcr/parks/trails/blue-hills-trail-map-2016.pdf

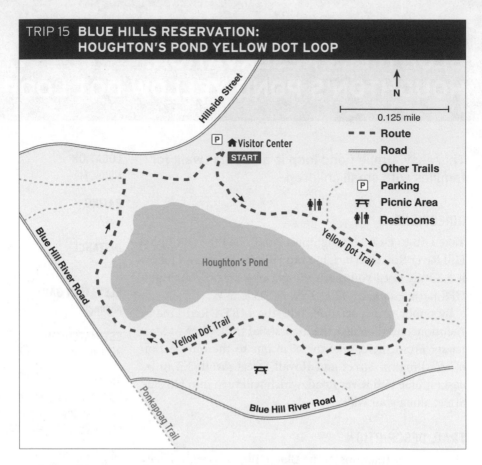

The trail begins at the main parking lot for the Houghton's Pond swimming area, off Hillside Street. Follow the path to the left, which leads east past the swimming beach on the pond's north shore, bearing right just after the bathhouse. A dirt road branches to the left and leads north toward the Bugbee Path and the Skyline Trail just east of Houghton Hill.

The path turns to the right to follow the pond's narrow eastern tip, where it briefly follows a dirt service road then continues west along the south shore, passing a picnic area. Great Blue Hill, the highest point in the Blue Hills Reservation, rises across the water to the west, and pine trees line the shore.

This trail is a great place to introduce children to some of the common wildlife we often take for granted. One of the most familiar creatures in these woodlands is the eastern chipmunk, which is most active during summer and fall, gathering food to store for the colder winter months. The chipmunks' metabolism slows during winter, and they go into a torporlike state in which they are mostly asleep, waking up periodically to feed on the food they have cached in storage areas. Chipmunks' varied diet includes fruits, nuts, seeds, insects, small rodents, and even snakes. In turn, they are an important prey species for predators, such as coyotes, foxes, and bobcats.

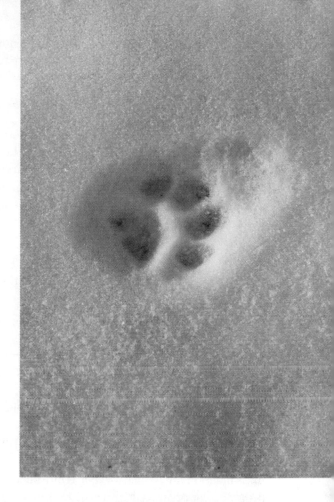

Houghton's Pond is a perfect day hike for families with dogs and young children. In summer, it's a popular swimming destination. Watch for animal tracks in winter.

One of the birds you may see on the pond is the double-crested cormorant, which is easily distinguished by its long, thin neck and black color. Although cormorants are now a familiar sight along New England's coast, they were largely eliminated from the region as recently as the early twentieth century. In Massachusetts, they were absent from the early nineteenth century until the 1940s, when breeding pairs were noted in the Boston area. Many commercial fishers once considered cormorants a threat to their livelihood—not for the volume of fish they ate but because they often broke up schools of fish at key fishing areas, diving and jumping into the water on their hunting rounds. Thanks to their adaptability, cormorants have strongly rebounded and are now seen even on some inland lakes.

Spring is an excellent time to watch for migratory waterfowl and songbirds. Due to the reservation's proximity to the coast and its concentration of forest in a heavily developed area, it is an important stopover point for birds flying long distances. Some of the colorful songbirds you may see or hear include pine warblers, scarlet tanagers, chestnut-sided warblers, and American redstarts.

The pond is a popular fishing area, and as you walk along the south shore, you'll probably pass several anglers. Fishers who frequent the pond report that it's a good place to catch trout, especially after the pond has been stocked. Other species include sunfish, perch, bass, pickerel, and carp. Fishing is allowed from the shore only.

The trail curves to the right around the pond's southwest corner, near Blue Hill River Road, where there are good views across the water to the east. From there, the trail crosses the pond's outlet and leads north past a field. You'll pass through a small swampy area at the pond's northwest tip, near Hillside Street. Complete the outing with a short walk east past a pavilion to the entrance and parking area. An interpretive sign marks a tree that was struck and damaged by lightning during a thunderstorm.

DID YOU KNOW

Many features of the Blue Hills, including the Eliot Tower, trails, and bridges, were constructed by the Civilian Conservation Corps in the mid-1930s. The workers, mostly veterans of World War I who had trouble finding employment during the Depression, lived in a rustic camp off MA 28 in Randolph. The site is marked by a piece of granite.

NEARBY

Convenience stores, a restaurant, and gas stations can be found on MA 138 near the intersection of Blue Hill River Road.

MORE INFORMATION

Blue Hills Reservation is open year-round from dawn until dusk. For more information, visit mass.gov/dcr or call 617-698-1802. Trail information and maps are available for $3 at the Trailside Museum, as well as at the reservation headquarters at 695 Hillside Street in Milton, behind the state police station. Mass Audubon operates two educational facilities within the reservation. The Trailside Museum on MA 138, 0.5 mile north of I-93, is open to the public Friday to Sunday, 10 A.M. to 5 P.M.; there is an admission fee. Call 617-333-0690 or visit massaudubon.org. Chickatawbut Hill Education Center offers workshops and programs for organized groups by reservation only.

16

BLUE HILLS RESERVATION: SKYLINE TRAIL

This trail is the longest in the Blue Hills, extending from Fowl Meadow in Canton east to Shea Rink on Willard Street in Quincy.

DIRECTIONS

Take I-93 to Exit 3 (Houghton's Pond). Go north onto Ponkapoag Trail, which becomes Blue Hill River Road, for 0.5 mile, then turn right onto Hillside Street and continue 0.7 mile to the reservation headquarters. *GPS coordinates:* 42° 12.820′ N, 71° 05.613′ W.

By public transportation, take the MBTA Red Line to Ashmont then take the high-speed trolley line to Mattapan. From there, take the #716 bus to the intersection of Washington Street and Royall Street. Walk 1.5 miles east on Blue Hill River Road, which will turn into Hillside Street along your walk.

TRAIL DESCRIPTION

For those looking for a true long-distance hiking experience within a few miles of downtown Boston, the Skyline Trail makes a 9-mile, east–west traverse of Blue Hills Reservation, passing over most of the major hills along the way. For much of its length, it is a one-way route, but from the summit of Great Blue Hill to Hillside Road, it splits into two branches, called the North Skyline Trail and the South Skyline Trail.

The Skyline Trail can be reached from any of the following streets: MA 138, at a parking lot on the west side, about 0.5 mile south of Mass Audubon's Blue Hills Trailside Museum; Hillside Street, at the reservation headquarters; Randolph Avenue (MA 28), where the closest parking is about 0.25 mile south of the trail crossing; and Willard Street, at the trail terminus at Shea Rink. You can also park at the Trailside Museum and follow the Red Trail (see

LOCATION
Canton, Milton, and Quincy, MA

RATING
Strenuous

DISTANCE
9 miles (full traverse); 2.4 miles (North and South Skyline trails loop)

ELEVATION GAIN
Approximately 700 feet cumulative, North and South Skyline trails loop

ESTIMATED TIME
6 hours (full traverse); 1.75 hours (North and South Skyline trails loop)

MAPS
USGS Norwood; online: mass .gov/eea/docs/dcr/parks/trails /blue-hills-trail-map-2016.pdf

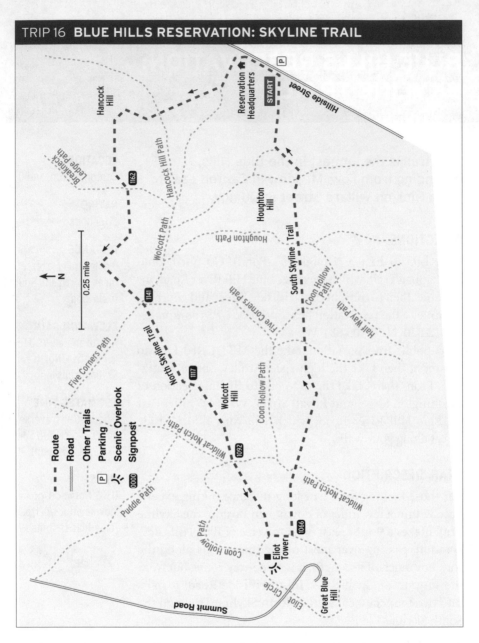

Trip 12) to the summit of Great Blue Hill then pick up either the North or South Skyline trail there. You should choose your route based on whether you can get a car pickup at some point on the trail, whether you have the time and energy for backtracking (one option is to follow some of the easier trails on the way out or back), or whether you need to return to your car.

For those looking for a shorter sampling that doesn't require backtracking or spotting cars at trailheads, the hike described here starts at the reservation headquarters on Hillside Street. It combines the north and south spurs of the

Skyline Trail to create a loop that includes the summit of Great Blue Hill, the reservation's highest point.

From the parking area of reservation headquarters, follow the North Skyline Trail, which makes a 0.25-mile beeline to the top of 510-foot Hancock Hill to the northwest. There are fine views from a ledge on the right, just below the summit. From the hilltop, continue to follow the light blue blazes. The trail descends to the west over rocky ground and crosses Breakneck Ledge Path at marker 1162. It then turns to the southwest as it descends a shoulder of Hemenway Hill.

You'll soon reach a six-way intersection at marker 1141, where the trail crosses Five Corners Path and Wolcott Path. A map is posted at this junction. Continue to follow the blue blazes straight across the junction. The trail then climbs out of the hollow and follows the ridge of Wolcott Hill. Stay straight at marker 1117, where a short side trail descends to Wildcat Notch in the valley between Great Blue and Wolcott hills. A short distance ahead is Wolcott Hill's 470-foot summit.

From Wolcott Hill, follow North Skyline Trail as it descends to Wildcat Notch, where it crosses Wildcat Notch Path at marker 1092. The trail then begins a rocky ascent up the northeast slopes of Great Blue Hill. After a steep but short climb, you'll reach the top of the hill near Eliot Tower and a stone bridge. There are fine views from the tower.

The return leg of this loop follows South Skyline Trail, which begins approximately 200 yards south of the stone bridge, at marker 1066. This trail, which is also well marked with light blue blazes, leads due east as it descends the eastern slopes of Great Blue Hill. You'll pass ledges offering fine views to the south and east across the reservation. The trail will lead you along a steep, rocky descent

This hike offers a true long-distance option within a few miles of downtown Boston. Skyline Trail's 9-mile, east-west traverse of the Blue Hills Reservation is a strenuous hike with fantastic views.

over Shadow Cliff. It then briefly follows a seasonal brook before crossing it at two large boulders. Continue to follow the blue blazes straight (east) at a junction with the southern portion of Five Corners Path.

After crossing Houghton Path, the trail leads up the western slopes of Houghton Hill then crosses the top of the hill just south of the summit. From here, complete the walk by descending the steep eastern slopes of Houghton Hill. The trail reaches Hillside Street approximately 200 yards south of the trailhead for North Skyline Trail. Turn left onto Hillside Street and walk north to the reservation headquarters and parking area.

DID YOU KNOW?

The Boston skyline is visible to the north on clear days. The tallest building in the city is the 790-foot, 60-story, glass-covered 200 Clarendon (formerly the John Hancock Tower) and the second-tallest building is a few blocks east, the 749-foot Prudential Tower. They are west of the cluster of buildings in downtown Boston, separated from them by the open spaces of Boston Common and the Public Garden.

MORE INFORMATION

Blue Hills Reservation is open year-round from dawn until dusk. For more information, visit mass.gov/dcr or call 617-698-1802. Trail information and maps are available for $3 at the Trailside Museum, as well as at the reservation headquarters at 695 Hillside Street, Milton, behind the state police station.

Mass Audubon operates two educational facilities within the reservation. The Trailside Museum on MA 138, 0.5 mile north of I-93, is open to the public Friday to Sunday, 10 A.M. to 5 P.M.; there is an admission fee. Call 617-333-0690 or visit massaudubon.org. Chickatawbut Hill Education Center offers workshops and programs for organized groups by reservation only. AMC's Ponkapoag Camp, on the eastern shore of Ponkapoag Pond, has cabins and seasonal tentsites available for overnights. Reservations are required; call 617-523-0655 or visit outdoors.org /lodging for more information.

NEARBY

The Adams National Historical Park on 135 Adams Street, in Quincy, is home to the birthplaces of presidents John Adams and John Quincy Adams, as well as the Stone Library, which has nearly 15,000 historical volumes. The U.S. Naval Ship Building Museum, on 739 Washington Street in Quincy, includes exhibits onboard the U.S.S. *Salem,* the world's only preserved heavy cruiser. There are many restaurants in Quincy on Hancock Street.

ENDANGERED PREDATOR: EASTERN TIMBER RATTLESNAKE

Eastern timber rattlesnakes are believed to have been widespread throughout eastern Massachusetts and the rest of New England during pre-Colonial times. Today, however, rattlesnakes inhabit only a handful of sites in Massachusetts, making them an endangered species protected by law. "Rattlers" are identified by a triangular head and a rattle at the end of the tail that makes a buzzing sound when vibrated. Body color ranges from yellow-brown to almost black, with dark, "V"-shaped bands across the back.

Because other dangerous creatures, such as mountain lions and wolves, have long been extirpated from New England, many people are surprised to find that poisonous rattlesnakes and copperheads still exist in the region. While both species have been decimated by habitat loss, hunting, and gathering by collectors, isolated populations remain in Massachusetts, Connecticut, Vermont, and New Hampshire. In Massachusetts, they are present in the Blue Hills, in the southern Berkshire Hills, and in Hampden County. A 2016 proposal to reintroduce rattlesnakes to an island in Quabbin Reservoir is now the subject of considerable debate in Massachusetts. State wildlife officials had planned to start a small colony of the endangered reptiles in a remote area, but residents objected, leaving the proposal in limbo as this guide went to press.

Ideal rattlesnake habitat includes isolated, south-facing hillsides; ridges; and rocky outcroppings that are surrounded by dense forest. This combination provides them with protected den sites as well as access to prey, such as mice, voles, shrew, rabbits, squirrels, chipmunks, and other small animals and birds. Rattlers are active from mid-spring into October and hibernate during winter. They usually bask during daytime and hunt at night, although they are more active during the day in cooler weather.

Because rattlesnakes and copperheads inhabit secluded areas and are able to hear approaching footsteps from a long distance away, hikers will rarely encounter them by chance on the trail. In the unlikely event you come across one while hiking, stop and back away slowly. In very rare instances, threatened poisonous snakes can deliver bites that, though not fatal, can cause physical damage. If you are bitten, remain calm and as still as possible to avoid spreading the venom. If you must move, limit the motion of the bitten limb and seek medical assistance as soon as possible.

Some nonvenomous Massachusetts snakes are often mistakenly believed to be poisonous. Milk snakes, which have a body size and color pattern similar to that of copperheads, shake their tails like rattlesnakes as a threatening gesture. Northern water snakes, which are relatively large, are regularly seen in wetlands.

NORTH OF BOSTON

The region north of Boston extending to the New Hampshire border includes the North Shore and adjacent inland communities. The topography is relatively gentle here, with no significant summits. There are, however, several low hills and drumlins (large mounds of debris left by re-

treating glaciers) that offer sweeping vistas, such as Ward Hill in Andover, where a hilltop meadow offers views to Boston and the Blue Hills. On nearby Weir Hill in North Andover, you can see Wachusett Mountain, Mount Monadnock, and the Wapack Mountains of southern New Hampshire.

Unlike in southeastern Massachusetts, where harsh soils support extensive pitch-pine and scrub oak woodlands, the forests here are predominantly of the oak-hickory type characteristic of much of southern New England. There are a few scattered groves of pitch pine and scrub oak along the North Shore, the largest of which is at Crane Beach.

Although suburbanization extending from Boston has led to development pressure, many of the inland communities have retained their rural character. At Appleton Farms in Hamilton, Bradley Palmer State Park in Hamilton and Topsfield, and Bald Hill in Boxford, trails wind through old farm fields and past building sites that offer a glimpse into the region's past, when much of the land was cleared for agriculture. The nearby Ipswich River Wildlife Sanctuary encompasses a cluster of wetlands along the Ipswich River, a short distance from the river's mouth.

Along the North Shore a series of coastal preserves comprise a variety of natural communities, some of which are uncommon. At the tip of Cape Ann—a small promontory that juts along the northern tip of Massachusetts Bay—is Halibut Point, home to rocky bluffs similar to those found in coastal Down East Maine. The point offers excellent tide pool habitat and is a good place to spot

Facing page: Snowy owls have been seen north of Boston recently due to an increased lemming population. Unlike other owls, snowy owls are not nocturnal and can be seen hunting any time of day or night.

wintering seabirds. There are views along the coast north to Mount Agamenticus in Maine. A rare magnolia swamp and rocky outcroppings are found at nearby Ravenswood Park in Gloucester.

A short distance north of Cape Ann is Castle Neck, a narrow slice of white-sand beach and dunes that extends between Castle Neck River and the Atlantic Ocean. Endangered piping plovers nest on the beaches, which are part of the Crane Beach Reservation.

Offshore from Newburyport near the New Hampshire border lies Plum Island, a 7-mile-long barrier island at the mouth of the Parker and Merrimack rivers. The bulk of the island lies within the Parker River National Wildlife Refuge, and its location and varied natural habitats make it one of the finest bird-watching locations along the eastern seaboard. During migration periods, it serves as a crucial rest area for great numbers of shorebirds, wading birds, songbirds, and raptors. The refuge and Castle Neck are part of the 25,000-acre Great Marsh, New England's largest salt marsh ecosystem.

17

WEIR HILL RESERVATION

This peaceful walk leads to scenic views along the shores of Lake Cochichewick and a meadow atop Weir Hill.

DIRECTIONS

From I-495, take Exit 42A and follow MA 114 east into North Andover for 1 mile. Turn left onto MA 133 east and continue 0.2 mile. At the traffic light, continue straight on Andover Street for 0.8 mile. At the traffic circle, continue straight on Great Pond Road then turn left onto Stevens Street and continue 0.8 mile to the entrance and parking on the right. *GPS coordinates:* 42° 41.839′ N, 71° 06.654′ W.

TRAIL DESCRIPTION

Weir Hill Reservation combines the best of woodlands, fields, and water. Hikers are treated to views not only from the hilltop but also from the shores of beautiful Lake Cochichewick, a water-supply reservoir. In 1715 settlers divided Weir Hill, establishing a series of farms along its slopes. The hill was cleared and used for sheep pastures. Although the forests have grown back, legacies of the property's agricultural past include miles of stone walls and scattered red cedar trees, which grew out of the abandoned fields. A handful of clearings are maintained throughout the reservation, including the meadow atop Weir Hill, where there are views west to the mountains of central New England.

From the parking area, take the wide main path, heading in a northeasterly direction, and turn right onto Stevens Trail at the first junction. (The return part of the loop is on the left.) A slow and steady climb takes you beneath huge oaks. After 1,500 feet, you will enter an upland meadow with magnificent views across the Merrimack River Valley to the west, including Wachusett Mountain, the Wapack Mountain ridge, and Mount Monadnock on the horizon.

LOCATION
North Andover, MA

RATING
Moderate

DISTANCE
2.3 miles

ELEVATION GAIN
170 feet

ESTIMATED TIME
1.5 hours

MAPS
USGS Lawrence; online: thetrustees.org/assets/documents/places-to-visit/trailmaps/Weir-Hill-Trail-Map .pdf

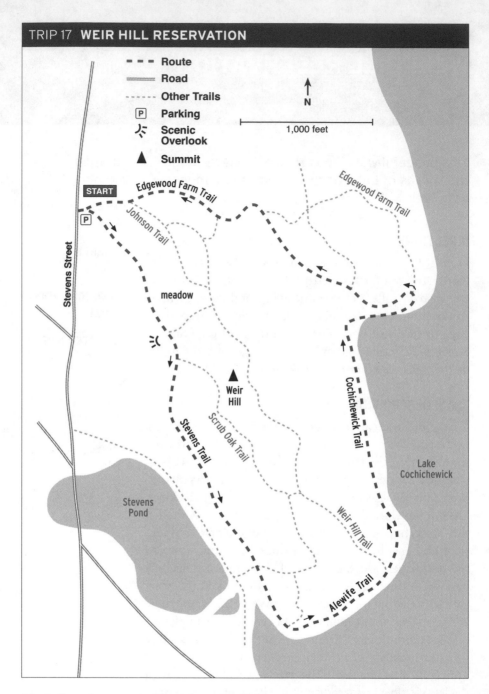

The hill you're on is a glacial drumlin that rises 300 feet above the surrounding countryside. Weir Hill, located a few hundred yards to the south, is roughly the same size. Walk the perimeter of the reservation by continuing on Stevens Trail southward toward Lake Cochichewick, a 2.5- to 3-mile walk.

After leaving the meadow, continue on Stevens Trail as it heads down the south side of the drumlin. From the meadow vista, walk 0.5 mile along Stevens Trail until it brings you to a strip of land that separates Stevens Pond from Lake Cochichewick. There is an interesting stone arch bridge at this spot. (To stay on Stevens Trail, bear left and do not cross the strip of land separating the bodies of water.)

As Stevens Trail passes Lake Cochichewick, its name changes to Alewife Trail. This quiet, peaceful walk by the banks of the lake is especially appealing in spring, when the shadbush blooms with white flowers.

One of the interesting features of this reservation is the difference in tree species between its east and west sides. The west side tends to be warmer and drier from the sun, while the east side stays cooler, with more moisture from the lake. You will notice a combination of oak and pitch pine along the western Stevens Trail, while on the east side are maple, beech, aspen, white pine, white birch, and shagbark hickory. The fruit of these trees, especially hickory and beech, provides food for a variety of animals that live on the reservation, including ruffed grouse, opossum, and raccoon.

In an eighth of a mile, the perimeter loop trail along the edge of the lake changes its name once again to Cochichewick Trail. After curving right to follow a small promontory, Cochichewick Trail intersects with a wider trail/dirt road; look for an old foundation on the shoreline. Go left, following this road as

The top of Weir Hill delivers an idyllic view of New England countryside.

it angles back, gradually climbing uphill and away from the water. You will pass an impressive stand of large white birch on your right.

Like many parts of New England, the land around Weir Hill at one time was open meadow, allowing sheep and cattle to graze. The settlers of North Andover began clearing the virgin forests in the seventeenth century. Their axes and saws were busy throughout the state, and today only small, scattered stands of old-growth timber remain, including groves in the Berkshire Hills and on Wachusett Mountain.

Stay left where the dirt road forks about 600 feet ahead. Just before the trail reaches the reservation boundary, turn left onto Edgewood Farm Trail, which passes over a wooden footbridge and beneath tall pines as it completes the loop. Backtrack to the parking area from the junction.

DID YOU KNOW?

Weir Hill Reservation got its name from the fish weirs American Indians once constructed in nearby Cochichewick Brook. The weir, usually a woven fence, would trap migrating fish on their way to the lake.

MORE INFORMATION

The reservation is open daily, sunrise to sunset. There is no fee; dogs are allowed on-leash. For more information, contact The Trustees of Reservations at 978-682-3580 or visit thetrustees.org.

NEARBY

The North Andover Historical Society preserves several old buildings on the village common, including Parson Barnard House, Carriage Barn, the Granary, Stevens Mills Depot, Hay Scales, and Johnson Cottage. Visit the society's website, northandoverhistoricalsociety.org, for more information. There are restaurants near the reservation on Chickering Road (MA 133/125).

18

WARD RESERVATION

Follow a short nature trail for close-up views of a quaking bog, a fascinating place to see rare and unusual plant life. Then explore the Solstice Stones and enjoy the abundant wildlife and long scenic views on Holt Hill.

DIRECTIONS

From I-93, take Exit 41 to MA 125 north and follow it for 5 miles. Turn right onto Prospect Road and follow it 0.4 mile to the parking area on the right.

From I-495, take Exit 42A to MA 114 east and follow it for 1.2 miles to the junction with MA 125. Continue straight on MA 114/MA 125 for 0.5 mile then turn right onto MA 125 south (Andover Bypass Street) and follow it for 1.6 miles. Go left onto Prospect Road and travel 0.3 mile to the parking lot on the right. *GPS coordinates: 42° 38.438′ N, 71° 06.721′ W.*

TRAIL DESCRIPTION

Featuring a quaking bog, fantastic vistas, and miles of woodland trails, Ward Reservation offers diverse attractions. The reservation is on the Bay Circuit Trail and its trail network includes several color-blazed loops. The two walks in this trip, which can be combined, include the bog; Holt Hill, which is the highest point in Essex County; and the northern section, which includes a mosaic of woodlands and wetlands.

Before or after the Holt Hill and Northern Section walk, take a short walk to the bog. From the parking area, follow the Red and Yellow trails past a grassy area and a private residence on your left. Follow both trails right and continue to marker 1 then bear right again on Yellow Trail. Be on the lookout for low-growing club mosses, poison ivy (with its three green leaves that shine in the sun), and

LOCATION
Andover, MA

RATING
Bog Trail, Easy; Holt Hill and Northern Section, Moderate

DISTANCE
Bog Trail, 0.6 mile; Holt Hill and Northern Section, 4 miles

ELEVATION GAIN
290 feet

ESTIMATED TIME
Bog Trail, 30 minutes; Holt Hill and Northern Section, 2 hours

MAPS
USGS Lawrence; online: thetrustees.org/assets/documents/places-to-visit/trailmaps/Ward_Reservation_TrailMap_2013.pdf

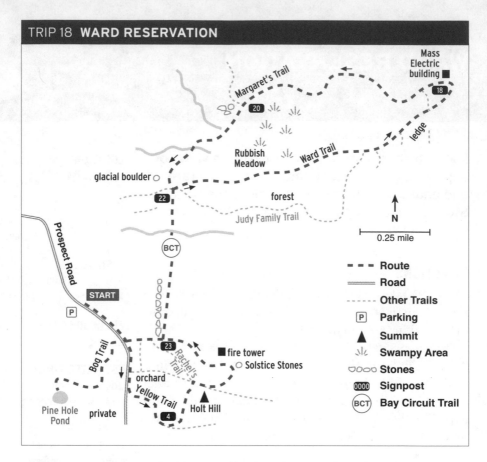

Indian pipe in the woods. The woodland trail goes only a short distance, and after a couple of minutes you will pass a wet area on the right. Shortly afterward, turn right onto a boardwalk at a "T" intersection.

As soon as you begin walking on the boardwalk, you will smell dank earth, spruce, and hemlock. The boardwalk rests on a mat of vegetation, below which is at least 19 feet of muck (as measured during the boardwalk's construction). Look for cattail; cotton grass, a member of the sedge family that has a cottony tuft in late summer; and highbush blueberries, which prefer the acidic soil of the bog. In just over a quarter-mile you'll reach the bog pond, where the boardwalk ends. Ringed by dark cedars, the bog is particularly appealing in fall, when the golden grasses along its edge frame the black water. To return to the parking area or to begin the Holt Hill and Northern Section walk, simply retrace your steps.

From the parking lot, go right on the paved road for 200 feet then follow Rachel's Trail, a footpath that climbs uphill, passing an apple orchard on the left. If you are here in the early morning, scan the orchard for deer, particularly when there is fruit on the trees. Shortly after rejoining Yellow Trail, turn left at the next junction (marker 4) onto the white-blazed Bay Circuit Trail. The wide path rises easily then turns to the right and enters the fields just below the summit of Holt

Hill. Look for bluebirds, bobolinks, kestrels (small hawks that primarily hunt insects), and other birds that prefer open meadows.

To your left, you will see a radio tower. Take the path through the meadow, and you will quickly arrive at the Solstice Stones and Holt Hill's summit. The Solstice Stones were assembled at the direction of the property's former owner, Mabel Ward, during the early twentieth century. They are laid out like a compass, with the largest stones indicating the four primary points. (The north stone is marked.) The narrow stone in the northeast quadrant points in the direction of the sunrise on the summer solstice, the longest day of the year, which is usually June 21. The view is breathtaking from Holt Hill, which, at 420 feet, is the highest hill in Essex County. Looking south, you can see the Boston skyline and Great Blue Hill in Milton.

After enjoying the view, walk toward the radio tower and follow the paved road downhill about a quarter-mile then turn right at marker 23, following the white-blazed Bay Circuit Trail and Red Trail. This trail runs north along a stone wall, indicating that this area was once pasture. Large white pines now grow here, and farther along the trail more oaks and maples appear. The trail gradually goes downhill, and after walking a little more than a quarter-mile, you will cross a tiny stream on wooden boards.

Check the forest floor for Indian pipe, a flowering plant that lacks the green pigment chlorophyll and is unable to manufacture its own food by photosynthesis. With the aid of a fungus that connects it to the roots of a nearby tree, Indian pipe collects its food from the host tree. Indian pipe grows 4 to 10 inches tall, and its nodding white or pink flowers are similar in shape to a pipe.

At the four-way intersection on the other side of the stream, continue to follow Red Trail by taking the second right onto Ward Trail. (Leave the Bay Circuit Trail, which continues left.) After about a quarter-mile, you will pass wetlands on the left. This is the unappealingly named Rubbish Meadow. (Wetlands, especially swamps, were historically regarded as undesirable, savage, or waste places, hence the name.) Watch for tree swallows, easily identified by their dark blue or green backs and their white bellies. In spring, they prefer to nest in cavities in standing timber and are attracted to backyard birdhouses near water. Tree swallows, each about 5 inches long, are very social birds and can provide hours of viewing pleasure as they dip and wheel in the sky, chasing one another or catching insects.

After 0.25 mile, you'll approach a ledge of granite on the right then pass through an area of small white pines that crowd the trail, creating a tunnel effect. Deer use this trail on their nocturnal rounds. See if you can spot their heart-shaped hoof prints in the ground.

At a four-way junction at marker 18, leave Red Trail and continue straight to another junction at the reservation boundary, near a Mass Electric building and posted trail map. Turn left to begin the loop back to the parking area on Margaret's Trail, which heads in a westerly direction along a stone wall.

The Solstice Stones are laid out like a compass, with a narrow stone in the northeast quadrant pointing toward the sunrise on the summer solstice, the longest day of the year. Boston's skyline rises to the south. Photo by Not on Your Nelly, Creative Commons on Flickr.

After walking roughly 0.5 mile on Margaret's Trail, continue straight at the first junction with Greg's Trail at marker 20, stepping up onto exposed bedrock. In another 200 feet or so, the trail forks. Stay straight (bearing right), following the trail to a tiny stream that drains the marsh on your left. Before crossing, you might want to go upstream to listen to the water making 4-inch drops over rocks. You can also explore the little side trail that loops back to a partial view of the wetlands by a semicircle of stones around a fire pit.

Look along the edge of the stream for animal tracks, such as those made by raccoons and minks, which both forage near wet areas. Minks can grow as long as 35 inches, including the tail, although the weight of a mink that size would be only about 2.5 pounds. They are crafty hunters and prey primarily on small rodents, but they will also eat birds, snakes, frogs, crayfish, and even muskrats.

Back on the main trail, just beyond the stream, you'll approach a fork. Follow the trail to the left, where it is crowded by pines. In about 300 feet, you'll arrive at another intersection. Bear left and cross another small stream at the outlet of a beaver wetland then continue across a short elevated boardwalk that offers fine views. A small glacial boulder rests on the ledge. After 0.25 mile, you'll return to the four-way intersection at marker 22; turn left on the white-blazed Bay Circuit Trail then follow Bay Circuit Trail and Red Trail right after 10 feet. Backtrack to the paved road then turn right to reach Prospect Road and the parking area.

DID YOU KNOW?

During the Revolutionary War, a large group of Andover townspeople climbed Holt Hill to watch the burning of Charlestown from the hill's summit.

MORE INFORMATION

The reservation is open year-round, 8 A.M. to sunset. There is no fee; there are no restrooms; and dogs are allowed. For more information, contact The Trustees of Reservations at 978-682-3580 or visit thetrustees.org.

NEARBY

The Addison Gallery of Landscape Art, part of Phillips Academy, is a museum dedicated to American art. Founded in 1931, its holdings include works by many prominent artists, such as John Singleton Copley, Winslow Homer, and John Singer Sargent. There are numerous restaurants in the center of Andover along and off Main and Elm streets.

THE LIFE AND TIMES OF A BOG

The bog at the Ward Reservation formed 12,000 to 14,000 years ago as the glaciers from the most recent ice age retreated across New England. The bog rests in a glacial kettle hole, a depression made when a huge block of ice from a glacier was left buried in the ground and then melted. Unlike in other bodies of water, decay in a bog is extremely slow due to the lack of active flowing water. As plants die, they accumulate at the bottom of the bog, forming a thick organic matter known as peat. Over time, the amount of open water in the bog gradually decreases as plants, such as leather leaf and sphagnum moss, take over. Sphagnum moss is very spongy and absorbent. First used by American Indians to line babies' diapers, it was later used by doctors as a dressing for wounds.

Both black spruce and tamarack, trees that are more common in northern New England, grow in the Ward Reservation bog. The trees are small but quite old, as it is difficult to harvest trees in these environments. Some of the rare plants here include rose pogonia, bog orchids, and two carnivorous plants: the sundew and the pitcher plant. (For more on the pitcher plant, see Trip 14 "Blue Hills: Ponkapoag Pond" on page 61.) The sundew is a much smaller plant, with round leaves and white or pink flowers. It, too, traps insects in sticky fluid, only this plant's leaves close around the insect. The insects provide the plants with some nutrients, such as nitrogen, that are lacking in the bog.

The low, shrubby vegetation bordering the bog is an excellent place to watch for dragonflies and damselflies, which together form the odonate order of carnivorous insects. One of the most visible species during midsummer is the blue dasher, a small and often abundant dragonfly. The males have light blue bodies, while females are brown, yellow, and black.

When exploring this and other bogs, be sure to stay on boardwalks and marked trails. Stepping onto the vegetative mats causes damage to these fragile environments. Doing so is also dangerous, as it is possible to break through the mat and sink deep into the mud and peat.

19

BALD HILL RESERVATION

Sprawled across three towns in central Essex County, Bald Hill Reservation protects 1,700 acres of forested hills and low-lying swamps as conservation land.

DIRECTIONS

From I-95, take Exit 51. At the end of the ramp, follow signs toward Middleton (south) then take the first right onto Middleton Road. Follow it 1.6 miles to a small roadside parking lot on the left at the Bay Circuit Trail crossing, where a sign welcomes you to Bald Hill. *GPS coordinates:* 42° 38.405' N, 70° 59.446' W.

TRAIL DESCRIPTION

The area encompassing Bald Hill and Crooked Pond is known as Bald Hill Reservation. It lies within the quiet, largely undeveloped town line of Boxford, near the Middleton and North Andover borders. The different tracts of conservation land here include the John C. Phillips Wildlife Sanctuary (where hunting is prohibited), Boxford State Forest, and Boxford Woodlots.

Bald Hill Reservation is an excellent destination for wildlife enthusiasts thanks to the wide habitat variety, including open hilltop meadows, rich forests, ponds, swamps, and beaver wetlands. Historians will also enjoy exploring the site of the former Russell Hooper Farm. Each season offers a new suite of attractions, including wildflowers, fall foliage, bird-watching, and animal tracks. Waterproof footwear is highly recommended in early spring and during other high-water periods, as the trails at Crooked Pond are susceptible to flooding. Trail junction numbers are marked on posts or blazes on trees.

To begin your hike, follow the main trail, which coincides with the white-blazed Bay Circuit Trail, away from

LOCATION
Boxford, MA

RATING
Easy to Moderate

DISTANCE
1.75 miles

ELEVATION GAIN
150 feet

ESTIMATED TIME
2 hours

MAPS
USGS Ipswich, USGS Lawrence; online: ecga.org/writable/ maps/file/baldhill_boxford.pdf

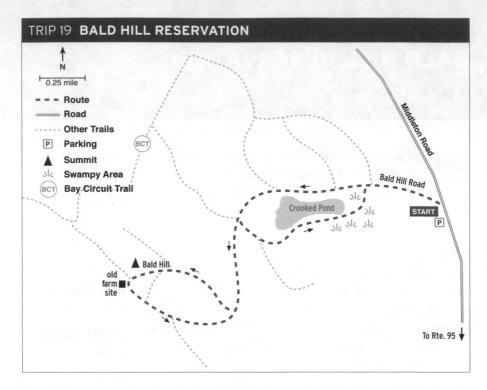

the parking area. Overhead, hemlock trees, some of which are infested with hemlock woolly adelgid, shade this wide, well-maintained trail as it heads in a westerly direction. About 0.25 mile into the walk, you will reach a junction at the east end of Crooked Pond, at the wildlife sanctuary boundary. This hike continues straight along the north side of the pond at marker 17, leaving the Bay Circuit Trail, which goes up the slope on the right. (If water levels are high, the trail on the left, which is an optional return route, may offer a drier path along the south shores.). Follow the footpath along the pond edge, where you can scan the shallow water for a variety of wildlife, including the resident beavers, great blue herons, and visiting ducks.

Oaks, maples, and pines begin to join the hemlocks as you walk parallel to the pond. At marker 14, bear left at the junction with a connecting trail to the Bay Circuit Trail, on the right. Beavers have built a dam along the trail at the pond's west end; cross this area carefully if the water is high. After you pass marker 13A, the walking becomes easier, as the main trail begins a gradual climb toward Bald Hill on a woods road. Blue blazes on trees indicate you've crossed the Boxford State Forest boundary. At marker 12, turn right to reach the crest of the hill in a short walk. Look carefully for old apple trees, a legacy of the preserve's agricultural past, amid the small maples and oaks. There are no spectacular views, but an open field stretches along the ridge, providing a nice sunny spot to picnic. It is especially inviting in autumn, when the trees bordering the field offer a vivid display of colors.

Wild calla wildflowers can be spotted around wetland edges at Bald Hill in spring.

Because there are nearly 2,000 protected acres in the reservation, wildlife abounds. Ruffed grouse, goshawks, barred owls, woodcocks, deer, fishers, and coyotes all live here. One of the more conspicuous birds is the pileated woodpecker, which is also one of the largest woodpeckers in North America and can be identified by its red head and loud, rasping call. Keep an eye out for wild turkeys, which have made a dramatic recovery after near-elimination during Colonial times.

One raptor to watch for is the northern goshawk, the largest member of the Accipiter genus of hawks. The goshawk is a rapid-flying hawk that feeds on birds and small mammals, including gray squirrels. It can negotiate its way through thick forest understory or fly just above the treetops. It is a magnificent and rather uncommon bird. If you are fortunate enough to see one, you won't forget the way it stares at you with its red eyes. Goshawks can turn anybody into an avid bird-watcher.

From the summit, bear left on a grass path that slopes downhill into the woods. You'll see another trail ahead that forks to the left. Follow the path on the right, which leads to a stone foundation marking the Russell Hooper Farmhouse site. After passing the foundation, continue to junction 10 and turn left onto a path along the field edge, with an old fireplace and chimney on the left. The trail leads away from the farm site then bears left and continues through the woods back to the intersection at marker 12. From here, retrace your steps toward Crooked Pond.

At marker 13A, you have the option of retracing your steps to the trailhead along the north side of the pond or turning right to make a loop along the south shore. For the latter, bear left at marker 13B and follow the narrow footpath along the southwest end of the wetlands, remaining close to the water on the left. Watch for wild calla blooming along the water's edge in midspring. After passing rock outcroppings, follow the trail as it bears left to complete the loop at the junction with the main trail and the Bay Circuit Trail. Turn right to return to the parking area.

DID YOU KNOW?

The Bald Hill area is known as one of the richest botanical sites in eastern Massachusetts. Preliminary surveys during 2008 and 2009 indicated 305 species of plants, including many associated with vernal pools, brooks, and other wetlands.

MORE INFORMATION

The reservation is open dawn to dusk; there is no fee. There are no restrooms. For more information, visit the Essex County Greenbelt Association website at ecga.org or the DCR Boxford State Forest website at mass.gov/dcr. Maps are available at nearby staffed DCR properties, including Bradley Palmer State Park and Harold Parker State Forest.

NEARBY

Witch Hollow Farm, located at the intersection of Main Street and Ipswich Road, was once the home of a woman tried in the infamous Salem witch trials of 1693. Pizza places are located on Georgetown Road and Joseph Smith Way; there are also several farm stands in town.

20

IPSWICH RIVER WILDLIFE SANCTUARY

This forested path circles a pond en route to the Rockery. Children will have fun exploring the maze of paths, bridges, and tunnels.

DIRECTIONS

From I-95, take Exit 50 for US 1 and go north for about 3 miles to its intersection with MA 97. Turn right (south) and proceed 0.5 mile then turn left onto Perkins Row. Go 1 mile to the entrance on the right. *GPS coordinates: 42° 37.875′ N, 70° 55.268′ W.*

TRAIL DESCRIPTION

The diverse habitats of the Ipswich River Wildlife Sanctuary include wetlands and unusual rock formations. Ten miles of trails wind through meadows, ponds, marsh, and forest, and alongside the Ipswich River. The area called the Rockery is a constructed maze of rocks and boulders formed into paths, bridges, and tunnels adjacent to a picture-perfect pond, surrounded by azaleas, rhododendrons, and mountain laurel.

The parking lot and nature center rest atop Bradstreet Hill, a glacial drumlin formed during the last ice age, when a glacier deposited debris and shaped them into a smooth, elongated mound. Also on the property are eskers, long ridges of sand and gravel. Eskers formed when meltwater streams in the glaciers deposited their debris in the ice, leaving raised streambeds after the ice melted.

The outing described here is a solid two-hour walk. If you are exploring with young children, you may want to shorten the route to its kid-friendliest features. In this case, walk to Waterfowl Pond and the Rockery, bypassing the Averill's Island loop (see map). Trail maps are available at the sanctuary headquarters.

LOCATION
Topsfield, MA

RATING
Easy to Moderate

DISTANCE
4 miles

ELEVATION GAIN
50 feet

ESTIMATED TIME
2 hours

MAPS
USGS Ipswich; online: massaudubon.org/content/download/8050/145205/file/ipswich_trails.pdf

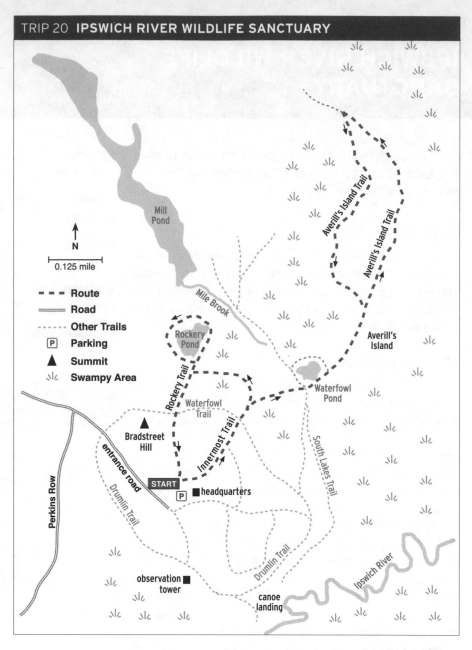

From the entrance, follow the path toward the headquarters and turn left onto the driveway by the red buildings. Look for a sign directing you to Innermost Trail. Follow this wide, grassy trail to the northeast, passing through a field of goldenrod, Queen Anne's lace, and milkweed, being careful of poison ivy. (Look for green leaves in groups of three that shine in the sun.) After walking roughly 50 feet, you will reach a junction at the edge of the field where you will bear left, following Innermost Trail downhill through foliage that has formed a tunnel.

After a few minutes, bear left at the junction with Ruffed Grouse Trail and continue to follow Innermost Trail beneath white pines and maples. In a couple of minutes, you will reach an intersection with Drumlin Trail but continue walking straight ahead on Innermost Trail. The trail crosses a boardwalk through a swamp of cattails, purple loosestrife, yellow flag iris, and swamp maples, soon reaching an intersection. Turn right, passing more wetlands where dead timber rises.

You will soon reach the intersection of several trails at a photogenic stone bridge. Turn left to get a good view of Waterfowl Pond from the bridge. Look for wading birds, such as great blue herons and night herons, and scan the water for frogs and painted turtles. Return to the junction and continue straight on Averill's Island Trail. A wooden observation platform on the left offers fine views across the water.

If you are visiting in May, inspect the edges of the path near the pond for recent signs of digging, indicating a snapping turtle may have laid its eggs in the dry ground adjacent to the pond. Once a female lays her eggs in the shallow depression, she covers them with dirt, but skunks and raccoons still manage to find many nests. Snappers play an important role in the health of ponds by eating dead fish, so teach children not to disrupt them or their nests. Much of the population in Massachusetts is at risk.

Look for yellow flag iris and swamp maples from this hike's boardwalks over the Ipswich River.

At the back of the pond, where the trail intersects with Averill's Island Loop Trail, go left. Passing beneath white pine, hemlock, and an occasional beech tree, the trail swings to the north. About a quarter-mile down is a fork in the trail where the loop begins. Bear right, passing towering white pines that give the forest an enchanted quality. In about half a mile, you will see an open marsh on the right and, just beyond that, the Ipswich River.

The trail now angles northwest through mixed woodland, where beech and oak trees display colorful fall foliage in late October. After about five minutes, you will reach the northern end of Averill's Island; turn left to complete your loop. (If you were to go right onto White Pine Loop Trail, you'd head into the northernmost end of the sanctuary; sometimes these trails are flooded from beaver activity.) Head south to arrive back at Waterfowl Pond in 0.75 mile, completing your loop of the island.

For the second part of the walk to the Rockery, bear right and retrace your steps past Waterfowl Pond, all the way to Waterfowl Pond Trail. Bear right again, and Waterfowl Pond Trail will take you through the heart of a marsh. In five minutes, you'll arrive at Rockery Trail. Turn right onto a boardwalk that brings you to Rockery Pond. Circle the pond in a counterclockwise direction by bearing right. Mountain laurel and rhododendrons make this an especially appealing walk in late spring. At the back end of the pond, cross a small bridge, walk through cedars and spruce, and arrive at the boulders of the Rockery. This spot offers a peaceful view of the pond's tranquil waters, and children will enjoy exploring its nooks and crannies. In one section, slabs of rock have been placed over the path, forming a dark tunnel. It's a magical spot, made more so by the many evergreens.

The Rockery was designed in 1902 by Shintare Anamete, a Japanese landscape architect. It was commissioned by Thomas E. Proctor, a former landowner, as a setting for his collection of exotic shrubs, trees, and flowers. It took seven years to build. Proctor bought rocks from surrounding farms because there were no boulders or glacial erratics on his property. Some of the boulders were transported more than 10 miles by horse and cart. Mass Audubon bought the sanctuary from the Proctor family in 1951.

To return to the parking lot, walk from the rock tunnel and retrace your steps over the boardwalk to the intersection of Waterfowl Pond Trail and Rockery Trail. Stay straight on Rockery Trail as it continues mostly uphill through woods and a field en route to the parking lot. It's about a half-mile walk from the Rockery to the parking area.

There are many more miles of trails to explore on future trips, including a walk to an observation tower overlooking Bunker Meadows and a trail to the banks of the Ipswich River.

DID YOU KNOW?

The sanctuary protects a particularly scenic 8-mile stretch of the Ipswich River, which is terrific for flatwater canoeing. Like other rivers in eastern Massachusetts, the Ipswich is threatened by water withdrawals, with fourteen communities drawing water from its basin. Water conservation measures are necessary to protect the river and its aquatic life from the stresses of reduced flow.

MORE INFORMATION

The sanctuary is open dawn to dusk, Tuesday through Sunday. It is closed Monday except for some holidays. There is an admission fee for nonmembers. Restrooms are available. The nature center provides programs, and members can rent canoes and cabins. For more information, contact the Ipswich River Wildlife Sanctuary at 978-887-9264 or email ipswichriver@massaudubon.org.

NEARBY

The Topsfield Fair has been held annually since 1818, with the exception of six years. The town was chosen for the agricultural festival due to its location in central Essex County, which made it easily accessible for stagecoach traffic. The fair is held for approximately ten days in early October. There are several places to eat in Topsfield on Main Street just west of the junctions of US 1 and MA 97.

21

BRADLEY PALMER STATE PARK

A network of well-maintained trails at a former estate leads to diverse attractions, including pastoral fields, forests, wetlands, and the Ipswich River.

DIRECTIONS

From the junction of US 1 and Ipswich Road in Topsfield, follow Ipswich Road east for 1.2 miles. Turn right onto Asbury Street and continue 0.25 mile to the entrance road on the left. Bear right at a sign for the mansion and follow the road to the main parking area. *GPS Coordinates: 42° 39.202′ N, 70° 54.405′ W.*

TRAIL DESCRIPTION

Situated amid a large expanse of conservation land in Essex County, Bradley Palmer State Park protects more than 720 acres in the Ipswich River watershed. The site was once the estate of Bradley Palmer, a prominent early-twentieth-century attorney who donated land to establish both the park and the adjacent Willowdale State Forest. Today the park is a popular destination for a variety of recreational users, including hikers, horseback riders, mountain bikers, and cross-country skiers.

The trail network includes an extensive network of old carriage roads and footpaths, some of which have been maintained and improved by the Essex County Trails Association. There are more than 75 numbered junctions marked on the DCR state park map, which is available at the park headquarters and on its website. The map is strongly recommended for those unfamiliar with the area due to the numerous intersections. In addition to the junctions noted on the map, there are several other numbered posts near the loop's start that can be confusing. This hike begins at the park's main entrance on Asbury Street and

LOCATION
Hamilton and Topsfield, MA

RATING
Easy

DISTANCE
3.3 miles

ELEVATION GAIN
255 feet

ESTIMATED TIME
2 hours

MAPS
USGS Cornwall; USGS West USGS Ipswich; mass.gov/eea/docs/dcr/parks/trails/bradpalm.pdf

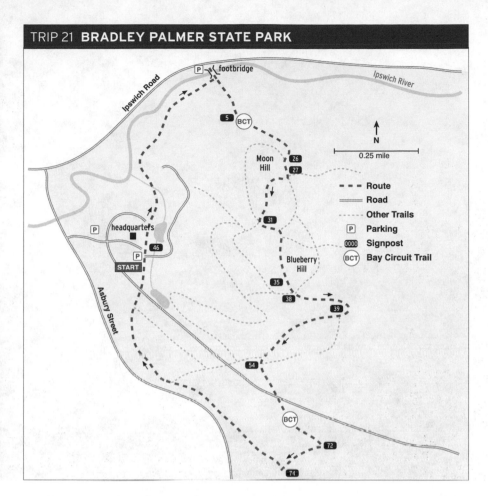

combines several trails, including a portion of the Bay Circuit Trail, to form a 3.3-mile loop. Walking on the well-maintained trails is easy, with the gentle climb of Moon Hill as the only elevation gain of significance.

From the parking area, walk to the headquarters then continue around the right side of the building to a trailhead at marker 46. Enter the woods on a footpath (part of the park's Healthy Heart Trail) that leads to the edge of a wetland associated with the Ipswich River, flowing a short distance to the west. Cross a footbridge providing a close-up view of a beaver dam. Bear right and continue over a low knoll then descend to a junction with a trail that parallels the Ipswich River. While this hike continues to the right, a short detour left leads to a bridge with fine views of the river and wetlands.

Follow the main trail northeast on a pleasant, easy route through the mixed oak, pine, maple, and beech woodlands bordering the river. After passing a field, reach a four-way junction (markers 4 and 21) adjacent to another footbridge over the Ipswich River at 0.7 mile. Here the long-distance Bay Circuit Trail (BCT) enters the park from the adjacent Willowdale State Forest and a parking area

Sharp-eyed hikers could spot a gray fox and other wildlife near field edges in Bradley Palmer State Park.

on Topsfield Road at the Topsfield–Ipswich town line. (This portion of the BCT is part of a connecting trail that joins the main BCT trail in Willowdale State Forest; the parking area is an alternative starting point for this circuit.)

Turn right onto the BCT and begin an easy ascent of the north side of Moon Hill, heading away from the river. This segment of the walk follows the BCT past numerous junctions. Watch carefully for the rectangular white blazes, as you'll also see markers for the Essex County Trails Association and the Discover Hamilton Trail; the latter is a long-distance trail that connects several conservation areas in the town of Hamilton. Cross a large, open field then reenter the upland woods and continue straight at marker 5, along an old carriage road. Old evergreen spruce trees shade the trail.

After a few minutes, you'll reach another large sunlit field at the top of Moon Hill, a 195-foot summit rising roughly 165 feet above the Ipswich River. These mixed forest-field habitats benefit a variety of wildlife, including eastern coyotes, red and gray foxes, white-tailed deer, and hawks and owls. Your best chance to see these and other species is in the early morning or evening, when they are most active on feeding rounds and there are fewer park visitors. Following the BCT and other blazes, bear left at marker 26 along the forest-field edge for a short distance then turn right at post 27 and continue across the heart of the meadow. Turn left at the next marker and follow the narrow grass path to the south side of the field.

At Marker 31, bear left again and follow the blazes along the field edge then reenter the woods and follow the BCT right at a fork along a gravelly woods road. One of the familiar year-round resident birds you'll likely see here is the white-breasted nuthatch, whose loud, nasal, yammering call belies its small size. Like other nuthatches, these are agile birds that often maneuver sideways or upside down along tree trunks. Thanks to its habitat diversity, the park is part of a designated Massachusetts Important Bird Area that encompasses the largest contiguous forest in northeastern Massachusetts.

Continue to follow the BCT south and east over Blueberry Hill. Pass junctions 35 and 38 then make an easy descent of the south slopes to the edge of another picturesque large meadow at marker 39. Bear right at successive intersections and continue along another old woods road lined by tall oak trees. After walking roughly 0.25 mile from the field, you'll reach a major junction in a small clearing where several roads and trails converge at marker 54. The hike continues left here, on the Bay Circuit Trail, which leads downhill and soon crosses the paved auto road. (You can also return to the entrance from the junction by heading right on the main woods road or by turning right onto the nearby paved park road at junction 52.) This section of the trail is especially colorful in late October and early November, near the end of the fall foliage season, when the numerous beech trees reach peak color. Beeches and oaks are the last of the main hardwood species to change color, and some trees even hold their dead leaves through winter.

You'll soon reach the edge of a large swamp at the park's southern end. (If the trail is flooded, you can backtrack to the paved road and return to the entrance.) At marker 72 turn right, off the BCT, and follow an unmarked trail through the heart of the wetland to a junction at a stone wall. Turn right again at marker 74 and follow the trail northwest along the park boundary, roughly parallel to Asbury Street. After passing more stone walls and a pastoral view across the road, the trail bends to the right and follows the edge of another clearing partially shaded by a large, spreading oak tree. After a quick descent, you'll reach a junction at a small pond near the entrance. Continue straight to complete the loop at the parking area.

DID YOU KNOW?

The former Bradley Palmer estate building has been rehabilitated by Willowdale Estates and is now used for weddings and other events.

MORE INFORMATION

The park is open dawn to dusk year-round. A seasonal parking fee ($5 for Massachusetts residents, $6 out of state) is charged at the main lot and wading pool areas. Restrooms are available at the headquarters. Contact the headquarters at 978-887-5931 or bradleypalmer@state.ma.us. Nearby Willowdale State Forest abuts the park and offers many miles of trails and swimming at Hood Pond. The woods roads are excellent for skiing in winter. There are restaurants in Ipswich center along and off Route 1A.

22

APPLETON FARMS GRASS RIDES

Easy walking trails that offer excellent cross-country skiing in winter meander through meadows, wetlands, and woodlands.

DIRECTIONS

From I-95, take Exit 20A. Go north on MA 1A for 4.5 miles then take a left onto Cutler Road and drive 2.2 miles to the intersection with Highland Street. Turn right onto Highland Street then quickly turn right again at the reservation's main entrance at Lamson Field. *GPS coordinates: 42° 38.971′ N, 70° 52.186′ W.*

By public transportation, take the Newburyport line of the MBTA Commuter Rail to Ipswich Station. The Ipswich Essex Explorer bus runs from the station to Appleton Farms roughly every two hours during normal weather conditions. Visit ipswichexplorer.com for schedules and hours of operation.

TRAIL DESCRIPTION

Appleton Farms is believed to be the oldest farm in continuous operation in the United States. Its plantings date to 1638, when the town of Ipswich granted the land to Thomas Appleton. The descendants of the original owner gave some of the land to The Trustees of Reservations in 1970, and the Appleton Farms Reservation opened to the public in 1998 with trails and community-supported agriculture.

The name Grass Rides came from the original use of the land as carriage roads. This usage of "ride" came from Europe, designating a path made for horseback riding. Horse-drawn carriages raced here in the late 1800s and early 1900s, which is why the main trails were designed as a loop.

LOCATION
Hamilton, MA

RATING
Easy to Moderate

DISTANCE
2.7 miles

ELEVATION GAIN
80 feet

ESTIMATED TIME
1.75 hours

MAPS
USGS Salem; online: thetrustees.org/assets/ documents/places-to-visit/ trailmaps/Appleton-Farms -Trail-Map.pdf

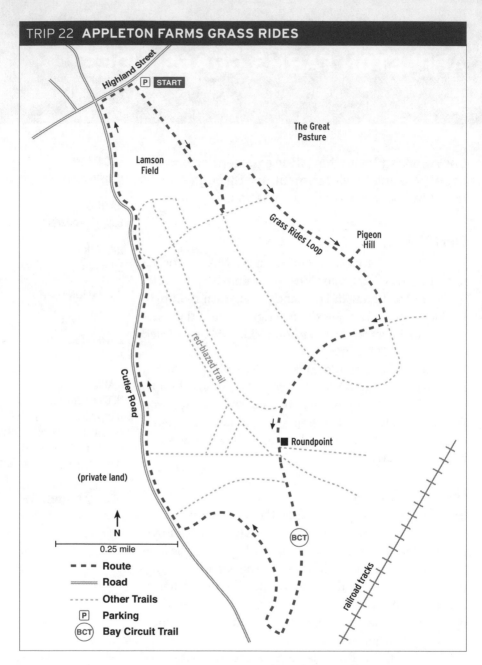

Highland Street
P START
The Great Pasture
Lamson Field
Grass Rides Loop
Pigeon Hill
red-blazed trail
Cutler Road
Roundpoint
(private land)
N
0.25 mile
BCT
railroad tracks

- - - Route
Road
----- Other Trails
P Parking
BCT Bay Circuit Trail

The reservation offers a nice combination of fields, wetlands, and wooded areas. This variety results in a wealth of ideal wildlife habitat, and the trails are so wide and the slopes so gentle that it is a perfect place for cross-country skiing.

The trail network includes several color-blazed loops and a portion of the Bay Circuit Trail. Allow yourself plenty of time before dark when embarking on this hike, as there are numerous junctions. This walk combines the

Cows graze and rest in the pasture at Appleton Farms. You can purchase cheese and milk from the farm store in the visitor center at the beginning of this hike. Photo by Massachusetts Office of Travel and Tourism, Creative Commons on Flickr.

red-blazed Grass Rides Loop and the Bay Circuit Trail, following both paths and roads in the Grass Rides.

From the parking area and entrance near the junction of Highland Street and Cutler Road, follow the main path, which is lined and shaded by a narrow strip of trees, across Lamson Field. During summer, watch for field wildflowers such as joe-pye weed, Queen Anne's lace, Saint-John's-wort, meadowsweet, and bluets.

The red-blazed trail soon enters the woods. Bear left at the first junction and follow the main path as it curves left around a small hill (an unmarked trail goes up the slope on the right) then turns sharply right to follow the woods along the edge of the Great Pasture. Rising above you is a mixed forest of pine, oak, maple, cedar, and majestic hemlocks. An entirely different suite of wildflowers grows in the forest, including lady's slipper, Canada mayflower, starflower, violet, and wild indigo. Unlike field wildflowers, these are most visible in mid- to late spring, before the deciduous trees fully leaf out and block light to the forest floor.

The forest-field edges are good places to catch a glimpse of wildlife such as foxes or coyotes, which visit in search of mice and other prey. While these predators are primarily nocturnal, they are occasionally seen during the middle of the day on hunting forays, particularly after their young are born in spring. Uncommon grassland birds, such as bobolinks, meadowlarks, and bluebirds, benefit from these clearings, which have declined with the regrowth of forests. Birds of prey that favor this habitat include American kestrels and red-tailed hawks.

You'll soon arrive at a small opening along the fence where you can walk to the left for a fine view of the pastures. A large concrete monument memorializes Francis Appleton, the ninth generation of the Appleton family to farm this land. After enjoying the view, continue to follow the trail for a short distance past a rest bench then take your first right at an unmarked junction onto a path that leads to the southeast, away from the field edge. The trail continues straight through a four-way intersection then makes a steep descent and passes between wetlands, where cattail reeds grow amid the low, shrubby vegetation. Take a moment to look for dragonflies and damselflies, yellow warblers, and red-winged blackbirds.

After a few more minutes of walking, you arrive at Roundpoint, a small, circular clearing where several trails meet that's marked by another large concrete monument. This hike continues straight on the white-blazed Bay Circuit Trail, which passes a swampy area and vernal pools. (For a 2-mile loop, turn right at Roundpoint and continue to follow the red-blazed trail.) At a junction with the reservation boundary at Cutler Road, turn right off the Bay Circuit Trail and follow the wide path parallel to the road.

The trail turns right and continues downhill past a wetland then bends left and right and returns to the road. Continue to follow the main trail north along Cutler Road, past numerous junctions on the right, to a gate. Turn right (north) and walk along Cutler Road (light traffic) for a short distance back to Highland Street and the Lamson Field entrance. Watch for deer along the edges of the fields at all hours of the day.

DID YOU KNOW?

Appleton Farms offers a community-supported agriculture (CSA) program that provides produce and other farm products to 650 shareholders. Visit thetrustees.org for membership information.

MORE INFORMATION

Both Appleton Farms Grass Rides and Appleton Farms are open year-round daily from sunrise to sunset. There is a $5 admission fee to the Grass Rides area for nonmembers of The Trustees of Reservations. Dogs are allowed only in the Grass Rides area at Appleton Farms, not elsewhere on the property, and an annual permit is required to walk dogs in Grass Rides or ride horses. The Appleton Farms visitor center is open Friday to Sunday, May through October, and on weekends in winter. Tours and programs are available periodically throughout the year. For more information, call 978-356-5728 or visit thetrustees.org.

NEARBY

Patton Park, named for the one-time Hamilton resident General George Patton, is located at the junction of MA 1A and Asbury Street and is home to a Sherman tank exhibit and a series of summer concerts. There are restaurants in South Hamilton along and off Railroad Avenue and MA 1A.

23

PARKER RIVER NATIONAL WILDLIFE REFUGE AT PLUM ISLAND

Plum Island is a premier destination for birding in the Northeast. These two short hikes feature the island's natural barrier beach; one hike takes you over a dune, and the other explores a marsh.

DIRECTIONS

From I-95, take Exit 57 and follow MA 113 east for 2.5 miles into Newburyport. At the junction with MA 1A, follow MA 1A south for 1.3 miles then turn left onto Rolfe's Lane at a traffic light and sign for the refuge. Follow Rolfe's Lane for 0.5 mile to its end then turn right onto Plum Island Turnpike and continue past the refuge visitor center on the right (opposite the Mass Audubon Joppa Flats visitor center). Cross the bridge over the Parker River then turn right onto Sunset Road and continue to the entrance gate and contact station. *GPS coordinates: 42° 44.045' N, 70° 47.509' W.*

TRAIL DESCRIPTION

The Parker River National Wildlife Refuge on Plum Island, a natural barrier beach, is a place nature lovers should visit in all seasons. It is one of the premier birding spots in the Northeast, as more than 270 species of migratory and resident birds have been spotted there. Spring and fall, when many migrants fly low over the dunes, are the peak seasons. But a winter walk—with white snow, golden-brown salt grass, and beach sand mixing together, can be a cure for cabin fever. Be aware that greenhead flies can be very unpleasant during July and early August.

The walk detailed here combines the two interpretive trails at the Hellcat area (parking lot 4), which is 3.8 miles down the entrance road from the main gate. There is also an observation tower on the dike near the parking area, and it's a good idea to stop here first to get the lay of the

LOCATION
Newburyport, MA

RATING
Easy

DISTANCE
1.4 miles

ELEVATION GAIN
40 feet

ESTIMATED TIME
1 hour

MAPS
USGS Ipswich, USGS Newburyport; online: fws.gov/refuge/Parker_River/map.htm

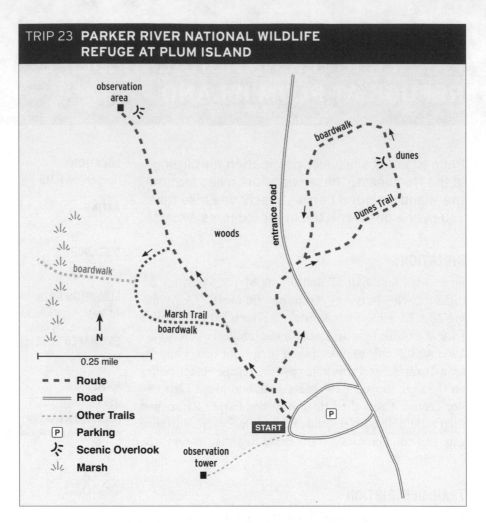

observation area

boardwalk

dunes

entrance road

woods

Dunes Trail

boardwalk

Marsh Trail
boardwalk

N

0.25 mile

- - - Route

Road

Other Trails

P Parking

Scenic Overlook

Marsh

START

P

observation tower

land and to see the wildlife in the freshwater marsh. The short path to the observation tower is at the rear of the parking lot. From the top of the tower you can see dunes, marshes, a beaver lodge, the ocean, and the mainland. Look for black ducks, green-winged teals, pintails, great blue herons, and green-backed herons in warmer months.

The Hellcat Swamp Nature Trail, most of which is a boardwalk, begins at the north side of the parking lot and forks only a couple of minutes down the trail. To first walk the dune loop, take the right fork through scrub oaks and freshwater marsh and follow it for 0.25 mile until you reach the entrance road. Cross the road and continue on the trail, which soon climbs stairs to a panoramic view of the dunes. If you are here in September, you may be rewarded with the sight of dozens of monarch butterflies migrating through the refuge. The open Atlantic is just 0.25 mile to the east from the top of the dune. A mounted spotting scope offers close-up views of birds and distant landmarks.

The overlook offers another excellent perspective of the island, which was formed by glaciers. Additional sculpturing occurred as the Merrimack River swept onto Plum Island. When the first Europeans arrived in the region, the island was covered with mature forest. Colonists quickly cleared the land, using white pine for ship masts and other lumber for wood fires, and set their sheep to graze on the rest of the vegetation. Today Plum Island once again has trees, but only a few approach 50 feet tall. The trees have gained a foothold in the hollows, where they are sheltered from the wind and are closer to groundwater. The plants nearest the beach are those that tolerate the salt spray: beach grass, seaside goldenrod, dusty miller, beach pea, and sea beach sandwort.

The steps and boardwalk continue as a short loop through the dunes and woodlands and along the small pockets of freshwater swamp. Complete the loop on the east side of the entrance road then cross the road and retrace your steps to the trail junction near the parking lot.

Turn right at this intersection, heading north on Marsh Trail. Stay to the right past two forks in the trail, and you will soon reach an observation area at the edge of a freshwater marsh, an excellent place to scan for birds and other wildlife.

From the observation area, retrace your steps to the south then turn right at the first intersection to continue the loop. A boardwalk will lead you through

With more than 270 species of birds spotted, Parker River National Wildlife Refuge at Plum Island is one of the premier birding locations in the Northeast.

wetlands where tall reed grass and cattails line the path. A side boardwalk leads farther out into the marsh. The purple-flowering plant that blooms in August is purple loosestrife, a nonindigenous plant that is taking over the wetlands. Fortunate observers may glimpse Virginia rails and soras, both uncommon marsh birds that are often well camouflaged. Once you have circled the marsh, the boardwalk returns you to the junction with the dune trail, where you will turn right to return to the parking lot.

For those who want to continue walking, there are many other exploration possibilities. A walk along the beach is always a good bet. You can examine the various flotsam that has washed ashore and listen to the surf—pounding and angry one day, gently lapping in rhythmic wavelets the next. Access to the beaches is restricted during the spring and summer shorebird breeding season; contact the refuge for updates.

Autumn is a good time to see rough-legged hawks and harriers hunting for small mammals and falcons wheeling in the sky as they migrate south. Lucky birders are sometimes rewarded in winter with the sight of a snowy owl, a visitor from the Arctic. Although snowy owls breed in the tundra, they move south at irregular intervals to winter in New England. Plum Island and the Boston Harbor Islands are two of the best locations to see them, particularly from December to the end of February. Some years they are fairly common at Plum Island, where they hunt in the open salt marshes, feeding on meadow voles and smaller birds.

Be on the lookout as well for the piping plover, an endangered bird that is successfully reproducing on Plum Island. Piping plovers are small sand-colored birds that nest on the beach and therefore are susceptible to being crushed by beach vehicles and disturbed by beachgoers. At nesting times in spring and early summer, sections of the beach may be closed for their protection. Harbor seals can also be seen bobbing in the surf beyond the breakers. Shorebirds, such as greater yellowlegs and willets, hunt along the shoreline and in tidal flats for invertebrates to feed on.

DID YOU KNOW?

The refuge is one of New England's most prominent migrant traps, or areas that are often visited by accidental or vagrant bird species. Some of the more unusual species spotted here include magnificent frigate birds, white pelicans, and western tanagers.

MORE INFORMATION

The refuge is open year-round. The headquarters and visitor center, located on the mainland across from the Mass Audubon Joppa Flats visitor center at the Plum Island Turnpike bridge, includes information, exhibits, and a gift shop.

There is a $5 fee, and annual passes are available. Restrooms are available at lot 4 and the main entrance; pets are prohibited.

During summer weekends, the refuge often fills to parking capacity early, and the entrance gate may temporarily close. (Visitors on foot or bicycle are admitted when parking lots are full.) Hunting is allowed at Nelson Island, which is closed to the public Monday through Saturday during hunting season.

The beach is often closed from April 1 through July or August to protect nesting shorebirds. For more information, contact refuge headquarters at 978-465-5753 or visit fws.gov/refuge/parker_river.

NEARBY

Sandy Point State Reservation, which abuts the refuge at the island's southern tip, offers additional beach trails and ocean views. The historical Newburyport waterfront is a popular tourist attraction. Free concerts are held in Waterfront Park on Friday evenings in season. There are restaurants in town on and off Water and State streets. Maudslay State Park, on Curzon Mill Road, encompasses the grounds of the former Moseley Estate on the banks of the Merrimack River. Visitors may enjoy the nineteenth-century gardens and plantings, as well as a large natural stand of mountain laurel.

24

CRANE BEACH LOOP

Five miles of trails wind through more than 1,200 acres of white sand beach and dunes along both sides of Castle Neck.

DIRECTIONS

From MA 128, take Exit 20A and follow MA 1A north for 8 miles to Ipswich. Turn right onto MA 133 east and continue 1.8 miles then turn left onto Northgate Road. Travel 0.7 mile, turn right onto Argilla Road, and drive 2.5 miles to the entrance at the end of the road. *GPS coordinates:* 42° 41.024' N, 70° 46.042' W.

By public transportation, take the Newburyport/Rockport line of the MBTA Commuter Rail to Ipswich Station, then take the Ipswich Essex Explorer bus. For schedule and rates, visit ipswichessexexplorer.com.

TRAIL DESCRIPTION

At the scenic Crane Beach Reservation, part of a network of preserves owned by The Trustees of Reservations, finger-shaped Castle Neck juts into the ocean at the mouth of the Castle Neck River and Essex Bay. An extensive pitch-pine forest, carnivorous plants, and cranberries can all be found here. The area is also known for its bird-watching and fall foliage.

This walk combines the reservation's Green and Red trails to form a 3-mile loop that explores the western portion of the neck. Although it isn't overly long and can be completed in less than two hours at a good pace, this isn't a hike to be underestimated. Most of the route traverses soft sand, exposed areas, and rolling terrain as the trails wind along and over a series of dunes. Visitors should bring plenty of water and sunscreen. For a shorter outing, you can walk Green Trail alone, or follow a portion of Red Trail to the beach and walk back along the shore

LOCATION
Ipswich, MA

RATING
Moderate

DISTANCE
3 miles

ELEVATION GAIN
270 feet

ESTIMATED TIME
2.5 hours

MAPS
USGS Ipswich, USGS Rockport; online: thetrustees.org/assets/documents/places-to-visit/trailmaps/Crane-Estate-Trail-Map.pdf

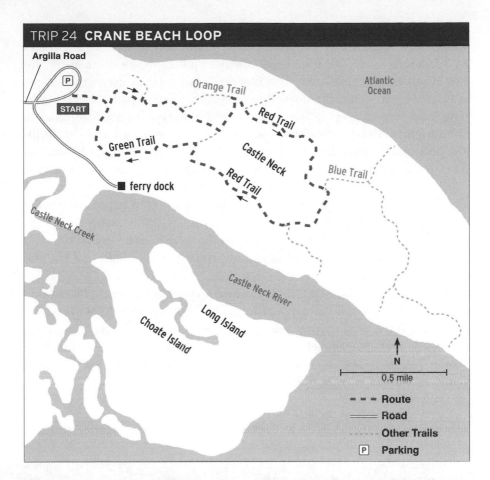

Argilla Road

P

START

Orange Trail

Red Trail

Green Trail

Castle Neck

Red Trail

ferry dock

Castle Neck Creek

Blue Trail

Atlantic
Ocean

Castle Neck River

Choate Island

Long Island

N

0.5 mile

- - - Route
——— Road
········ Other Trails
P   Parking

to the entrance. The trails are well marked, with numerous numbered posts and maps at key junctions.

The trail begins on the east side of the large parking lot, across from the beach offices and walkways. The path enters the woods and follows a short boardwalk then arrives at the start of the Green Trail loop in an open area, where you will turn left. The ocean soon comes into view to the north, with Crane Beach's wooden walkways visible on the left. The trail curves to the right, and beautiful views unfold as it crosses the dunes. This area is ecologically fragile; the dunes, which prevent the land from being engulfed by the sea, are held together by long, connected plant roots. Stay on the marked trail and do not walk along the crests of the dunes or step on the vegetation.

After a few minutes of walking, you'll arrive at a fork at marker 2. Turn right here and continue to follow the loop trail as it descends into a patch of woods. Here the path is shaded by pitch pine and scrub oak. This forest type is common on Cape Cod and the southeast Massachusetts coast, less so along the North Shore. These trees are well adapted to the sandy soils that few other species can tolerate.

The trees and shrubs offer food and cover for a variety of wildlife that call Castle Neck home. Eastern coyotes are fairly common; watch for their tracks and droppings along the trail, especially near junctions within their territories. Another midsize predator that is present, but quite elusive, is the bobcat, which makes its dens in remote areas well off the beaten path. Bobcat tracks have been seen throughout the year by park rangers. From midsummer to late autumn, watch for meadowhawk dragonflies flittering around the shrubs along the path, especially near wet areas. The hardy yellow-legged meadowhawk is the last of the state's 170 dragonfly species that remains active as the warm weather winds down. You might see it in late November or even early December when conditions are right. The beach itself is an important nesting site for endangered piping plovers and least terns. (To protect shorebirds, dogs are not allowed between April 1 and September 30.) Keep an eye on the sand for the tiny tracks of mice, which, along with cottontail rabbits, are prey for coyotes and bobcats.

Follow Green Trail straight through a junction where an orange-blazed trail leaves left and continue through a grove of overhanging pitch pines to another open area. You'll soon arrive at a junction where the Green and Red trails meet and briefly overlap. Although this hike continues to the left on Red Trail, for a shorter outing, you can go right and return to the parking area via the Green Trail loop for a 1.7-mile round-trip.

A favorite of locals and visitors alike, Crane Beach is home to protected dunes and sandy beaches.

Red Trail crosses a series of dunes as it leads you back toward the ocean. Beach grasses and shrubs, such as beach rose, help stabilize the dunes, which exist in a variety of ever changing shapes and sizes. The path curves to the east at the second junction with the orange-blazed trail, and the ocean again comes into view. Just beyond the junction, a side trail on the left offers a five-minute walk to the beach. (Another option for a short walk is to take this path then turn left and walk along the beach back to the parking area.) The loop continues to the right and follows moderately rolling terrain over a series of dunes along the north side of the neck. At the crest of the climb, there are fine sweeping views. Watch for red admiral and monarch butterflies in the patches of shrubs.

The trail curves away from the ocean and winds to a "Y" junction. At this intersection, roughly an hour's walk from the trailhead, Blue Trail leaves left to connect with other one-way trails that explore the remote eastern portion of Castle Neck—options for a longer adventures; be sure to have plenty of water. This hike continues along Red Loop, which follows rolling terrain across the heart of the neck. Bear right again at the next marked junction (marker 21), where a one-way trail branches to the south. Just beyond this junction, a short but steep climb up a dune rewards you with a beautiful panoramic view overlooking the mouth of Castle Neck River and its associated marshlands to the south.

The path descends the dune and continues to the northeast along more rolling terrain and soft sand. After another short but steep climb, it weaves along Wigwam Hill, where American Indians once built signal fires at overlooks. You'll pass a view of the ocean to the right (north), and more vistas unfold as the trail descends the hill and rejoins Green Trail at marker 25.

Turn left here onto Green Trail and continue past marker 6 into a pine grove that offers a much-needed break from the sun and a stretch of easy walking. Note the lack of plant diversity, the result of the sandy soils and acidic pine needles in the grassy woods here. The path emerges back onto another open dune and curves to the right (north) to cross the center of the neck. At the close of the loop, turn left and make the short walk along the connector path to the parking area.

MORE INFORMATION

The reservation is open year-round from 8 A.M. to sunset. Admission fees, as much as $25 per car on summer weekends, are charged year-round. Reduced rates and a yearly parking sticker are available for Trustees of Reservations members. Fees are lower for cyclists, walkers, and those visiting after 4 P.M. Visit thetrustees.org for more information.

During peak season (Memorial Day through Labor Day), Crane Beach is a popular swimming beach, especially on weekends, with lifeguards and rangers on duty. In-season amenities include bathhouses, showers, picnic tables, refreshments, merchandise, drinking-water fountains, and transportation for mobility-impaired and -challenged visitors. Portable toilets are available in the off-season. Horseback riding is allowed from October through March by permit and fee. Dogs are allowed from October through March with a Green Dogs permit, free for Trustees members and Ipswich residents.

DID YOU KNOW?

The Castle Neck area was actively farmed from the time of European settlement through the early twentieth century. Salt hay cut from the marshes was used to feed cattle.

NEARBY

Castle Hill, just west of the beach at the end of Argilla Road, is home to the historical Crane Estate and its beautifully landscaped grounds. The nearby Crane Wildlife Refuge consists of 697 acres of islands, salt marsh, and intertidal environments. More than 3 miles of trails explore this area, where more than 200 species of birds have been observed. For more information about both areas, visit thetrustees.org. There are restaurants in the center of Ipswich along and off MA 133 and MA 1A.

25

COOLIDGE RESERVATION

Easy trails lead to an overlook, a pond, and a beach. The historical Ocean Lawn, open Friday to Monday, offers additional magnificent views.

DIRECTIONS

From MA 128, take Exit 15 and follow signs to Manchester. In 0.5 mile, at the small white sign for Magnolia and Gloucester, take a left onto Lincoln Street. Go about a half-mile to its end. At the stop sign, take a left onto MA 127 north. Proceed 2 miles to a parking area on the right. *GPS coordinates: 42° 34.791' N, 70° 43.554' W.*

TRAIL DESCRIPTION

Established in 1992, Coolidge Reservation is named for the Coolidge family, who donated 41.6 acres in 1990 and 1991. In 1992, Essex County Greenbelt Association donated an additional 16.2 acres. With these gifts, most of the original land purchased by Thomas Jefferson Coolidge is now protected by The Trustees of Reservations for conservation and historical preservation.

Within its compact 66 acres, this preserve encompasses two very different parcels of land connected by a right-of-way for walkers. The northern portion adjacent to the entrance features hilly woodlands and a pond, while the southern section (open Friday through Monday) includes the Ocean Lawn, an awe-inspiring open space above the sea. Walking is easy on the well-maintained trails and is flat, except for the path to the summit of Bungalow Hill. Even if your visit is during the middle of the week, when access to the Ocean Lawn is restricted, the reservation's other trails and features are well worth the visit.

Start your walk by entering the woods at the trail adjacent to the signboard at the back of the parking lot. A short distance from the trailhead is a "Y" junction; follow the

LOCATION
Manchester-by-the-Sea, MA

RATING
Easy

DISTANCE
3 miles

ELEVATION GAIN
150 feet

ESTIMATED TIME
2 hours

MAPS
USGS Salem; online: thetrustees.org/assets/ documents/places-to-visit/ trailmaps/Coolidge -Reservation-Trail-Map.pdf

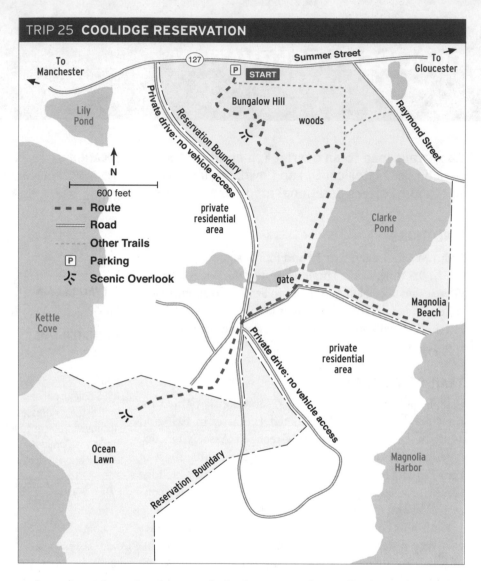

path on the right and make a quick climb up Bungalow Hill. The trail is shaded by the forest and passes an exposed granite ledge and small boulders. Pass a faint trail on the left, a shortcut to the hilltop, continuing on the wider trail, which soon curls around the crest of the hill and leads to a small overlook. The view is to the southeast, toward Magnolia Harbor, with the ocean on the horizon.

To descend the hill and connect with the reservation's main trail, watch for a narrow path that continues through the woods to the left of the overlook. This trail snakes downhill, passing fern-capped rock ledges, a giant pine tree that was blown down in a storm, and a closed trail on the right. At the junction with the main trail, turn right and follow the path along the edge of Clarke Pond, passing through a tunnel-like canopy of small trees and bushes. This 12-acre salt pond, which is rejuvenated by tides twice daily, has benefited from recent tidal restoration efforts in this watershed.

The trail continues for roughly 0.25 mile along the pond's edge to a small stone bridge at the outlet of the pond, where there is an intersection at a metal gate. Here the trail to the left leads east to Magnolia Beach (also known as Gray Beach), while the path to the Ocean Lawn is straight ahead. This hike continues along the former, which reaches the west end of Magnolia Beach in an easy quarter-mile. The beach, open May to September for walking only (no sunbathing), is a good place to listen to the surf and enjoy fine panoramic views, including a series of high rocks to your right.

Retrace your steps to the metal gate, and if the Ocean Lawn area is open, go left. After about 300 feet, the path crosses a road onto private property, so please stay on the designated trail. Follow the trail for roughly 0.25 mile to a breathtaking view above the ocean. Acres of rolling lawn and magnificent trees are in front of you. This is the Ocean Lawn, with Kettle Cove to the northwest and the Atlantic Ocean to the south.

Thomas Jefferson Coolidge, the great-grandson of President Thomas Jefferson, purchased the Ocean Lawn in 1871 for $12,000. He built a large white clapboard country home in 1873 and also sold several lots to relatives, friends, and business associates. In 1902, Coolidge had a grand cottage, known as Marble Palace, built on the Ocean Lawn. It featured the Roman columns favored by President

This hike passes the colorful rocks of Magnolia Beach in Coolidge Reservation.

Jefferson. The entire brick and white-marble house measured 230 feet in length. The structure was razed during the 1950s to make room for a new house, which was subsequently demolished in 1989.

The lawn slopes gently down to the ocean, and at the water's edge is a concrete breakwater that makes an excellent walkway. Picnicking is allowed on the Ocean Lawn, and there are a few large trees, one of which is an enormous beech with spreading branches that provides a shady spot to spread a blanket. If you walk to the tree's trunk and look up, you will see that the main branches of the tree are wired together to prevent splitting.

Another especially scenic spot is the very southern tip of the Ocean Lawn, where a granite bluff offers sweeping views of the offshore islands. Scan the water for harbor seals and birds, such as eiders, scoters, and cormorants. Few places are as peaceful and scenic as this.

From here, end the walk by retracing your steps to return to the parking area. You can bypass the Bungalow Hill paths by simply following the main trail all the way back to the entrance; turn left just before reaching Summer Street.

DID YOU KNOW?

Among the numerous dignitaries who were guests at Marble Palace during its heyday were President Woodrow Wilson and his wife, Edith, who were given use of the house for a week in 1918.

MORE INFORMATION

The trails near Clarke Pond and the entrance are open year-round from 8 A.M. to sunset. There is no admission fee. There are no restrooms. Dogs are allowed on woodland trails only, not on the Ocean Lawn. The Ocean Lawn is open Friday through Monday, 8 A.M. to sunset. For more information, contact The Trustees of Reservations at 978-526-8687 or visit thetrustees.org.

NEARBY

The center of Manchester is home to a cluster of shops and the Trask House Museum on Union Street (MA 127). Several restaurants are located on and off MA 127.

26

RAVENSWOOD PARK

This ecologically diverse slice of wilderness includes a magnolia swamp, rocky ledges and boulders, and a large forest.

DIRECTIONS

From MA 128, take Exit 14 to MA 133. Follow it east for 3 miles to MA 127. Turn right and proceed south for 1.9 miles to the reservation entrance on the right. *GPS coordinates:* 42 35.493′ N, 70 41.911′ W.

TRAIL DESCRIPTION

Ravenswood is a pocket of forested wilderness within the suburbs of the North Shore. Large hemlock trees, miles of winding trails, and a rare magnolia swamp are all reasons to visit the 500-acre property, which is owned by The Trustees of Reservations. History lovers will enjoy the story of Mason A. Walton, the Hermit of Gloucester, who lived in Ravenswood Park for 33 years. Samuel E. Sawyer, a wealthy merchant who summered here, preserved this land. In 1889, Sawyer's will created Ravenswood Park as a property "laid out handsomely with drive-ways and pleasant rural walks." Following his death, the property was managed by a dedicated group for 104 years. It was then transferred to The Trustees of Reservations in 1993.

This 2.5-mile walk first goes through Great Magnolia Swamp then leads to the hermit cabin site before looping back to the parking area through old trees and rocky terrain. A detailed trail map is posted on the sign at the parking area. The walking is mostly easy, over mildly rolling terrain.

From the parking lot, follow Old Salem Road, a wide historical carriage road, into the woods. Within 0.25 mile, turn left at Junction 1 (opposite Ledge Hill Trail) and follow the narrow, yellow-blazed Magnolia Swamp Trail

LOCATION
Gloucester, MA

RATING
Easy to Moderate

DISTANCE
2.5 miles

ELEVATION GAIN
Minimal

ESTIMATED TIME
2 hours

MAPS
USGS Gloucester; online:
thetrustees.org/assets/
documents/places-to-visit/
trailmaps/RavenswoodPark
_TrailMap_2016.pdf

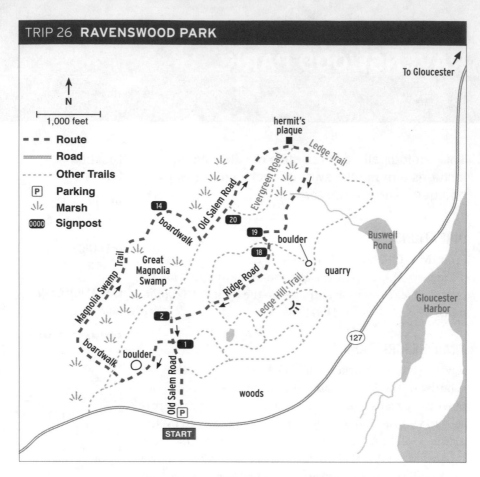

beneath large hemlocks as it winds its way up and down small hills in a south-westerly direction. Just 300 feet down the trail, a narrow trail enters on the left, but you should continue straight. In another 300 or 400 feet, you'll arrive at an exposed ledge of rock where a car-sized glacial boulder is perched on the bed-rock. Such boulders are known as glacial erratics due to the haphazard way they were deposited by glaciers roughly 15,000 years ago.

Follow the rocky trail to the right of the boulder as the path curls to the right, heading toward the swamp and passing through an understory of mountain laurel and blueberries. You soon reach an intersection. Going straight will bring you to a narrow boardwalk that traverses the ferns and thick foliage in the wet area of the swamp. Red maples and sweet pepper grow along the boardwalk, and the low-lying swamp has a decidedly different feel than the upland trail. The regionally uncommon magnolia trees for which the swamp and the nearby village of Magnolia are named also grow here. In the mid-nineteenth century, Henry David Thoreau visited the swamp to see the magnolias.

During the 1800s and early 1900s, many magnolias were taken from the swamp, and the population was on the verge of extinction before protective measures and

Red maple trees grow along the boardwalk in Ravenswood Park.

replanting ensured the survival of a limited number of specimens. (They are on the state's endangered species list.) In this northern climate, the magnolias do not grow very tall and can be difficult to distinguish from the other trees. Perhaps the best time to spot one is in June, when their creamy white flowers are blooming, giving off a delicate scent. The species growing here is the sweet bay magnolia (*Magnolia virginiana*), a primarily southern species that is native to lowlands and prefers rich, moist soil. Please be sure not to bend the trees' branches to see the flowers up close, as this can damage growth.

The narrow boardwalk continues 0.25 mile before reaching dry ground. The trail bears right and follows the edge of the swamp in a northerly direction for about 0.5 mile, with more large hemlocks, boulders, and rocky outcroppings visible. At junction 14, where the blue-blazed Fernwood Lake Trail enters from the left, turn right onto a shorter boardwalk that crosses the swamp. The path continues uphill, past more hemlocks with winterberry growing below, then joins Old Salem Road.

Turn left here onto Old Salem Road and continue past the lower junction with Evergreen Road at marker 20, following the main road to the left. Look for a few yellow birches off to your left, followed by another wet area where red maple and a few white pines grow. Stone walls lace the woods, indicating this was once pasture or farmland. Chances are, the soil was too stony for growing crops and was used instead for sheep or cattle pasture.

After walking 0.5 mile from the Magnolia Swamp Trail junction, you'll arrive at a boulder with a plaque dedicated to the Hermit of Gloucester, Mason A. Walton. This scholarly man initially came to Gloucester to cure himself of tuberculosis after his wife and child died early in his marriage. As his health improved, and with the permission of the landowner, he built a cabin on the north side of Ravenswood in 1884 and spent his days writing and studying wildlife. People came to his cabin to listen to him discuss the flora and fauna of the area, and he contributed to the magazine that became *Field and Stream*. He died in 1917 at age 79; the cabin was destroyed by a fire in 1948.

One of the animals that was absent in Walton's day but is increasingly common now is the fisher, a large member of the weasel family. Its muzzle is pointed, its ears are broad and rounded, and its legs and feet are stout. Its glossy coat is brownish-black, with small white patches on the neck. Fishers are one of the few animals that kill and eat porcupine. They do so by circling the porcupine, biting its exposed face, and tiring it out before moving in for the kill. The hemlocks along the trail are a chief food source for the porcupine, and the exposed ledges offer good denning areas.

From the hermit site marker (junction 23), begin the return leg of the loop by turning right off Old Salem Road onto Evergreen Road, another wide carriage road that leads southwest. About five minutes farther down this road, the trail passes over a tiny stream where a nice stand of mountain laurel grows beneath the canopy of tall hemlocks. After 0.25 mile of walking, you will reach a road on the left at junction 19. Turn left and continue about 75 feet farther to junction 18 then bear right on Ridge Road. (On future trips, you may want to take an even longer walk by turning left here to visit a small former quarry, returning to the parking area via Quarry Road and the orange-blazed Ledge Hill Trail—a narrow, snaking path through very rocky terrain.) This hike stays on the well-maintained Ridge Road for about 0.5 mile, passing beneath more impressive pines and hemlocks, until it intersects Old Salem Road at junction 2. To reach the parking lot, turn left and follow the road for 0.25 mile.

DID YOU KNOW?

Ravenswood contains many relics of Cape Ann history, from American Indian burial mounds and artifacts, to rock walls and cellar holes built by early settlers, to the old carriage roads that are now park trails.

MORE INFORMATION

The park is open year-round, dawn to dusk. There is no fee (a donation is recommended) and no restrooms. Dogs are allowed. Mountain biking is allowed in designated areas except during the March and April mud season. Call The Trustees of Reservations at 978-526-8687 or visit thetrustees.org.

NEARBY

The Gloucester Fisherman's Memorial on South Stacey Boulevard was established in 1925 in recognition of both the town's 300th anniversary and its many sailors who have been lost at sea. There are restaurants on Main and Rogers streets near the waterfront.

27

HALIBUT POINT STATE PARK AND RESERVATION

Enjoy magnificent views of the ocean, a historical quarry, and a walk along the rocky coastline at the tip of Cape Ann.

DIRECTIONS

Take MA 128 (Yankee Division Highway) to Gloucester. After crossing the Annisquam River bridge, turn north at the Grant Circle rotary on MA 127 (Washington Avenue), following signs for Annisquam and Pigeon Cove. Follow MA 127 for 6.1 miles, then turn left onto Gott Avenue, where you will see the state park entrance. If you are coming from Rockport Center, take MA 127 north for 0.5 mile to Gott Avenue and turn right. *GPS coordinates:* 42° 41.199′ N, 70° 37.902′ W.

By public transportation, Cape Ann Transit Authority (CATA) offers bus service, but riders must request Halibut Point (between the Pigeon Cove post office and the Rockport train station), as the park is not a scheduled stop. For more information, contact CATA at 978-283-7916 or visit canntran.com.

TRAIL DESCRIPTION

On the rockbound Cape Ann coastline, which is more reminiscent of Maine than Massachusetts, Halibut Point offers walkers, beachcombers, birders, and history buffs a wonderful network of trails to explore. The state park and the adjacent shoreline owned by The Trustees of Reservations collectively form a unique area of open space on this rocky headland known as Halibut Point. From 1840 until the mid-twentieth century, Halibut Point was the site of numerous quarry operations sourcing granite as old as 450 million years.

The trail begins across the street from the parking lot at an informational sign. Dense foliage crowds the path,

LOCATION
Rockport, MA

RATING
Easy

DISTANCE
1.5 miles

ELEVATION GAIN
Minimal

ESTIMATED TIME
1 hour

MAPS
USGS Rockport; online: mass.gov/eea/docs/dcr/parks/north/halb.pdf, thetrustees.org/assets/documents/places-to-visit/trailmaps/Halibut-Point-Reservation-Trail-Map.pdf

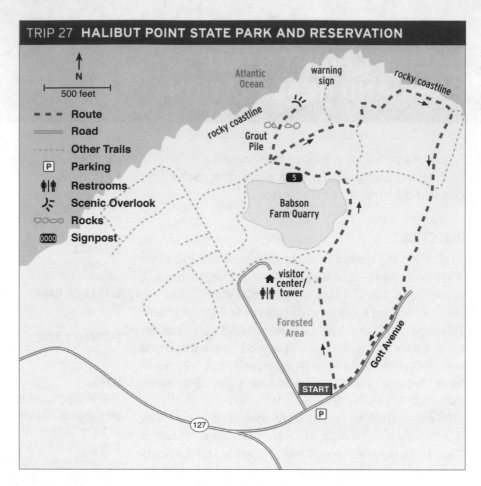

forming a tunnel of green as you walk in a northerly direction heading toward the open Atlantic. The trail is wide and flat, with a covering of wood chips. Red cedars, wild apples, dogwoods, oaks, mountain ash, wild cherry, and the draping vines of grapes line the path. Watch for eastern cottontail rabbits here, especially early and late in the day. After 0.25 mile, you will reach a "T" intersection overlooking Babson Farm Quarry, now filled with water.

Turn right at the quarry and follow the path, which is marked with several interpretive signs, along the quarry's edge. One of the pieces of granite on the left has visible grooves that were created by past cutting and drilling. Follow the path halfway around the quarry, just past marker 5 (the number is painted on a rock on the right), to a fork in the trail. Turn right and follow a sign to an overlook. The jumble of rocks you are standing on is called the Grout Pile, where discarded pieces of granite were dumped over the years and now form the perfect vantage point to view the coastline and ocean. On clear days, you can see the New Hampshire coast, including the Isle of Shoals, and the low profile of Mount Agamenticus in Maine. With binoculars, you can scan the shoreline for seals or watch the lobster anglers checking their traps. Should you see a seal on the rocks below, do not approach it. Young harbor seal pups often rest on the rocks while their mothers continue to feed offshore. The pups will nap then later return to the sea and join their mothers.

During winter, the point is an excellent place to watch for wintering seabirds and waterfowl, including northern gannets, loons, scoters, red-breasted mergansers, red-necked and horned grebes, common eiders, and purple sandpipers. The common loon winters off Halibut Point. It does not make its haunting cry in winter, and its distinctive black-and-white-patterned plumage is replaced by a dull brown color on its back, with its throat and chest white. Loons migrate in small flocks and continue to dive beneath the water surface, hunting for fish. A distinctive seabird to watch for is the razorbill, which bears a resemblance to penguins in its shape and color. Be sure to bring binoculars or a spotting scope, as the birds may be far out at sea or hidden in the coves.

Once you have enjoyed the overlook, retrace your steps 200 feet to the intersection near the quarry, this time following the path with the sign that reads, "To Ocean." The path slopes downward, first through an area of small scrub oaks and shadbush, then to a more open area of large rocks. Use caution when exploring the ocean shoreline, as the pounding surf can sweep over the rocks and make walking hazardous, especially after storms. Look for wildflowers—trout lily, violet, aster, goldenrod—growing in the rocky soil.

As you walk the point, you'll be exploring a landscape unique to the southern New England coast. Cape Ann is the largest outcrop of rocky headland between Cape Cod and Maine's Cape Elizabeth. These ledges are resistant to

Hikers of all ages enjoy exploring the tide pools on Halibut Point.

wave erosion, unlike the sand spits and dunes that constitute the rest of the Bay State's coastline. The slablike granite rocks and toppled ledges at Halibut Point are a testament to the ice sheet that moved through the land 10,000 years ago. The bedrock tended to break along parallel cracks, which is why the granite slabs look layered. Just a few hundred feet farther inland, evidence of the glaciers is seen in the huge, round boulders that litter the landscape. The boulders, called glacial erratics, were deposited haphazardly by the retreating glaciers, and Cape Ann has an abundance.

The rocky ledges offer some of the finest tide pool habitat in Massachusetts, and during low tide, you will be able to observe the marine organisms—starfish, barnacles, algae—that survive this harsh environment by clinging to the rocks.

Once you have enjoyed exploring the rocks near the ocean, follow the path back up to the intersection and head east (to your left when facing away from the water, right if facing the ocean). Carefully cross the open rocks and walk parallel to the ocean for about a quarter-mile toward a lone house you can see farther down the coast. You'll soon arrive at a sign that marks the reservation boundary and points to Sea Rocks, a right-of-way path along the water owned by the town of Rockport. Turn right here onto a narrow path that leads away from the ocean through a grove of low trees. After five to ten minutes of easy walking, turn right onto Gott Avenue and complete the loop by walking 0.25 mile back to the parking area. Please respect the private residences along the road.

DID YOU KNOW?

The Halibut Point area was originally called "Haul About" by sailors because they had to carefully tack around the treacherous, rocky shoreline.

MORE INFORMATION

The park is open year-round, dawn to dusk. There is a $5 parking fee payable at a self-serve station; admission is free for Trustees of Reservations members, pedestrians, and cyclists. Portable restrooms are available. The state park visitor center closed for renovations in 2016 and is scheduled to reopen in 2017. There is no bicycling; pets are allowed on-leash. Natural history programs are offered year-round, and tours of the quarry are offered on Saturdays from Memorial Day to Labor Day. Contact the state park headquarters at 978-546-2997 or visit mass.gov/dcr. Contact The Trustees of Reservations at 978-526-8687 or visit thetrustees.org.

NEARBY

The historical and scenic Gloucester waterfront is a short drive from Halibut Point. Cape Ann is home to five lighthouses, including the Eastern Point Lighthouse at the tip of Eastern Point in Gloucester and the Annisquam Lighthouse, off MA 127 near the Gloucester–Rockport town line. There are restaurants along and off MA 127A in the center of Rockport.

WEST OF BOSTON

The area from the Worcester Hills east of Wachusett Mountain to the outer suburbs of Greater Boston is often referred to as Metro West. Spread throughout this landscape are a number of low, rocky hills, ridges, and outcroppings. While none approaches the 2,000-foot heights of Wa- chusett Mountain and Mount Watatic to the west, many offer surprisingly long views across the region. Several of these are clustered in an area just west of the Route 95 and 128 corridor, including Noon Hill and the Rocky Woods in Medfield; Noanet Peak in Dover; the Rocky Narrows of the Charles River Valley in Sherborn; and Nobscot Hill, the highest point of the Bay Circuit Trail, in Sudbury and Framingham.

Among the major rivers that course through this region are the Nashua, Concord, Sudbury, and Assabet. A series of national wildlife refuges along these waterways, including the Oxbow Refuge in Harvard and Great Meadows in Concord and Sudbury, are managed for the benefit of migratory birds and other wildlife, and they offer trails where visitors may easily explore a variety of habitats. The Nashua River also serves as the source for the Wachusett Reservoir, which was created as a water supply for Boston in 1905. The reservoir is the second largest freshwater lake in Massachusetts after the Quabbin Reservoir and is home to common loons and bald eagles.

Although the Metro West area generally is more developed than most of western and central Massachusetts, it boasts a considerable amount of forested land. This is evidenced by the return in recent years of moose, black bears, and fishers, all of which require large blocks of forested habitat. The woodlands mostly lie within the transition zone between New England's northern and southern forest types and feature a mix of species, including oaks, white pine, birches, and maples. Familiar woodland wildflowers include pink lady's slipper, painted trillium, trailing arbutus (also known as mayflower), and violets.

Despite their proximity to the outer suburbs of Greater Boston, the towns of Concord and Lincoln are home to a number of conservation areas, many of which are also significant historic sites. Perhaps the best known of these is Walden Pond in Concord, once home to Henry David Thoreau and now the site of popular walking trails and a swimming beach. At nearby Minute Man National Historical Park, Battle Road Trail winds through a mosaic of forests, wetlands, farm fields, and historic buildings associated with the American Revolution. In the nearby Sudbury River Valley, Mount Misery is part of an extensive network of protected land and trails managed by the town of Lincoln.

28

WACHUSETT RESERVOIR AND RESERVATION

More than 4,000 acres of water and woods, maintained by the Department of Conservation and Recreation, offer outstanding hiking, snowshoeing, and wildlife watching.

DIRECTIONS

From I-190, take Exit 5 and follow MA 140 south for 2.4 miles, passing the reservoir's Thomas Basin. Turn right at the junction with MA 110 and MA 12, cross the bridge, drive another 0.2 mile, and park in the lot on the left, at gate 25. GPS coordinates: 42° 22.204' N, 71° 46.915' W.

TRAIL DESCRIPTION

Wachusett Reservoir was created in 1905 as part of the water supply for Greater Boston. Along with the Quabbin Reservoir, to which it is connected, it also serves as an important wildlife reservation.

The 4,135-acre reservoir's forest buffer includes a network of unmarked, informal trails, most of which lead to its shores. This 4.2-mile, one-way walk follows the southwest shore, with many fine views across the water. It is but one of many options for visitors here. The woods and wetlands offer excellent wildlife habitat, where common loons, bald eagles, wild turkeys, migrating songbirds, and a variety of waterfowl can be seen.

From the parking area, walk around gate 25 and follow the dirt road across the wide power-line clearing. The mixed habitat of field, open water, and forest is a good place to look for wildlife, including white-tailed deer, wild turkeys, and a variety of songbirds: common yellowthroats, wood thrushes, and prairie warblers. The road curves left, crosses a small brook, then follows a straight and level course through a pine plantation. Several narrow side paths on the left lead to the reservoir.

LOCATION
West Boylston, MA

RATING
Easy

DISTANCE
4.2 miles

ELEVATION GAIN
225 feet

ESTIMATED TIME
2.25 hours

MAPS
USGS Hudson, USGS Marlborough, USGS Worcester North; online: mass.gov/eea/agencies/dcr/massparks/region-central/wachusett-reservoir.html

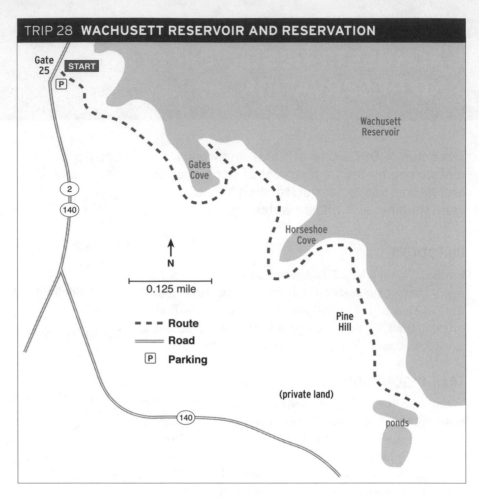

Gate 25
START
P

Wachusett
Reservoir

Gates
Cove

2
140

Horseshoe
Cove

N

0.125 mile

Pine
Hill

- - - Route
——— Road
P   Parking

(private land)

140

ponds

After ten to fifteen minutes, you'll cross a bridge over Scarlett's Brook then continue up the hill above the stream. At the crest of the climb, bear left at a junction and descend the hill to another intersection at marker 306. Turn left here to make a short one-way detour to Gates Cove. From the shoreline at the trail's end, there are fine views across the water to the historical Old Stone Church and Wachusett Mountain.

Due to its size, Wachusett Reservoir attracts many birds, including bald eagles and nesting pairs of common loons. The common loon can be identified by a long, pointed bill on a sleek black head and black-and-white markings on its back. If you are lucky, you might hear one or more of its calls. At night it tends to emit a mournful wail, while in the daytime you are more apt to hear its tremolo, which sounds like a demented laugh. Both can send shivers up your spine.

Watching a loon is fascinating, whether it is taking off, flying, or diving. It is a large bird, weighing about 9 pounds, and has difficulty getting into the air. That's why you never see a loon on a small body of water. It needs up to

Wildlife sightings are frequent in Wachusett Reservoir. Here, common loons swim the southwest shore.

a quarter-mile to flap its wings, running along the lake's surface to become airborne. Once in the air, the bird is at home, traveling at speeds in excess of 60 MPH. Equally impressive is the loon's ability to dive underwater in search of fish. It uses its wings to propel itself underwater and usually stays beneath the surface for about 40 seconds, although loons have been known to stay submerged for up to five minutes.

The adjacent forests are home to wildlife, including coyotes, deer, and bobcats. Some say the cougar, considered extinct in New England, might roam these woods. There have been many reported sightings in New England, including several at Quabbin Reservoir, although people may be seeing an animal that was illegally released from captivity. It's fun to speculate, but until one is captured or a high-quality photo is taken and clearly defined tracks are found, we can only speculate.

To continue the hike, backtrack to marker 306 and follow the wide main dirt road through the woods. After approximately ten minutes, the trail curves to the left, crosses a small brook lined with skunk cabbage, and follows the shore at Horseshoe Cove. Check the low vegetation on the left for more songbirds and colorful dragonflies. There are approximately 170 species of odonates—or the collective order of dragonflies and damselflies—active in Massachusetts throughout the warm months. After a few minutes, the road splits. Follow the left fork along the shore, with more good views of the reservoir. Stay straight where the road narrows and continue to follow the path along the shore. The trail soon curves to the right and rejoins the main dirt road near a small sand beach.

The reservoir's deep, clear waters offer anglers excellent opportunities for catching lake trout, brown trout, salmon, and some very large smallmouth bass. No boating is allowed, but shore fishing is permitted at gates 6 through 35 and at Thomas Basin. (It is prohibited in the northern area near the dam.) The fishing season runs from April (if the ice is out) to November 30; other regulations are posted at mass.gov/dcr.

Continue on the road, with the water to your left and the steep slopes and outcroppings of Pine Hill on the right. The trail continues above two ponds in the ravine on the right then reaches marker 312 at a fire hydrant and the pumping station building. A narrow path drops down to the edge of the ponds, and a short trail leads to the reservoir's edge. This marks the endpoint of this hike, although more woods roads and trails stretch beyond this area for those with more time to explore. Backtrack to the parking area, making sure to keep the water on your right as you retrace your steps. At marker 306, you can save time by bypassing the side trip to the shore.

DID YOU KNOW?

At the time of its creation, Wachusett Reservoir was the world's largest artificial reservoir. Anticipating the need for further sources, state water-supply planners included an aqueduct intake from the west, which eventually became Quabbin Reservoir.

MORE INFORMATION

The Department of Conservation and Recreation (DCR) manages the lands surrounding the reservoir, protecting the water quality and enhancing the ecological integrity of this valuable natural resource. Trails are open from one hour before sunrise to one hour after sunset. There is no fee; dogs are prohibited. For more information, call 978-365-3800 or visit mass.gov/dcr. Maps and information are available at the administration building on 180 Beaman Street (MA 140) in West Boylston. Hiking is allowed in any area unless posted otherwise. Entrances currently open are gates 6 through 16 along MA 70, gates 17 through 24 along MA 140, and gates 25 through 42 along MA 12 and 110. The bluffs at the reservoir's south end can be reached by parking on MA 140 (just west of MA 70) and walking along the shoreline, heading to the right, or from gates 13 through 15 off MA 70. From here, you can get a sense of just how large the reservoir is.

NEARBY

For history buffs, the place to go is West Boylston's Old Stone Church, located on the shores of the reservoir just off MA 140, about 200 yards past where it splits from MA 12. (The street name for MA 140 here, along the Thomas Basin section of the reservoir, is Beaman Street.) Only the church's stone exterior remains, as the church had to be abandoned when the reservoir was created. Although its interior has been stripped bare, it is still a beautiful structure and a good starting point for a stroll around Thomas Basin. Large maples and pines dot the shoreline path, and waterfowl can often be seen resting in the basin.

The popular Wachusett Mountain State Reservation and Ski Area, featuring 17 miles of hiking trails and long views from the region's highest summit, is a short drive north along Route 140, in Princeton. There are restaurants in the center of Clinton, reachable via MA 62, 70, or 110, along and off High Street.

MASSACHUSETTS' WATERSHED WILDERNESS

The history of the water supply in Massachusetts is as old as the state itself. In the years following European settlement, the city of Boston used a variety of local sources for drinking water, including Jamaica Pond. As the region's population rapidly grew, the ponds proved incapable of meeting the increased demand, and state planners began searching outside of the metropolitan region for future sources.

A series of reservoirs west of the city reached their capacity by the end of the nineteenth century, so planners recommended creating an extensive water-supply network in central Massachusetts. In 1897 construction began on Wachusett Reservoir, which was formed by the impoundment of the south branch of the Nashua River, near Worcester. The work was completed by 1905, and when the new reservoir was filled to its capacity in 1908, it became both the world's largest artificial reservoir and the largest freshwater body in Massachusetts. Water was delivered from Wachusett Reservoir to Weston Reservoir, near Boston, via a long aqueduct. In order to build Wachusett Reservoir, several neighborhoods in the towns of West Boylston and Clinton had to be abandoned and flooded. Today, one building from these neighborhoods, the Old Stone Church in West Boylston, remains standing near the water's edge; it is one of the town's best-known landmarks.

In spite of Wachusett Reservoir's size, it was only a matter of time before more regional water sources would be necessary. During the early 1920s, the state began planning for the much larger Quabbin Reservoir in the Swift River Valley. This was an especially controversial project, as it called for four towns—Enfield, Dana, Prescott, and Greenwich—to be abandoned and flooded. Roughly 3,500 people were dislocated, buildings were razed, and in 1938 the towns officially ceased to exist. Although residents were compensated by the state, the amount they received for their land was low. The 40-square-mile reservoir was filled during the mid-1940s.

With the completion of Quabbin Reservoir, Boston's water needs seemed secure. But due to the prolonged drought of the 1960s, water supply again became an issue, and a proposal was put forward to divert portions of the Connecticut River to Quabbin. This time there was considerable sustained opposition from a variety of interests in western Massachusetts, and the project was never approved. A fortunate byproduct of the debates was the adoption of water-conservation measures in eastern Massachusetts, which have significantly reduced the region's water demand in recent decades.

29

MOUNT PISGAH CONSERVATION AREA

Hike along old stone walls and woodland streams to the summit of Mount Pisgah and enjoy views of Hudson, Marlborough, and the Worcester Hills.

DIRECTIONS

From I-290, take the Church Street/Boylston/Northborough exit (Exit 24). At the end of the exit, follow signs toward Boylston. Turn right onto Ball Street at the sign for Tougas Family Farm. Follow Ball Street for 1.7 miles to its end. Turn left onto Green Street, traveling 0.5 mile to where the road forks, and bear right onto Smith Road. Travel 0.3 mile to the parking area on the right. *GPS coordinates: 42° 21.587′ N, 71° 40.267′ W.*

TRAIL DESCRIPTION

Mount Pisgah is located in the hilly northwest section of Northborough, adjacent to the Berlin town line. It is the highest point in Northborough and offers scenic views across the hills of southern Worcester County. A mix of narrow footpaths and old dirt roads traverse a forest of red oak, white pine, maple, and beech. Other features, such as forest streams and stone walls marking the old farms that once operated on these grounds, also await your discovery. The 83-acre Mount Pisgah Conservation Area abuts other conservation land, including a 92-acre tract owned by the Massachusetts Division of Fisheries & Wildlife, that forms a fairly large patch of contiguous second- or third-growth forest with habitat for a variety of wildlife. The reservation's trails also connect to other recreational trails in the town of Berlin. This hike is a fairly easy circuit that includes a short climb to the ridge of Mount Pisgah. The route combines several of the reservation's well-marked trails.

LOCATION
Northborough, MA

RATING
Easy

DISTANCE
1.75 miles

ELEVATION GAIN
115 feet

ESTIMATED TIME
1.5 hours

MAPS
USGS Marlborough; online: svtweb.org/sites/default/files/MountPisgah.pdf

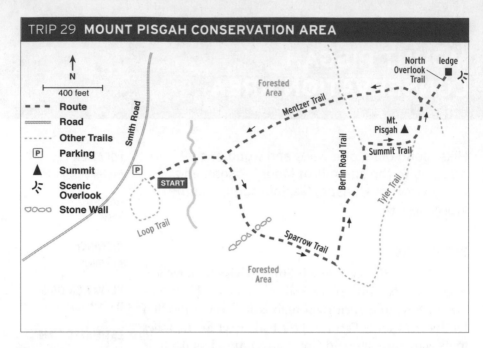

From the parking area, follow the yellow-blazed Mentzer Trail east, passing beneath tall white pines. A couple of minutes in, on your left will be a small grove of young trees that has sprung up from what was once a field cleared for agriculture. Opportunistic (also known as "early successional" or "pioneer") tree species, including gray birch, poplar, pine cherry, and white pine, are the first to establish themselves in such areas, later to be followed by oaks and maples. Look for eastern cottontail rabbits in the tangle of undergrowth and in the thick grasses.

Within 0.25 mile, the trail crosses Howard Brook then splits. Go right on the red-blazed Sparrow Trail. Red maples, oaks, and pines line this path, which is rocky in places. On the forest floor are blueberry bushes, sheep laurel, and herbaceous plants, such as partridge berry, mosses, and princess pine. After another 0.25 mile, the path comes to a stone wall and curls to the left, following the wall.

Go along the stone wall for a couple of minutes then continue to the right through an opening in the wall. The path now heads primarily eastward again and soon intersects with an old logging road called Berlin Road Trail. Turn left onto the logging road and follow it for 0.25 mile until you come to Summit Trail on the right. Take this right and go about an eighth of a mile to a "T" intersection then turn left onto Tyler Trail. You are now on the spine of a ridge. Look for a rock a few feet off the trail to the left embedded with the U.S. Geological Survey marker indicating the summit of Mount Pisgah. The vista from the ridge requires about five more minutes of walking to the next "T" intersection, where Mentzer Trail, which is your return route, comes in on the left. Here you should turn right and go 20 feet to where the trail forks. Bear left, proceeding about 200 feet to the exposed rock ridge, where there's a view overlooking Hudson and Marlborough to the east.

The walk down from the hilltop is a more direct route to the entrance and takes only about 20 to 25 minutes. From the overlook, backtrack to the intersection of Tyler and Mentzer trails and continue straight on the latter, following yellow markers. Continue straight where the trail crosses Berlin Road Trail. The path will lead through a stand of hardwoods where white birches soon become more numerous.

It is not uncommon to come across deer and raccoon tracks. The elusive fisher, a large member of the weasel family, has also been spotted here. Fishers are great hunters of squirrels, porcupines, rabbits, mice, and birds. Barred and great horned owls have been seen here, along with hawks, deer, and foxes. Of the two foxes that live in Massachusetts, red foxes are fairly common, while gray foxes, which have catlike claws enabling them to climb trees, are somewhat shier and more elusive. They occasionally establish dens close to human dwellings, including in barns and backyards.

The trail you are on soon enters the shade of a pine grove then, 0.3 miles from the Berlin Road Trail crossing, returns to the stream junction you crossed at the start of the hike. Turn right here and cross the stream to return to the parking lot.

Easterly views from central Massachusetts' Mount Pisgah can extend as far as Boston.

DID YOU KNOW?

The conservation area's trails are named for families with historical connections to the land. The Mentzer, Sparrow, Bennett, and Tetreault families all operated farms in the area, and legacies of their activity, such as stone walls and old farm equipment, remain along the trails.

MORE INFORMATION

Mount Pisgah Conservation Area is open year-round, dawn to dusk; there is no fee. There are no restrooms. Dogs are allowed, but owners must clean up after them. Visit svtweb.org for more information. The Mentzer farmhouse is still standing near the town center on Green Street.

NEARBY

Much of the land surrounding Mount Pisgah is still actively farmed. From June to November, the nearby Tougas Family Farm offers fruit picking, including apples, strawberries, peaches, raspberries, and blueberries. There are also animals for children to visit and a kitchen that serves country dishes. Contact the farm at 508-393-6406 for more information. There are restaurants along US 20 and MA 9.

30

OXBOW NATIONAL WILDLIFE REFUGE

Part of the Eastern Massachusetts National Wildlife Refuge Complex, the Oxbow National Wildlife Refuge protects wetlands and forests along the Nashua River.

DIRECTIONS

From MA 2 in Harvard, take Exit 38A and follow MA 110/111 south for 1.6 miles. At Harvard Center, turn right and continue on MA 110 for 2 miles to the village of Still River. At the post office, turn right onto Still River Depot Road, following signs for the refuge. After passing the refuge's open fields, cross the railroad tracks then bear right to the main parking area, where maps, brochures, and restrooms are available. *GPS coordinates: 42° 29.744' N, 71° 37.565' W.*

TRAIL DESCRIPTION

If you're an enthusiast of wetlands and wildlife, you'll enjoy the Oxbow National Wildlife Refuge, a nearly 1,700-acre complex of wetlands, forests, and fields along the banks of the Nashua River in the picturesque town of Harvard. From 1917 until 1974, much of the refuge was part of the Fort Devens military reservation, and the Department of Defense still has land holdings on the other side of the river. You may hear target practice and drills during your visit.

This hike follows the refuge's 1.9-mile interpretive trail, which comprises three short paths, each exploring a different habitat. Along the way, you'll have continuous views of a variety of habitats, including the river and its associated swamps, ponds, and beaver wetlands; floodplain and upland forests; and fields, which sustain a diverse wildlife community. Numbered posts correspond to an interpretive flyer available at the information kiosk. Portions of this route, especially near the junction of the river and the

LOCATION
Harvard, MA

RATING
Easy

DISTANCE
1.9 miles

ELEVATION GAIN
Minimal

ESTIMATED TIME
1.25 hours

MAPS
USGS Ayer; online: fws.gov/refuge/oxbow

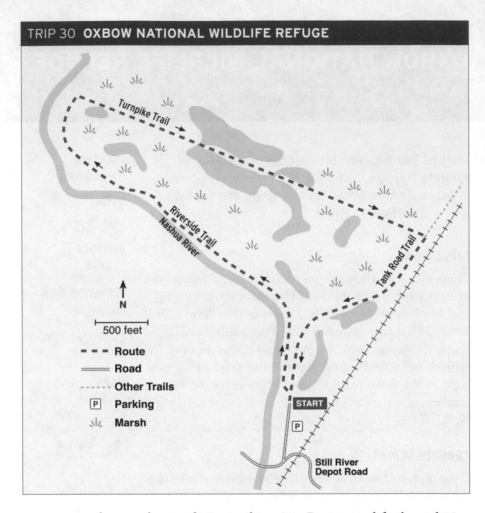

Turnpike Trail

Riverside Trail
Nashua River

Tank Road Trail

N

500 feet

- - - **Route**
——— **Road**
- - - - - **Other Trails**
P **Parking**
ᴽᴸ **Marsh**

START

P

Still River
Depot Road

causeway paths, may be wet during early spring. Be prepared for bugs during late spring and summer.

From the information kiosk at the parking lot, walk around the metal gate to your right onto Tank Road Trail then quickly bear left at a marked junction onto Riverside Trail. This narrow path follows the east bank of the Nashua River, offering fine views across the water. Walk quietly, and you may well see a great blue heron or a flock of ducks here. Along the banks is a cluster of silver maples, one of the trees characteristic of floodplain forests. Riverside Trail parallels Tank Road Trail, which is a short distance through the woods to your right, for 0.2 mile (a short crossover path connects the two trails) then bears left to follow a bend in the river.

You'll soon pass a large clearing on the right maintained as a field for the benefit of wildlife. Before the military acquired it, the refuge was productive farmland, as the valley offered much more fertile soil than the surrounding rocky hills. Among the many upland species that benefit from mixed habitats are eastern coyotes, red and gray foxes, white-tailed deer, bluebirds, monarch butterflies, and numerous birds of prey. Field wildflowers, such as Queen Anne's lace and goldenrod, bloom during summer and nourish a variety of insects.

From the field, the trail continues north along the river. Another tree that grows in the floodplain is shagbark hickory, whose overlaying sections of bark indeed give it a shaggy appearance. During late spring and early summer, you'll likely see many ebony jewelwing damselflies—easily identified by their brilliant, dark green bodies and black wings—flitting around the vegetation that borders the river. Damselflies are distinguished from dragonflies by their smaller size and their practice of perching with their wings folded vertically. (Dragonflies spread theirs out horizontally.) Another insect to watch for is the small, orange-and-black pearl crescent butterfly. Frogs and toads scamper across the grassy path below.

At 0.8 mile from the trailhead, the path turns sharply to the right at marker 6 and leads away from the river to explore the adjacent floodplain. You are now walking on Turnpike Trail, originally built by farmers to transport hay out of the wet meadows. This portion of the walk is prone to flooding in early spring, and if it is impassable, you can backtrack to the start and walk the rest of the hike in reverse. The muddy areas here offer plenty of opportunities to look for animal tracks; some of the most common are those of white-tailed deer and

Beaver wetlands and floodplain forests make up a large portion of Oxbow National Wildlife Refuge.

raccoons. The trail crosses a series of wood bridges and short boardwalks then continues east in a straight line along a causeway.

The path passes close by two large beaver lodges, offering excellent close-up views of their architecture. Hard as it may be to believe now, beavers once were nearly eliminated from much of Massachusetts and the rest of New England due to unregulated hunting and trapping. Wars and settlement of North America were influenced by access to beavers and their pelts. Look carefully for trees that have been cut by beavers, the animal that affects this landscape more than any other, apart from humans. Wading birds and waterfowl benefit from beaver-created wetlands; keep an eye out for great blue herons, green herons, and wood ducks.

A few minutes farther along, a short side trail on the right leads to an enclosed wooden observation blind at the edge of a wetland where you can watch for ducks, birds, river otters, turtles, raccoons, and muskrats. The main trail continues along the north shore of this pool then ends at a three-way junction with Tank Road Trail, 1.5 miles from the trailhead and 0.7 mile from the river.

Here you have the option of continuing the loop by turning right, or extending the outing by making a one-way detour on Tank Road Trail. For the latter, the road continues north for approximately 0.8 mile to a beaver pond and the Route 2 overpass. On the north side of the overpass, the road connects with the recently established Goddard Trail and a trail to Mirror Lake, a kettle pond that abuts the refuge (follow signs at junctions).

For those following the circuit, Tank Road Trail—the name of which is a holdover from the old military reservation—leads past a grove of large white pines and briefly parallels the Boston and Maine Railroad tracks, then follows the edge of another wetland. Black-eyed Susans and daisy wildflowers grow along the road's edge in summer. The river and Riverside Trail soon come into view on the right, and for a last view of the water, you can take the short crossover trail on the right. After 0.4 mile of easy walking from the Turnpike Trail junction, you'll be back at the main parking area.

DID YOU KNOW?

Biologists at the refuge monitor a variety of wildlife species, including birds, reptiles, amphibians, and mammals. Their findings are used to plan future management practices for this and other refuges, such as creating freshwater impoundments for waterfowl and fields for American woodcock and bluebirds.

MORE INFORMATION

The refuge is open year-round from dawn to dusk. There is no visitor center onsite; restrooms, maps, and brochures, including a bird checklist, are available at the parking lot. A boat launch is near the parking area. Camping, fires, and swimming are prohibited; fishing is allowed in the river but not in ponds or wetlands; skiing is allowed. The refuge is part of the Eastern Massachusetts National Wildlife Refuge Complex, the headquarters and visitor center for which are at the Great Meadows National Wildlife Refuge Sudbury Unit in Sudbury. For more information, call 978-443-4661 or visit fws.gov/refuge/oxbow. A map of Mirror Lake is available at harvardconservationtrust.org.

NEARBY

The Fruitlands Museum, a short distance from the refuge at 102 Prospect Hill Road, is a National Historic Landmark with exhibits related to New England's landscape. This was also the site of a utopian experiment by Bronson Alcott and Charles Lane in 1843. The museum is open from mid-April to mid-November; visit fruitlands.org for more information. There are restaurants on Ayer Road (MA 110/111) north of the junction with MA 2.

31

GREAT BROOK FARM STATE PARK

Great Brook Farm offers a wide variety of flora and fauna for nature study and groomed trails for cross-country skiing.

DIRECTIONS

From I-495, take exit 32. Take MA 225 and follow it to Carlisle Center. At the rotary bear right on Lowell Street (following the sign for Chelmsford) for 2 miles to the park entrance on the right. *GPS coordinates:* 42° 33.365′ N, 71° 20.889′ W.

TRAIL DESCRIPTION

Purchased by the state in 1974, Great Brook Farm is rich in history and has more than 10 miles of trails. The popular Pine Point Loop trail, named for its passage beneath towering white pines, is a pleasant 2-mile ramble around Meadow Pond. A designated Healthy Heart Trail, Pine Point Loop is marked with blue markers and painted blazes. At numbered junctions, it connects with numerous less-traveled park trails, including Tophet Swamp Loop at the southern end of the property.

From the parking area, walk around a small pond toward the red farm buildings. Turn right onto Lantern Loop Trail near a kiosk (maps may be available), bike rack, and sign for the ice cream stand. Continue a short distance to North Road. Cross the road in front of the farm and begin Pine Point Loop at a sign reading, "Trails Open to Hiking," with a blue blaze. Follow the path about 600 feet then bear right onto a dirt farm road and continue past an arm of Meadow Pond, a shallow body of water with fingers stretching in various directions. The trail is wide and flat, making it an excellent place for cross-country skiing. Picnic tables are scattered about the fields and woods, including one that rests on a point of land jutting toward the water.

LOCATION
Carlisle, MA

RATING
Easy

DISTANCE
2.25 miles (Pine Point Loop),
3 miles (with extension)

ELEVATION GAIN
Minimal

ESTIMATED TIME
1.5 hours

MAPS
USGS Billerica; online: mass
.gov/eea/docs/dcr/parks/trails/
greatbrook-summer.pdf

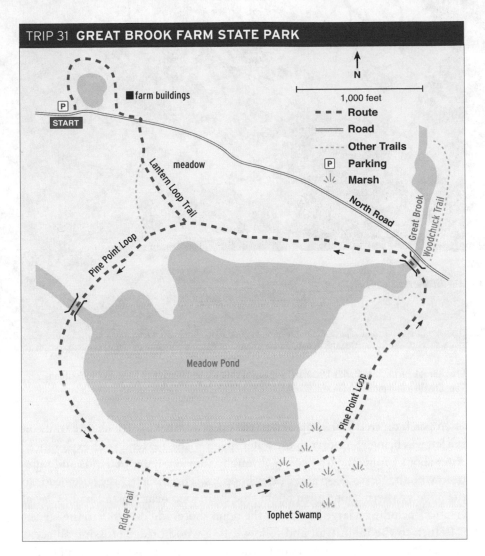

Keep an eye out for great blue herons, which can blend in perfectly with dead trees at the edge of Meadow Pond. Another fascinating bird sometimes seen here is the wood duck. Nesting boxes have been erected on posts in the ponds to help these colorful birds reestablish in New England. They had declined due to both hunting and the widespread cutting of the large trees in which they nest. The males are especially beautiful, with iridescent greens, purples, and blues, and a white chin patch. Females are a grayish-brown color with a white eye ring. Their habitat includes wooded rivers, ponds, and swamps. They are fast flyers and are quite agile as they navigate airborne between trees.

Follow the main trail past wetlands then bear left at a cornfield on the right at marker 21. In past centuries, American Indians planted corn and other crops in the fertile meadows here. Listen for the screeches of the red-tailed hawks that

Great Brook Farm State Park's 1,000 acres features more than 20 miles of trails. Photo by Joanna Poe, Creative Commons on Flickr.

often perch on tree limbs adjacent to the open cornfield. Various side trails on the left will bring you closer to the water if you wish to extend your exploration. After about 1 mile, the trail passes through more low-lying wetlands and junctions with the Keyes Loop and Beaver Loop trails on the left. (The latter leads to the pond's eastern shores then rejoins the main loop near North Road.) Glacial erratics, including a large boulder at the pond shore, add diversity to the scene.

Return to the main trail and follow it to a wood bridge crossing adjacent North Road, where the waters of Great Brook tumble over a dam and out of the pond. Next to the bridge is a small parking area with access to the trail. (A parking pass is required in season.) Here you have the option of detouring off the pond loop to explore the trails on the opposite side of the road at marker 13. If you follow Woodchuck Trail across the road and along Great Brook, it soon reaches the site of an old mill on a small pond. At the back end of the pond, the water cascades over a waterfall lined with stones erected by the settlers. Try to imagine the work that must have gone into its construction. The pattern of the lichen-covered rocks and the whitewater below makes for an interesting scene.

In 1691, John Barrett built one of the first cloth-fulling mills in America here, to clean and thicken cloth. A sawmill and a gristmill were erected in the early 1700s. The power of Great Brook was also put to work in the 1800s, when mills made wheels, nail kegs, and birch hoops. The mill site is still visible at the northeastern end of the property, just beyond where Great Brook passes under North Road.

As you retrace your steps toward North Road, notice a small sign for the garrison, where the pioneers erected a stone house for protection. If the approximately 15-foot-wide cellar hole was the entire size of the house, it must have been cramped inside, but tight quarters would have been the least of the settlers' worries during a raid.

To complete the hike, return to Pine Point Loop and follow the path past a small field and through the woods on the north side of the pond. (You can also walk along North Road for 0.5 mile, back toward the parking area.) You'll soon return to the junction with the dirt road at the start of the loop. Bear right and retrace your steps to the farm and the parking area. Along the way, you will have the pleasure of seeing the farm and pastures. Children enjoy seeing the cows in the fields and the ducks in the pond near the barn. You can top off your trip with a visit to the ice cream stand at the back of the farm.

DID YOU KNOW?

There are several American Indian sacred sites on the grounds, and agriculture has been practiced here for centuries. Holstein cattle have been kept on-site for the past 60 years, through present day.

MORE INFORMATION

Great Brook Farm is open dawn to dusk; there is a $2 parking fee from April 1 to December 1. For more information, call 978-369-6312 or visit mass.gov/dcr.

The Great Brook Ski Touring Center is open from December 1 to March 20 (snow conditions permitting) on Mondays, Wednesdays, and Fridays from 10 A.M. to 5 P.M.; Tuesdays and Thursdays from 10 A.M. to 9 P.M. (with night skiing on Lantern Loop); and weekends and holidays from 9 A.M. to 5 P.M. It offers ski rentals and a lodge and snack bar. Call 978-369-7486 or visit greatbrookski.com.

NEARBY

Carlisle is a small, rural town with little development. Fern's Country Store, a classic New England general store that has operated at its present location on the village-center rotary since 1844, offers sandwiches, soups, salads, and dinners. Ice cream is available at the nearby Kimball Farm Ice Cream Stand on 343 Bedford Road (MA 225).

32

GREAT MEADOWS NATIONAL WILDLIFE REFUGE

The trails at Great Meadows, one of the region's richest wildlife areas, offer continuous views of the Concord River, its floodplain, and two ponds.

DIRECTIONS

From the center of Concord, follow MA 62 east for 1.4 miles then turn left onto Monsen Road. Continue 0.3 mile to a sign for the refuge then turn left and follow the refuge entrance road to the parking area. *GPS coordinates*: 42° 28.507' N, 71° 19.770' W.

By public transportation, take the Fitchburg line of the MBTA Commuter Rail to Concord, walk to the town center, and follow MA 62 to Monsen Road. The refuge is approximately 2.3 miles from the Commuter Rail station.

TRAIL DESCRIPTION

The 3,800-acre Great Meadows National Wildlife Refuge comprises two divisions, known as the Concord and Sudbury units, that include portions of the Concord and Sudbury rivers. It's part of the Eastern Massachusetts National Wildlife Refuge Complex, which also includes the nearby Assabet River and Oxbow National Wildlife Refuge. These three preserves protect more than 7,000 acres of habitat for wildlife in the heart of New England's most populous region. The visitor center is located at the Sudbury Unit. (See "More Information," on page 151.) The route described here follows Dike Trail at the Concord Unit, an easy circuit through prime wildlife habitats.

At the start or finish of your walk, be sure to climb the observation tower adjacent to the parking area for sweeping views across the refuge. Dike Trail begins at a gate next to an information sign across the parking lot from the tower and follows a straight causeway between the

LOCATION
Concord, MA

RATING
Easy

DISTANCE
1.7 miles

ELEVATION GAIN
Minimal

ESTIMATED TIME
1 hour, plus time to watch wildlife

MAPS
USGS Maynard; online: fws .gov/refuge/great_meadows

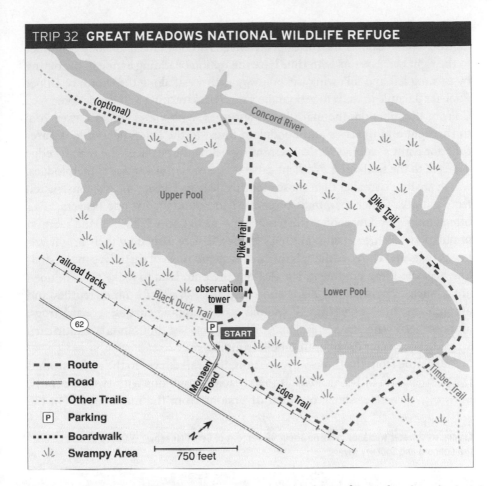

Upper and Lower pools. The impoundments are drained into the river during summer, opening up extensive mudflats that are heavily used by southbound migratory waterfowl and songbirds.

This is one of the region's richest wildlife areas. More than 220 birds have been recorded here, including the tiny but loud marsh wrens that breed at only a handful of other sites in Massachusetts. Watch for them in clumps of cattails during warm months. Thanks to an active nest box program, the refuge hosts a healthy population of wood ducks, which have recovered from decline caused by hunting and the loss of mature nesting trees. Other breeding waterfowl include blue-winged teals, mallards, grebes, black ducks, American coots, and Canada geese, while American wigeons and gadwalls pass through during migrations. During spring and late summer, you may see migrating shorebirds, such as dunlins, greater and lesser yellowlegs, and sandpipers, in muddy areas. The often elusive marsh birds include soras, Virginia rails, great blue and green herons, and black-crowned night herons. Characteristic songbirds of wetland edges include northern water thrushes, swamp sparrows, yellow warblers, and great-crested flycatchers.

After 0.4 mile, the trail arrives at a three-way junction on the narrow strip of land between the pools and the Concord River. Although the main loop continues to the right here, visitors with time have the option of adding a mile to the outing by turning left and following the one-way path west, along the shores of Upper Pool, for 0.5 mile to the refuge boundary then backtracking to the junction.

From the junction, the main loop continues, with views across Lower Pool to the right and the river and floodplain forest to the left. Stop and look carefully for giant snapping turtles swimming below the surface. The marshy edge adjacent to the trail offers excellent close-up views of muskrats and their lodges, which are much smaller than those made by beavers and are mostly constructed from cattails. Other mammals present in the wetlands include beavers, river otters, minks, and raccoons. The refuge is home to one of New England's largest populations of threatened Blanding's turtles, distinguished by their bright yellow throats and chins. Although the turtles spend most of their lives in the shallow, vegetated impoundment, females venture onto land to make nests in open areas, such as agricultural fields and backyards. Watch for other reptiles and amphibians, including painted, spotted, and snapping turtles; leopard frogs; and northern water snakes. In late April, you may see thousands of exotic carp attempting to enter the impoundment from the river.

At 0.6 mile from the three-way junction, the trail curves to the right, around the northern tip of Lower Pool. It then reaches junctions with two side trails, both of which offer short, optional diversions from the main route. On the

Crucial freshwater wetlands make up about 85 percent of Great Meadows' 3,600-plus acres along the Concord and Sudbury Rivers.

right is the 0.35-mile-long Edge Trail, which explores the woods along the edge of Lower Pool. To the left is Timber Trail, which makes a 0.4-mile loop through oak, pine, and maple woodlands. The oak-pine woods add to the refuge's habitat diversity and are home to red foxes, white-tailed deer, and songbirds (northern orioles, red-breasted grosbeaks, scarlet tanagers, phoebes, and eastern wood peewees). Year-round residents include great horned and eastern screech owls, red-bellied and pileated woodpeckers, and wild turkeys.

At 1.3 miles, Dike Trail joins the Bay Circuit Trail at a junction near the refuge boundary. Turn right and follow both trails southwest along the old Boston and Maine Railroad line for 0.4 mile to the refuge entrance road. The Bay Circuit Trail continues south from the refuge to Minute Man National Historical Park and Walden Pond.

DID YOU KNOW?

The Concord and Sudbury rivers have a long history of human use, as evidenced by relics of American Indian activity dating to 5,500 BCE. In pre-Colonial times, the meadows were used as agricultural fields and burned to create habitat for game animals.

MORE INFORMATION

A parking fee ($4 weekly, $12 annual) is now charged at the Concord Unit. Passes may be purchased at a self-serve pay station, at the Great Meadows and Assabet River refuge offices, or by phone or internet. Other federal passes, including Duck Stamps, are accepted. The trails close at sunset.

The refuge headquarters and visitor center are located at the Sudbury Unit. From MA 27 on the Sudbury–Wayland town line, turn north onto Old Water Row and continue 1.9 miles to a right onto Lincoln Road. Follow Lincoln Road 0.4 mile then turn left onto Weir Hill Road and continue 0.3 mile to the refuge entrance road. There are two short interpretive trails at the Sudbury Unit that can be combined into an easy 1-mile circuit exploring wetlands along the Sudbury River and a low glacial hill along its banks.

Boat launches are available on the river roads near both divisions. A launch for cartop boats is available at the Sudbury Unit; it requires a five-minute walk from the entrance over easy terrain. For more information, call 978-443-4661 or visit fws.gov/refuge/great_meadows.

NEARBY

The Great Meadows Concord Unit is a short drive from Minute Man National Historical Park (Trip 33) and Walden Pond (Trip 34). The Old North Bridge and the Minute Man Statue, which mark the site of the first battle in the American Revolution, are just west of the refuge off Monument Street. There are restaurants in Concord Center.

33

MINUTE MAN NATIONAL HISTORICAL PARK: BATTLE ROAD TRAIL

This historic woodland-and-meadow trek doesn't stray far from settled areas but is quaint and pleasant nonetheless, particularly in spring and fall.

DIRECTIONS

From I-95, take Exit 30B for MA 2A west to Concord. Follow MA 2A approximately 0.3 mile. You will enter the park and see signs directing you to the Minute Man Visitor Center located less than 1 mile from I-95/MA 128. From the visitor center, follow MA 2A west 1.9 miles then bear right onto Lexington Road and continue 0.9 mile to Meriam's Corner in Concord. Turn right onto Old Bedford Road then enter the parking area on the right. *GPS coordinates*: 42° 27.606' N, 71° 19.424' W.

By public transportation, take the Fitchburg line of the MBTA Commuter Rail to the Concord stop. Walk along Sudbury Road to the center of town (Sudbury Road converges with Main Street) and take a right onto MA 2A. Stay left when, after the Alcott House, the Cambridge Turnpike diverges to the right. You'll pass the Wayside Visitor Center on your right and soon will come to Meriam's Corner, where this hike begins. The trailhead is 2.5 miles from the Commuter Rail station.

TRAIL DESCRIPTION

Congress created Minute Man National Historical Park in 1959 to preserve and interpret the events, ideas, significant historic sites, structures, properties, and landscapes associated with the start of the American Revolution.

The theme of this trail is the Battle of April 19, 1775, which launched the American Revolution, but the trail interprets the broader story of the people whose lives were altered by the events that took place here, including their

LOCATION
Concord, Lincoln, and Lexington, MA

RATING
Moderate

DISTANCE
5 miles

ELEVATION GAIN
Minimal

ESTIMATED TIME
3 hours

MAPS
USGS Maynard; online: nps.gov/mima/planyourvisit/maps.htm

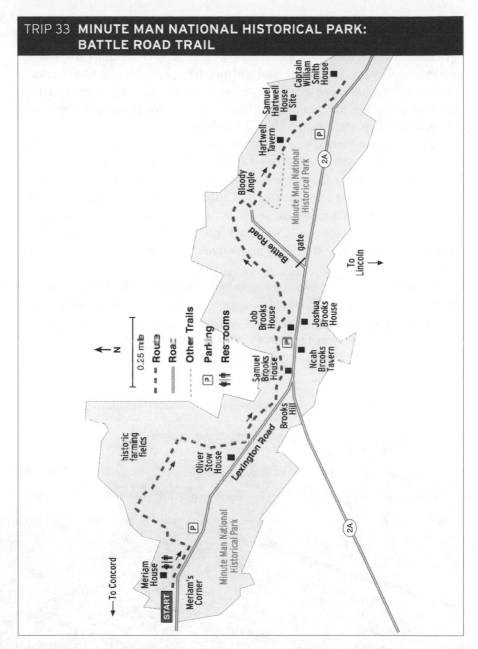

relationship with the landscape. Much of the trail follows remnants of the Battle Road, although some sections leave the historic road to follow the route of the Minute Men, traversing a mosaic of farming fields, wetlands, and forests. Fall foliage can be particularly spectacular here, but it can also bring crowds on weekends. Winter is quieter, and the park's trails are great for snowshoeing. The route as described here is a 5-mile round-trip hike that returns you to your car. It takes you from the Meriam House to the Captain William Smith House.

From the Meriam House, follow the path as it winds to the east. The route soon passes a series of historical farm fields that have been continuously used for agriculture since the seventeenth century. By the turn of the eighteenth century, approximately 90 percent of the land within what is now Minute Man National Historical Park had been converted to agricultural use. Although extensive meadows existed in the area prior to European settlement, acres of forest were cleared to create pasture and cultivated cropland.

The trail turns right and winds south toward MA 2A, passing the first of two so-called Bloody Angle historical sites and crossing a boardwalk over protected wetlands as it nears the Job and Joshua Brooks houses. After passing the houses and briefly paralleling MA 2A, the trail turns northeast and follows another boardwalk. Here you'll follow the route of the Minute Men northeast through woods of sugar and silver maple, white oak, and American beech. The dominant shrubs in the understory are mostly nonnative species, including buckthorn and honeysuckle.

Although history is a main attraction here, there is plenty for naturalists to observe as well. The park's habitats support a wide variety of terrestrial and freshwater aquatic wildlife. Common mammals include species typically associated with rural and developed areas, such as eastern cottontail, gray squirrel, deer mouse, beaver, red fox, coyote, and white-tailed deer. Less-common species,

Captain William Smith House is one of several notable homes in Minute Man National Historical Park.

such as bobcat and fisher, also inhabit the area. All told, roughly 70 species of birds, 12 species of fish, and more than 30 species of reptiles and amphibians have been documented in the park. Bird-watching is especially good in spring, when many migratory species are present.

Continue to follow the trail as it bears right along a stone wall and soon arrives at the second Bloody Angle site, where it joins Battle Road. You'll pass by Hartwell Tavern, a restored eighteenth-century home and tavern that was standing on Battle Road at the start of the war and is therefore known as a witness house. A short distance farther along is the Captain William Smith House, another witness house, which was built in the late seventeenth century and was the home of Captain Smith, who was commander of the Lincoln Company.

The Smith House marks the end of this one-way walk, although the trail continues to the eastern boundary of the park in Lincoln. As you retrace your steps to the parking area near the Meriam House, you can explore the other trails that branch off Battle Road, such as Vernal Pool Trail near the second Bloody Angle.

DID YOU KNOW?

The British militia was in Concord in April 1775 because it had been sent to seize military stores and ammunition kept by colonists. The British general Thomas Gage was under pressure from his superiors in England to maintain control of Massachusetts.

MORE INFORMATION

Visitor centers in the park include the North Bridge (174 Liberty Street in Concord), Minute Man (250 North Great Road, Lincoln), Hartwell Tavern, Whittemore House, and Wayside. Some are open only seasonally. The grounds are open sunrise to sunset, at which time the parking lot gate closes. Pets are allowed in the park and in all visitor centers but must be on a leash no longer than 6 feet at all times. For more information, contact park headquarters at 978-369-6993 or visit nps.gov/mima.

NEARBY

The Old North Bridge and Minute Man Monument, which mark the site of the war's first battle, are off Monument Street. Another historic feature of note adjacent to the bridge is the Old Manse, at 269 Monument Street. Built in 1770 for minister William Emerson, it then served as a meeting place for mid-nineteenth-century transcendentalists, such as Henry David Thoreau, Bronson Alcott, and Margaret Fuller. It is now a National Historic Landmark and is managed by The Trustees of Reservations. The long distance Bay Circuit Trail passes by the bridge and house. There are restaurants in Concord Center.

34

WALDEN POND

Although Walden Pond is not remote and you won't be alone, on a quiet day you will feel miles away from civilization. Indeed, you are at the heart of the beginnings of the American conservation movement.

DIRECTIONS

From I-95, take exit 29B for MA 2 west toward Acton. Follow MA 2 west about 9 miles then turn left onto MA 126. The Walden Pond State Reservation parking lot will be on your left in a quarter-mile. *GPS coordinates:* 42° 26.451′ N, 71° 20.123′ W.

By public transportation, take the Fitchburg Commuter Rail line to Concord Station, which is near the corner of Thoreau Street and Sudbury Road. Walk away from town on Thoreau Street, cross MA 2 (carefully), and Walden Pond State Reservation will soon be on your right. The pond entrance is about 1 mile from the station.

TRAIL DESCRIPTION

Starting in 1845, Henry David Thoreau lived at Walden Pond for two years, two months, and two days. He wrote *Walden* after his experiment to live "deliberately" and simply in the woods. Today the park is run by the state. It includes the pond, trails, a swimming area, a boat launch, and a replica of Thoreau's cabin. The Thoreau Society runs a gift shop where you will find trail maps, souvenirs, and other information about the reservation.

This route takes you around the pond and up to a vantage point from which you can view the area. For decades, the trails and slopes around the pond have been eroded by overuse. In recent years, major efforts have been made to quell the erosion and restore the vegetation. A visit reveals

LOCATION
Concord, MA

RATING
Easy

DISTANCE
Approximately 3 miles

ELEVATION GAIN
100 feet

ESTIMATED TIME
1.5 hours

MAPS
USGS Maynard; online: mass .gov/eea/docs/dcr/parks/trails/ walden.pdf

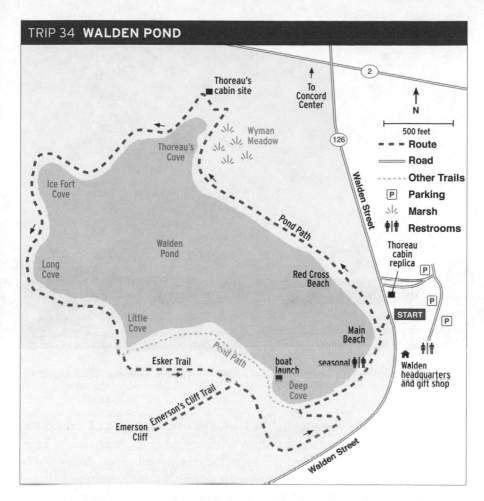

To Concord Center

2

N

500 feet

- - - Route
=== Road
---- Other Trails
P Parking
Marsh
Restrooms

Thoreau's cabin site

Wyman Meadow

Thoreau's Cove

Ice Fort Cove

Walden Pond

Long Cove

Little Cove

Esker Trail

Pond Path

Red Cross Beach

Walden Street

126

Thoreau cabin replica
P

P

START
P

Main Beach

boat launch

seasonal

Deep Cove

Emerson's Cliff Trail

Emerson Cliff

Walden headquarters and gift shop

Walden Street

their success but will also show that restrictions are still warranted. Stay on the designated trails and roads or on the beach.

From the parking lot, cross the road to the ramp down to the pond's beach area. Turn right and walk along Red Cross Beach or on the path just above it, but as the beach ends, make sure you are following the path, not the shore. You are now skirting the north shore of the pond on Pond Path.

Walden Pond is one of many kettle-hole ponds in eastern Massachusetts. These were formed more than 10,000 years ago, when ice blocks melted in sand or gravel deposits, leaving behind depressions that filled with water and became the ponds we see today. Kettle holes usually have no streams flowing in or out of them, and this is true of Walden Pond.

The path turns right (north) along a cove. This is Thoreau's Cove, and the site of his cabin is just off the main Pond Path here. When Thoreau lived here, Walden was surrounded by one of the few remaining woods in the area, the other lands having been cleared for farming. By the time the state bought the property in 1922, much of this forest had been cut. Now the woods have grown back and

At times, Walden Pond evokes the tranquility that inspired Henry David Thoreau. Photo by Matthew Grymek.

include berry bushes, sumac, pine, hickory, and oak. Thoreau had planted 400 white pines beyond his cabin, but these were leveled in the hurricane of 1938. The stone chimney that marked the site of the original cabin was discovered in 1945 by an archeologist after a three-month search.

As you walk along the trail, keep an eye out for the reservation's wildlife, including squirrels, chipmunks, rabbits, skunks, raccoons, red foxes, and white-tailed deer. Many of these animals were present in Thoreau's day, although some, such as deer, were nearly eliminated by hunting and habitat loss due to forest clearing. Scan the trees for chickadees, red-tailed hawks, and migratory songbirds (present from spring to early fall), and check the pond for kingfishers, geese, and flocks of migratory waterfowl. The pond is stocked by the state and otherwise would have few fish. The best time to see wildlife at this well-trafficked spot is in the early morning or evening.

From the cabin site, Pond Path turns south and ascends uphill slightly. To the right are the train tracks you traveled along if you took the Commuter Rail from Boston. The tracks originally were laid by the Boston and Fitchburg Railroad in 1844, just one year before Thoreau moved to the cabin. Pond Path then winds south and west along the western shore of the pond, passing Ice Fort Cove and Long Cove. After Long Cove, Pond Path turns east. At Little Cove, the trail dips southward, and there is a side path to the right leading to Esker Trail. Here you have the option of continuing left on Pond Path and following it to Deep Cove or going right to explore the overlook and Esker Trail.

To climb to the overlook, take the side path and turn left onto Esker Trail, which runs parallel and just uphill of Pond Path. Soon Emerson's Cliff Trail leads to the right and uphill to an overlook. In summer, the view can be obscured by vegetation. Trace your steps back to Esker Trail and turn right onto it, following it as it parallels Route 126 to the boat-launch ramp. Turn left and walk down the ramp to the beach at Deep Cove. From here, reconnect with Pond Path. Pond Path leads to the main beach and the ramp, back up to the road and parking lot.

DID YOU KNOW?

After he lived in it, Thoreau's cabin was acquired by farmers who moved it to the other side of Concord to use for storage. It was dismantled in 1868.

MORE INFORMATION

A new solar-powered visitor center with a bookstore, a gallery, and a slate of interpretive programs is your on-site hub for information, including an introduction to Thoreau's experiences. You can visit a replica of his cabin at the park headquarters.

Hours vary according to season, and visitors are encouraged to call ahead for hours. There is an $8 parking fee for Massachusetts residents and a $10 fee for others; the lot fills up early on summer weekends. A 1,000-visitors-per-day cap has been set, so it's advisable to plan ahead and go early, or to call first to determine if a visit is feasible. All organized groups must make advance reservations. There are seasonal restrooms by the main beach and portable restrooms by the parking area. No dogs (except working dogs), fires, camping, bikes, or alcoholic beverages are allowed in the park. There are no trash receptacles or picnic tables. For more information, contact park headquarters at 978-369-3254 or visit mass.gov/dcr.

NEARBY

Thoreau Farm, the site of Thoreau's birth, in 1817, is located at 341 Virginia Road in Concord. It was built around 1730 and was part of an active farm into the twentieth century. It is now managed by the Thoreau Farm Trust; visit thoreaufarm.org for information on tours. There are restaurants in Concord on Thoreau and Walden streets, and other roads near the town center.

If this easy hike around Walden Pond doesn't sate your thirst, consider seeking out the Adams Woods and Wright Woods trails on adjacent land to the southwest (see concordnet.org). Crossing the Commuter Rail tracks is dangerous and should be done with extreme caution, but the risk is rewarded with quieter, less populated hiking trails overlooking the Sudbury River and Fairhaven Bay.

HENRY DAVID THOREAU: NATURALIST, EXPLORER, AND WRITER

Walden Pond is well known as the site of the esteemed writer Henry David Thoreau's mid-nineteenth-century retreat. From his self-built cabin, he wrote, observed nature, and explored the area, often heading south-southwest along the Sudbury River toward Fairhaven Bay and the hilly region of Mount Misery.

In his essay "Walking," Thoreau wrote, "I can easily walk ten, fifteen, twenty, any number of miles, commencing at my own door, without going by any house, without crossing any road except where the fox and the mink do: first along by the river, and then the brook, and then the meadow and the woodside."

Thoreau would walk every day and wondered how anyone could stay indoors: "I confess that I am astonished at the power of endurance, to say nothing of the moral insensibility of my neighbors who confine themselves to shops and offices the whole day for weeks and months, aye, and years almost together." Thoreau probably would be even more astonished by our society's development and commercialization of open space, but at least the acres around Walden Pond, Mount Misery, and many other places in eastern Massachusetts have been saved.

Thoreau was born in Concord in 1817. He attended Harvard University during the 1830s and lived in the cabin at Walden Pond, on land owned by Ralph Waldo Emerson, from 1845 to 1847. During this time, he recorded detailed observations about the natural year that ultimately served as the source for essays he wrote later in life. *Walden*, published in 1854, was not widely acclaimed at first but is now regarded as one of the classics of American nature writing.

Thoreau's interest in natural history and travel increased during the 1850s. He visited Cape Cod several times, and his detailed descriptions of a treeless, barren landscape with long, open views are an invaluable record of what the Cape's landscape looked like following centuries of intensive timber harvesting. His other travels in New England included expeditions to the Katahdin–Moosehead Lake region of Maine and to the White Mountains. He visited New Hampshire's Mount Monadnock several times and wrote one of the first detailed natural descriptions of the mountain.

After contracting bronchitis in 1859, Thoreau spent his final years writing and editing essays, such as *The Maine Woods*, and his journals. He died in 1862 at age 44.

35

LINCOLN CONSERVATION LAND

The conservation land surrounding Mount Misery provides excellent views of the Sudbury River and Fairhaven Bay, as well as of forests, ponds, and marshes.

DIRECTIONS

From I-95, take Exit 26 for US 20 east. Turn left onto Stow Street then turn left again onto MA 117 west (West Main Street). Follow MA 117 for 5.9 miles until you reach the Lincoln Conservation Land–Mount Misery parking entrance on the right (0.7 mile after MA 117 crosses MA 126). *GPS coordinates:* 42° 25.054′ N, 71° 21.236′ W.

By public transportation, take the Fitchburg line of the MBTA Commuter Rail to Lincoln. Walk 0.5 mile southwest on Lincoln Road and turn right onto MA 117. Walk another 0.5 mile to its intersection with MA 126. Continue to follow MA 117 west 0.7 mile, to the parking area on the right.

TRAIL DESCRIPTION

The quiet, rural town of Lincoln is home to numerous conservation areas that protect approximately one-third of its total acreage, with more than 60 miles of trails for hikers to explore. At the Mount Misery conservation area, well-marked trails offer views of the diverse habitats of 284-foot Mount Misery, one of the prominent hills of the Sudbury Valley. This walk, which includes a portion of the Bay Circuit Trail, circles the base of Mount Misery then loops westward toward the Sudbury River.

The trail begins on the east side of the main parking lot on MA 117. From gate post 4 and the bike rack, follow the white-blazed Bay Circuit Trail along the north shore of a small pond then turn right at the first junction and

LOCATION
Lincoln, MA

RATING
Moderate

DISTANCE
3 miles

ELEVATION GAIN
50 feet

ESTIMATED TIME
1.5 hours

MAPS
USGS Maynard; online:
lincolnconservation.org

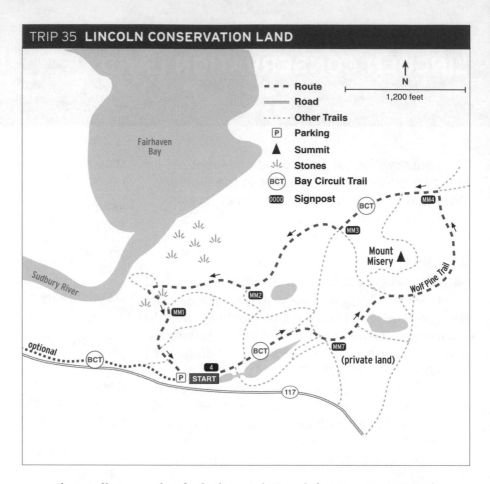

cross the small stream that feeds the pond. Turn left at junction MM7 then go left again at the next intersection, continuing past the western shore of another pond (the water will be on your right) to a four-way junction at the base of Mount Misery.

Turn right here onto an old cart road. (The trail continuing straight ahead makes a quick climb to the summit of the hill, where trees block almost all of the views, then descends to rejoin the route described here on the north side of the hill.) The cart road draws an easy, nearly level circle around the base of Mount Misery, passing rock ledges and a beaver wetland. White-tailed deer are sometimes seen at dusk in the field on the right. Oak, white pine, and the occasional white birch and beech compose the woods. (Many hemlock trees have been killed by the pest known as the hemlock woolly adelgid.) After walking about 1.5 miles from the parking lot, rejoin the Bay Circuit Trail at junction MM4, at the edge of a large field. Turn left and continue straight past the next junction, where the aforementioned trail over Mount Misery's summit comes in on the left.

Keep an eye out for barred owls, which nest in the tree cavities of mature forests and forested wetlands, such as those at Mount Misery. Barred owls often roost by day then make their hunting rounds at night. Their call, which sounds like *who-cooks-for-you*, is one of the most distinctive bird songs. Northern goshawks have also been seen in the area. These hawks are relatively uncommon and feed on birds, such as grouse, and mammals, such as squirrels. The goshawk is identifiable by its long tail, its short wings, and its broad, white eye-stripe.

Continue west on the Bay Circuit Trail to junction MM3 then turn right onto another old cart path. Bear right at junction MM2 and follow the trail, which winds west to the edge of a broad marsh and floodplain along the Sudbury River, with good views across the wetlands. The trail soon leads to the river itself, where you can watch for waterfowl flying up and down it. After enjoying the view, follow the main trail away from the river to junction MM1 then bear right and continue for a short distance to complete your loop and return to the parking area.

DID YOU KNOW?

Mount Misery was named in the 1780s when, according to local lore, two yoked oxen wandered there and wrapped themselves around a tree. Unable to escape, they perished on the hill.

Wild turkeys evade a young hiker on Lincoln conservation land. Photo by Maury Eldridge.

MORE INFORMATION

The conservation land is open dawn to dusk; there is no fee. Dogs are allowed. A boat launch is located at Farrar Pond on MA 117, 0.2 mile west of the conservation area. You can walk along the Bay Circuit Trail to the pond. See the posted information sign for the most recent rules. For more information, contact the Lincoln Conservation Commission at 781-259-2612 or lincolntown.org, or visit the Lincoln Land Conservation website, lincolnconservation.org.

NEARBY

Mass Audubon's Drumlin Farm is a great place to take children. It is located on MA 117 in Lincoln, 4.5 miles west of the MA 117 overpass at I-95. Children will love the farm animals. The 180-acre property also includes trails that wind through fields, pastures, ponds, and woods; a gift shop; and a nature center where programs are held. Restaurants are located in the center of Concord.

36

NOBSCOT HILL AND TIPPLING ROCK

The rocky ridges of Nobscot Hill, the highest point on the Bay Circuit Trail, and Tippling Rock offer outstanding views and wildlife habitat.

DIRECTIONS

From I-495 in Marlborough, take Exit 24 (24A if you're traveling north; 24B if you're traveling south). Follow US 20, which becomes Boston Post Road, east for 7.8 miles. After passing Nokomis Road on the right, turn right and enter the parking area on the south side of the highway. (Watch for a small sign denoting town of Sudbury conservation land and the Tippling Rock Trail.) If you reach the quaint Barnstead Shoppes shopping center, you've gone too far. *GPS Coordinates:* 42° 21.638' N, 71° 26.498' W.

TRAIL DESCRIPTION

Nobscot Hill, which at 602 feet is the highest point along the entire 231-mile Bay Circuit Trail, is part of a series of rocky hills and ridges in Sudbury and Framingham, the heart of the Metro West region. From viewpoints near its summit and from the nearby open ledges of Tippling Rock, hikers enjoy long views to Mount Monadnock, Wachusett Mountain, and Boston.

Several contiguous conservation areas, including the Weisblatt and Nobscot conservation lands (managed by the town of Sudbury), the Nobscot Scout Reservation (owned by the Knox Trail Council), and DCR's Nobscot Hill tract (marked as Callahan State Park on some maps), collectively protect more than 700 acres. This hike begins at Weisblatt Conservation Land and follows the Bay Circuit Trail over Tippling Rock to the summit of Nobscot Hill. There are numerous junctions with other trails, and carrying a map is strongly recommended. See the "More

LOCATION
Sudbury and Framingham, MA

RATING
Moderate

DISTANCE
4 miles

ELEVATION GAIN
515 feet

ESTIMATED TIME
2.25 hours

MAPS
USGS Framingham; online: svtweb.org/sites/default/files/Nobscot.pdf

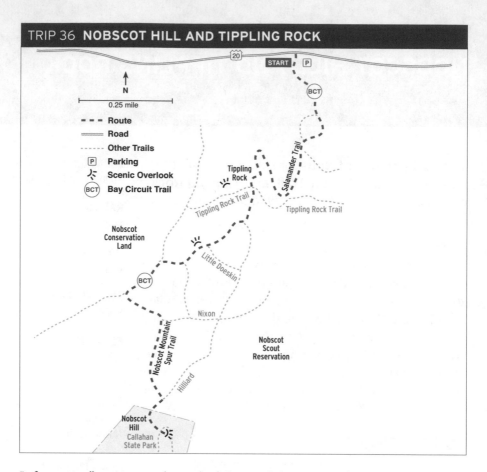

Information" section at the end of this trail description for landowners' rules and contact information.

Begin at the Weisblatt Conservation Land trailhead by following the Bay Circuit Trail (BCT) and Salamander Trail south on an easy ascent through the property's northwest corner. Salamander Trail is aptly named for the conservation area's vernal pools, one of which you can view a short distance from the trailhead. These wetlands offer critical breeding habitat for wood frogs, spring peepers, and spotted salamanders. Large, undeveloped, and roadless areas are especially important for vernal pool wildlife, as they offer protected travel corridors that enable animals to safely disperse in an otherwise heavily developed region.

After Salamander Trail leaves to the left, looping back to the parking area, continue to follow the BCT southwest toward the boundary of the adjacent Nobscot Scout Reservation, which you'll reach at roughly 0.5 mile. Bear right and follow the BCT as it briefly bends northwest and ascends the base of a ridge then curves sharply left and continues south along the ledge.

This rocky habitat, which is relatively uncommon in eastern Massachusetts, offers ideal denning habitat for wildlife, such as fishers, porcupines, coyotes, and bobcats. Like many other species, fishers were extirpated from Massachusetts during Colonial times but have returned to the region in recent decades. While the animals themselves are rarely seen, their tracks are visible in the winter forest and around stone walls, where they hunt porcupines and other small mammals.

At 0.8 mile, after roughly 20 to 25 minutes of walking, you will reach the rocky crown of Tippling Rock at the south end of the ridge. At 426 feet, it is the highest point in the town of Sudbury. (Nobscot Hill is just across the town line, in Framingham.) Local lore has it that a farmer split this giant boulder to keep it from tipping onto his cattle. From this vantage point, there are easterly panoramic views across the Metro West region to the Blue Hills and the tall buildings of downtown Boston. To the west is a partial view of the sloping profile of 2,006-foot Wachusett Mountain, the highest point in Massachusetts east of the Berkshires.

After enjoying the views, continue to follow the BCT down the west end of the rocky ridge, following the white plastic BCT markers carefully at junctions. After the junction with Tippling Rock Trail, turn right and continue over an adjacent ridge. A stone chimney just off-trail marks the site of an old cabin. Pass a memorial boulder then turn right and descend into the northeast corner of Nobscot Conservation Land, a 118-acre tract also managed by the town of Sudbury. Follow the blazes left again at a junction. (The trail straight ahead continues 0.3 mile to a parking area off Brimstone Lane.)

A wooden shelter at Nobscot Hill mimics the patterns in the wilderness beyond. Photo by MGStanton, Creative Commons on Flickr.

After another 0.1 mile, reenter Nobscot Scout Reservation at the base of Nobscot Hill. After crossing a stream, turn sharply right at the next junction and begin a moderately steep ascent of the northeast slopes. Amid the dense woodlands, the stone walls you see offer evidence of this landscape's past, when even the rocky hills were cleared for agriculture. A forest fire in 1930 burned a large portion of the reservation, but the forests have rebounded strongly over the past 85 years. Early morning and evening are the best times to watch for wildlife, such as migratory songbirds and owls, which often nest in the tall pines.

Shortly after crossing the Framingham town line, continue past two more trail junctions and enter DCR land on the upper slopes. At 1.9 miles from the trailhead, you'll reach the 602-foot summit of Nobscot Hill, which is capped by communications towers and a fire tower. Although there are no views from the summit proper (unless you're invited up by rangers during the fire tower's seasonal operations), you can follow the trail to the left roughly 125 yards to reach a ledge with a partial easterly view of the Boston skyline. Another overlook on the south side of the summit offers clear-day, long-distance views of Wachusett Mountain to the west, Mount Monadnock to the northwest, and distant Mount Kearsarge in central New Hampshire to the north.

From the summit, retrace your steps along the Bay Circuit Trail to Tippling Rock and the trailhead. You can explore the other trails, but be sure to have a map and follow markers carefully at the numerous junctions.

DID YOU KNOW?

The Nobscot Scout Reservation is divided into two management areas. The Open Space Zone, which includes the Bay Circuit Trail, is a wildlands area. The Program Zone hosts scout activities and is managed for wildlife habitat and firewood.

MORE INFORMATION

Skiing is not permitted on Weisblatt Conservation Land. Skiing and biking are allowed at Nobscot Scout Reservation, but swimming, wading, and horseback riding are prohibited; pets must be leashed; and visitors must keep away from buildings, facilities, and campsites. For more information, visit the Sudbury Valley Trustees website at svtweb.org, call 978-443-5588, or visit the Bay Circuit Trail website at baycircuit.org.

NEARBY

Longfellow's Wayside Inn, a nonprofit historic landmark, offers many attractions, including a photogenic gristmill that was built by Henry Ford in 1929, a restaurant and inn with overnight lodging, and a 125-acre park. It is located on Wayside Inn Road off US 20. There are restaurants on US 20 (Boston Post Road) in Sudbury.

37

BROADMOOR WILDLIFE SANCTUARY

Broadmoor is a sanctuary rich in both natural and human history. Walk past the remains of a gristmill and a sawmill and along fields that were farmed for hundreds of years.

DIRECTIONS

From Route 128, take Exit 21 to Route 16 west. Travel 7 miles into South Natick. The parking lot and signs welcoming you to Broadmoor will be on your left. The sanctuary is located on Route 16 (280 Eliot Street), 1.8 miles west of the center of South Natick. *GPS coordinates: 42° 15.368′ N, 71° 20.421′ W.*

TRAIL DESCRIPTION

Broadmoor Wildlife Sanctuary is a popular hiking destination due to its diversity of terrain and wildlife. This sanctuary is home to more than 150 varieties of birds, including 60 breeding species. At the nature center building, you can pick up a map detailing the site's 9 miles of trails. The trails have color-coded markers, with blue taking you away from the parking lot and yellow leading you back. The most scenic area is at the eastern end of the property, with Mill Pond–Marsh Trail taking you past the pond and mill sites, and Charles River Trail leading down along the river. Even when the parking area is full, the trails leading to the western end of the property rarely have more than a few hikers. One such trail is Indian Brook Trail, which leads to the even more secluded Glacial Hill Trail.

Begin your walk by checking in at the visitor center and then turning right a few feet down the main trail onto Indian Brook Trail, near the boardwalk (signpost 2). The beginning of Indian Brook Trail passes through a beautiful open field where kestrels, kingbirds, mockingbirds, cedar waxwings, and indigo buntings can be seen, in

LOCATION
Natick, MA

RATING
Moderate

DISTANCE
3 miles

ELEVATION GAIN
50 feet

ESTIMATED TIME
1.5 to 2 hours

MAPS
USGS Framingham; online: massaudubon.org/content/download/7967/144652/file/broadmoor_trails.pdf

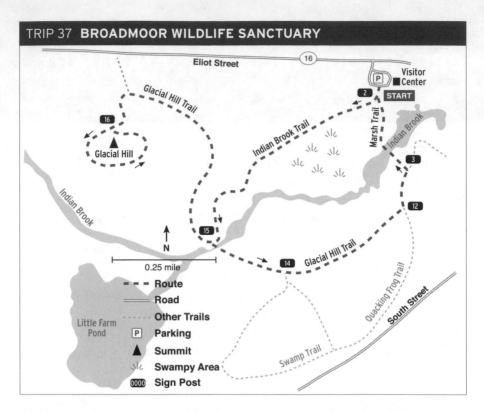

addition to the resident woodchucks. A short spur trail on the left is an extension of All Persons Trail, which leads to an observation platform overlooking the field. Soon Indian Brook Trail leads into a wooded area of oaks on the right and Indian Brook Swamp on the left. A short boardwalk on the right offers close-up views of a vernal pool.

Indian Brook Swamp and the sanctuary's other wetlands are home to wood ducks, painted turtles, kingfishers, great blue herons, raccoons, muskrats, and river otters. In 1989, beavers moved into Indian Brook Swamp. This was big news for Charles River watershed lovers, as these were apparently the first beavers to inhabit the area in many years. This beaver family built a dam at the junction of Indian Brook Trail and Glacial Hill Trail then built a lodge a short distance upstream.

At signpost 15, you'll reach a junction with Glacial Hill Trail. This hike continues to the right (northwest) along the northern portion of Glacial Hill Trail. (You will return to this junction after looping over Glacial Hill.) The trail winds its way through the oaks for about a half-mile before reaching a little hill, or drumlin—a doughnut-shaped glacial deposit rising up from the swampy forest below. Common but often elusive inhabitants of these woodlands include deer, foxes, great horned owls, and wild turkeys.

After crossing a wetland at the base of the hill (an area that may be flooded during spring's high water), Glacial Hill Trail runs along the top of the hill, forming a small loop before bringing you back to the main path. Retrace your steps to Indian Brook Trail at junction 15.

From here you can take a left and retrace your steps back to the parking lot, or you can continue the loop by taking a right across Indian Brook and following the southern portion of Glacial Hill Trail. Follow Glacial Hill Trail left at junction 14 (Swamp Trail makes a quick loop to the right here) and continue to the junction at post 12, at the edge of a clearing. Turn left here then bear left again on Marsh Trail at junction 3.

As the trail winds back to the nature center, it crosses a boardwalk with fine wetland views. Shortly before reaching the center, be sure to make the short detour onto the All Persons Trail boardwalk. This is an excellent wildlife viewing area, where muskrats, northern water snakes, and large groups of basking painted turtles may be seen at close range.

Another little-known section of the sanctuary is Little Farm Pond, a 23-acre kettle pond located just over the town line, in Sherborn. To reach this pond from the main parking lot, drive 1.1 miles west on MA 16, turn left onto Lake Street, and continue 0.8 mile to Farm Road. Turn left onto Farm Road and look for a small parking area on the left side of the road, about 100 yards from the intersection of Lake Street and Farm Road. From here you can hike down the dirt road to the pond and explore unmarked trails along its west side. This

The painted turtle (*Chrysemys picta*) is commonly found in sunny, shallow bodies of water throughout Massachusetts and can spend as many as six hours a day basking in the sun.

is a special place, quiet and rich with wildlife and unusual plants, such as carnivorous sundews and pitcher plants.

DID YOU KNOW?

The nature center is a state-of-the-art building with 128 solar panels for electricity and heating. Composting toilets save an estimated 100,000 gallons of water annually, and rainwater is collected to water landscape plants.

MORE INFORMATION

The wildlife sanctuary is open Tuesday through Sunday, dawn to dusk; it is closed on Mondays except for holidays. Admission is free for Mass Audubon members; for others, there is a fee ($5 for adults, $4 for children ages 2 to 12 and seniors); dogs are prohibited. The nature center is open Tuesday through Friday, 9 A.M. to 5 P.M., and Saturday, Sunday, and Monday holidays, 10 A.M. to 5 P.M. For more information, contact Broadmoor Wildlife Sanctuary at 508-655-2296 or broadmoor@massaudubon.org.

NEARBY

Restaurants are located in Natick Center along and off Main Street. The historical (circa 1881) Bacon Free Library is located in a pleasant setting along the Charles River in South Natick, at 58 Eliot Street (Route 16). It is the home of the Natick Historical Society. The Center for the Arts in Natick, located in the former Central Fire Station, hosts a variety of musical and theatrical performances.

38

ROCKY NARROWS RESERVATION AND SHERBORN TOWN FOREST

The rugged hillsides of the remote Rocky Narrows, reachable by foot or by canoe/kayak, are a highlight of the Charles River Valley.

DIRECTIONS

From I-95, take Exit 16B and follow MA 109 west 8 miles to the junction with MA 27 in Medfield. Turn right on MA 27 north and continue 3.1 miles to the junction with MA 115 in Sherborn. Continue on MA 27 0.3 miles past the reservation's south entrance on the right then turn right on Snow Street. After 0.4 mile, bear right on Forest Street and continue another 0.4 mile to the parking area (room for six cars) on the right. *GPS coordinates: 42° 13.557′ N, 71° 21.241′ W.*

TRAIL DESCRIPTION

The contiguous Rocky Narrows Reservation, owned by The Trustees of Reservations, and the Sherborn Town Forest offer hikers a relatively wild section of more than 400 acres of woodlands to explore. One highlight is King Philip's Overlook, an open ledge atop a steep valley (see essay on page 177) that affords a fantastic view of the Charles River. Hemlock trees cover much of the hillside in the reservation, and a walk here feels more reminiscent of northern New England than suburban Boston. Although this route is fairly straightforward, this area has many trails, and carrying a map is strongly recommended for first-time visitors. Maps are also posted at the trailhead and at some junctions.

This hike, which begins at the Rocky Narrows Reservation Forest Street entrance, combines the Red and Blue Trails and the long-distance Bay Circuit Trail. The walking is mostly easy, with a couple of quick climbs. A handful of areas may be muddy or wet, depending on the season, although the largest of these can be bypassed easily.

LOCATION
Sherborn, MA

RATING
Moderate

DISTANCE
2.7 miles

ELEVATION GAIN
165 feet

ESTIMATED TIME
1.5 hours

MAPS
USGS Medfield; online: thetrustees.org/assets/documents/places-to-visit/trailmaps/RockyNarrows_TrailMap_2014.pdf

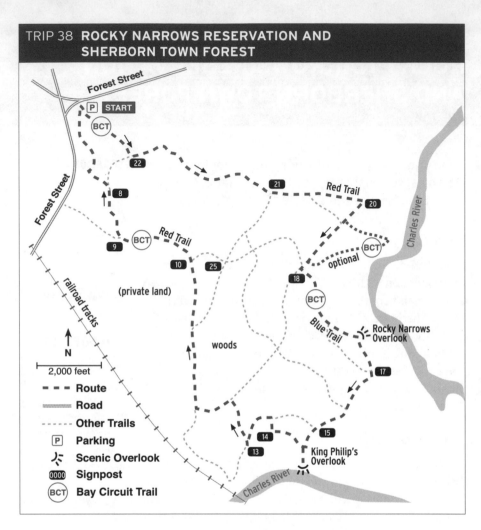

Forest Street

START

BCT

22

8

Forest Street

Red Trail

21

20

9

BCT

Red Trail

10

25

(private land)

railroad tracks

18

BCT

optional

BCT

Rocky Narrows
Overlook

Blue Trail

woods

N

2,000 feet

17

- - - **Route**
—— **Road**
····· **Other Trails**
P **Parking**
⅄ **Scenic Overlook**
0000 **Signpost**
BCT **Bay Circuit Trail**

14

15

13

King Philip's
Overlook

Charles River

Charles River

Follow the path across the field adjacent to the parking area then bear right onto a gravel road. After passing more fields, the trail, marked with white Bay Circuit Trail blazes and red blazes, enters the woods at marker 22 and descends to a small wetland. These areas, where different habitats meet, are especially rich in wildlife. Skunk cabbage blooms in abundance in early spring, and frogs will likely jump off the path into the water as you approach.

Continue to follow the route east, through woods of oak, pine, and scattered hemlock, bearing left at junction 21. At junction 20, turn sharply right opposite a wetland, where in spring and summer you'll likely hear the distinctive *conk-la-ree* call of red-winged blackbirds. When you come to a junction after another 500 feet, you can turn left to follow the Bay Circuit Trail to a canoe landing on the bank of the Charles River or, if conditions are wet, simply continue straight on Red Trail to junction 18, where it rejoins the Bay Circuit Trail.

There is a healthy population of white-tailed deer here. During spring, you might see their heart-shaped tracks in the damp earth of the trail. The narrow part of the print is made by the front of the deer's hoof and indicates the direction the animal was traveling. Another large mammal in residence is the coyote, which can be found throughout Massachusetts. Coyotes are very adaptable, eating whatever food source is available, including house cats. They are secretive animals and do most of their hunting at night. A coyote howl in the wee hours is a sound you won't soon forget.

At marker 18, turn left off of Red Trail and follow Blue Trail and the Bay Circuit Trail upslope along a stone wall. Continue high above the west bank of the Charles River, passing through shady groves of large eastern hemlock trees. The Rocky Narrows Overlook and other viewpoints provide vistas across the valley. The woods on the far side of the river are part of Medfield State Forest. Hemlocks thrive in these rocky ridges and ravines, growing to a height of 70 feet in cool, moist spots. To distinguish hemlocks from other evergreens, examine the needles closely. Hemlock needles are flat with blunt tips, typically half an inch to a quarter-inch long—shorter than spruce and fir needles. There are usually several needles upside down on the branchlet, and while they are dark green on top, the undersides are silvery. Because the needles are acidic, there is often little undergrowth beneath trees where needles have fallen year after year. Hemlocks have brown cones, about 0.75 inch long, which hang from the tips of the branches. They mature in the fall and stay on the tree until spring. Another way

Fall foliage, seen here from King Philip's Overlook, makes for a stunning hike in Rocky Narrows Reservation.

to distinguish the hemlock from fir trees is to look at the crown of the tree. The hemlock will be rounded, while the fir comes to a sharp, dense point. Unfortunately, hemlock is declining significantly in southern New England due to infestation of the hemlock woolly adelgid (see page 38).

At junction 17, bear right and follow the Blue and Bay Circuit Trails away from the river, entering Sherborn Town Forest. At marker 15, bear left and follow the white-blazed Bay Circuit Trail on a quick descent to King Philip's Overlook. Enjoy the fine view south across the valley, taking in the fields and more of the Medfield State Forest. A railroad bridge is visible to the right. This is a good place to look for hawks soaring above the river. Great blue herons also make their way up and down the river. Their population has increased due to cleaner rivers and because the proliferating beaver population has led to more ponds with standing timber, the herons' preferred nesting spot.

Begin the return leg by following the left fork of the Bay Circuit Trail to junction 14, where you'll rejoin Blue Trail. Turn left here then bear right at a posted map at junction 13 and continue to nearby junction 10, where Blue Trail ends at its second junction with Red Trail. Turn left and follow the combined Red Trail and Bay Circuit Trail downhill to a large wetland along Seawall Brook, then turn right and follow the Red and Bay Circuit Trails north along the wetland edge to marker 10. After passing the wetland, bear right (marker 9) then left (marker 8) at successive junctions to return to the parking area. One note: If the trail at marker 10 is flooded during spring, you can avoid a wet crossing by going right at junction 10 then left at junction 25, continuing to Red Trail at junction 21 then going left to the reservation's entrance.

DID YOU KNOW?

As you follow the trail atop the Rocky Narrows, you're traversing a landscape that is 650 million years old. Colonists referred to the Narrows as "the Gates of the Charles."

MORE INFORMATION

Rocky Narrows Reservation is open year-round, dawn to dusk. There is no fee or restrooms; dogs are allowed on-leash. For more information, call 508-785-0339 or visit thetrustees.org.

NEARBY

The centers of Medfield and Sherborn have many historic buildings. A number of these old homes were part of the Underground Railroad in the nineteenth century and have trap doors, secret rooms, and hidden passages. There are restaurants in Medfield Center along Main Street (MA 109) and North Street.

KING PHILIP'S WAR: AN EARLY AMERICAN CONFLICT

Rocky Narrows is one of several nature preserves in eastern Massachusetts that also have historical connections to King Philip's War. The conflict began in 1675, when Metacom, an American Indian leader whose English-given name was Philip, led an uprising of Wampanoags, Nipmucks, and Narragansetts in an effort to regain tribal lands from European settlers. The war, which cost the lives of an estimated 600 colonists and 30,000 American Indians, eliminated or severely weakened many native tribes. Although more than half of New England's then-90 established towns were damaged by the battles, colonists rapidly rebuilt.

King Philip's Overlook at Rocky Narrows is one of many hilltops, vistas, and rock formations in Massachusetts named for the American Indian leader. Medfield, which lies in front of you as you look across the river from the overlook, was hard hit by the uprising. Many homes were burned and several settlers were killed, but the American Indians could not overpower the colonists' garrison.

Another site of interest is today part of the nearby Noon Hill Reservation. Many historians believe that King Philip launched his raid on the town of Medfield from Noon Hill. Others argue the raiders amassed on the west side of the Charles River. No matter where the attack came from, this was an important area for the American Indians, who preferred to situate near the confluence of major streams and rivers. Here, Stop River enters the Charles River below Noon Hill.

After the American Indians withdrew from Medfield, one fighter who had learned English left a note near a burned bridge over the Charles River that read: "Know by this paper, that the Indians that thou hast provoked to wrath and anger, will war this twenty-one years if you will: there are many Indians yet, we come three hundred this time. You must consider the Indians lost nothing but their life; you must lose your fair houses and cattle." Despite these bold words, the American Indians were outnumbered by the British.

The attack on Medfield occurred in February 1676. By August of that year, so many American Indians had been killed, including Philip, that the war ended. Ironically, Philip was the son of Massasoit, the Wampanoag leader who had showed kindness to the Pilgrims during their first disastrous year in Plymouth.

39

NOANET WOODLANDS

An extensive network of trails leads to a millpond and a waterfall, and up to modest Noanet Peak, where there are views across forested hills to the Boston skyline.

DIRECTIONS

From I-95, take Exit 17 onto MA 135 west. Drive 0.8 mile and turn left onto South Street, just after crossing the Charles River. Go 1.1 miles on South Street and turn left onto Chestnut Street. Follow Chestnut Street 0.3 mile and bear right onto Dedham Street immediately after re-crossing the Charles River. Continue 1.9 miles to the parking lots on the left at Caryl Park, which is managed by the town of Dover and provides access to the Noanet trails from the north. (See "More Information" following the trail description below for directions to the new Noanet Woodlands main entrance, which is not part of this hike but provides access to other trails.) *GPS coordinates:* 42° 14.878′ N, 71° 16.161′ W.

TRAIL DESCRIPTION

The diversity of terrain makes Noanet Woodlands so special. Swamplands, brooks, millponds, a waterfall, upland forests, and a 387-foot hill are all found here. These features provide for excellent nature study, as well as hiking, jogging, and cross-country skiing on the reservation's extensive trail network. The property abuts Powisset Farm, also owned by The Trustees of Reservations, and the privately owned Hale Reservation, creating a contiguous wildlife refuge.

The trail network includes four main blazed trails and other unnamed paths. This hike begins at Caryl Park, which abuts the reservation, and combines portions of Caryl Loop, Peabody Loop, and Noanet Peak trails. The

LOCATION
Dover, MA

RATING
Moderate

DISTANCE
3.5 miles

ELEVATION GAIN
230 feet

ESTIMATED TIME
1.75 hours

MAPS
USGS Framingham, USGS Medfield; online: thetrustees.org/assets/documents/places-to-visit/trailmaps/Noanet-Wayfinding-May-2014.pdf

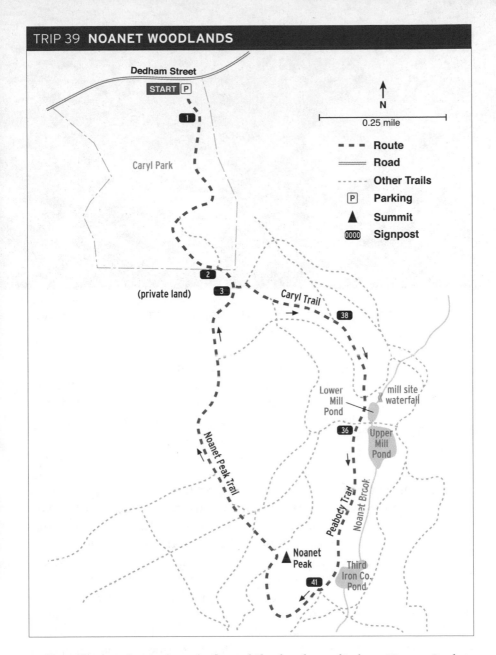

Dedham Street

START P

N

0.25 mile

Route

Road

Other Trails

P **Parking**

▲ **Summit**

0000 **Signpost**

Caryl Park

1

2

3

(private land)

Caryl Trail

38

Lower Mill Pond

mill site waterfall

36

Upper Mill Pond

Noanet Peak Trail

Peabody Trail

Noanet Brook

▲ Noanet Peak

Third Iron Co. Pond

41

walk to the ponds is relatively flat, while the short climb to Noanet Peak is steep in spots.

From Caryl Park, follow the main trail, which begins on the south side of the east parking lot at junction 1 and leads south into the woods. After about 1,000 feet, it turns to the right and soon reaches a "T" junction with a woods road. Turn left and follow the road past a small stream and a glacial boulder at marker 2; go left at the next fork, at marker 3. (Noanet Peak Trail, which is the

The site of the former Dover Union Iron Mill in Noanet Woodlands serves as a historical waypoint on this hike. Photo by Mike Halsall, Creative Commons on Flickr.

return loop, branches to the right here.) At this point, you'll exit Caryl Park and enter The Trustees of Reservations land. The trail then splits again at the start of the Caryl loop. Go right here on the loop's right branch, marked by red discs. Continue following this trail straight through a junction in an open area where a trail comes down from the right. Bear left at the next junction and continue on Caryl Trail. The path follows the base of a bridge then bends left and right near marker 38.

After about a quarter-mile, you will see a sparkling waterfall cascading from Lower Mill Pond on the left side of the trail. (You can make a short detour here on paths that circle the pond.) This was once the site of the Dover Union Iron Company, which operated from 1815 into the 1830s. The brook was too small to adequately power the mills, and the company eventually went out of business. The original dam was destroyed by flooding in 1876 but was reconstructed in 1954 by Amelia Peabody, who later bequeathed the land to The Trustees. The holding ponds above the dam are a perfect place to sit and have lunch, serenaded by the sound of falling water and singing birds. Painted turtles, frogs, and blue-gills inhabit the various ponds and wetlands. The setting is made complete by the large pines, oaks, maples, and beeches that surround the ponds.

Next you'll leave Caryl Trail and follow Noanet Peak Trail to marker 36. From here, continue on Peabody Trail (blue blazes) as it passes between Noanet Brook, far on the left, and forested slopes to the right. Follow the trail in a southerly direction for about 0.4 mile. Just beyond Third Iron Company Pond, you will come to a four-way trail intersection at junction 41. To reach Noanet Peak, take the unnamed trail on the right that climbs the hill. After about 50 yards, the trail bears left and makes a steep but short climb up the south slope. Follow this trail for about a quarter-mile. By bearing right at the next intersection, onto Noanet Peak Trail, you will reach the summit in a couple of minutes of walking. The top of the peak grants an excellent view of the Boston skyline and the hills to the east. Powisset Peak, part of the nearby Hale Reservation, is also visible. In fall, the hilltop is a good place to see migrating hawks flying south.

From Noanet Peak, retrace your steps for about 50 feet then bear right downhill on an unnamed trail that descends to the west. Stay straight on this trail for a quarter-mile until it rejoins Noanet Peak Trail, marked with yellow disks. Bearing right on Noanet Peak Trail, you'll pass private residences to the left, near the reservation's western boundary, before completing the loop at junction 3. From here, turn left and backtrack 0.5 mile to Caryl Park and the parking area.

DID YOU KNOW?

Amelia Peabody was well known in Dover for her conservation efforts. She originally purchased a farm near the present Noanet Woodlands in 1923, then subsequently added hundreds of acres over the next six decades.

MORE INFORMATION

Noanet Woodlands is open sunrise to sunset; there is no fee. Dogs are allowed, but you must follow posted leash rules. Mountain biking requires a free permit. For information, contact The Trustees of Reservations at 508-785-0339 or visit thetrustees.org. The reservation's new main entrance is on Powisset Street. *GPS coordinates:* 42° 13.682' N, 71° 15.401' W. To reach it from I-95, take Exit 16B and follow MA 109 west for about a mile then turn right onto Dover Road and continue 2.3 miles to the entrance. Parking is restricted at Caryl Park during peak athletic field use: weekdays in April and May from 3 to 8 P.M.

NEARBY

The historic Benjamin Caryl House, home of Dover's first minister, is located at 107 Dedham Street. The house, which was added to the National Register of Historic Places in 2000 and is now owned by the Dover Historical Society (incorporated in 1900), was built in 1777 and includes eighteenth-century furnishings. Restaurants are located in the center of Needham on Highland Avenue, Great Plain Avenue, and Chestnut Street.

40

ROCKY WOODS RESERVATION

This expansive reservation offers a choice of walks exploring ponds, rocky outcroppings, and boulders, with opportunities to fish, picnic, and cross-country ski.

DIRECTIONS

From I-95 take Exit 16B for MA 109 west. Follow it 5.5 miles through Westwood to Hartford Street in Medfield. Take a hard right onto Hartford Street. Follow it 0.6 mile to the entrance and parking lot on the left. *GPS coordinates:* 42° 12.386' N, 71° 16.601' W.

TRAIL DESCRIPTIONS

Rocky Woods is one of the largest properties owned by The Trustees of Reservations, and it offers a wide variety of year-round recreational activities. The name Rocky Woods is appropriate; the land is a series of uneven ridges with many rocky outcrops, including Whale Rock, which resembles the back of a whale rising from the forest floor. The reservation is rich in wildlife, and early-morning hikers are often treated to the sight of a fox, a ruffed grouse, or a great blue heron wading in one of the ponds.

Described here are two hikes that explore this large area. These may be done separately or combined as a longer outing. Both start at the main entrance.

Southern section: From the south end of the parking lot near the gatehouse, follow Yellow Trail along a wide, well-maintained path for a short distance to Echo Pond Trail, at junction 1. Continue straight on the Yellow Trail, which skirts the shallow waters of Echo Pond. Stop for a moment on the wooden footbridge to look for frogs, turtles, and waterfowl. Then leave Yellow Trail and continue straight on Echo Pond Trail, heading in a southwesterly

LOCATION
Medfield, MA

RATING
Easy to Moderate

DISTANCE
Southern section, 3.5 miles; northern section, 3.1 miles

ELEVATION GAIN
Southern section, 180 feet; northern section, 360 feet

ESTIMATED TIME
Southern section, 1.5 hours; northern section, 1.75 hours

MAPS
USGS Medfield; online: thetrustees.org/assets/documents/places-to-visit/trailmaps/Rocky-Woods-Fork-Factory-Brook-Trail-Map.pdf

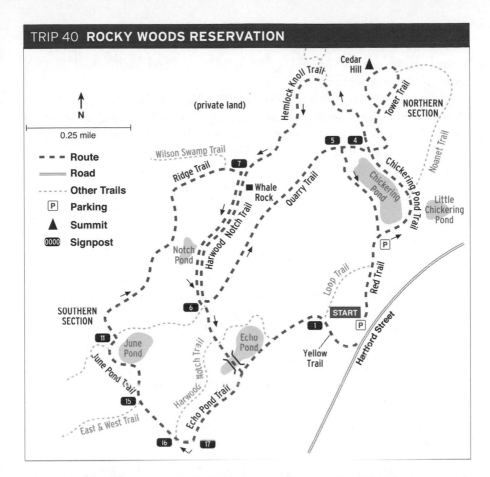

direction. This wide path is excellent for cross-country skiing, with just enough slopes for excitement.

At the next intersection (junction 17), turn right; pass junction 16 and bear right at junction 15 onto June Pond Trail. This short path soon passes the west side of June Pond, which is often all but dry by midsummer. At the pond's north-west corner (junction 11), bear left onto the 0.7-mile Ridge Trail. You will notice both the trees and the terrain begin to change here. Beech and birch appear, and granite boulders—dropped during the retreat of the glaciers—fill the woods. You'll appreciate the origin of the name Rocky Woods.

Walk along Ridge Trail until you come to Harwood Notch Trail, on the right at junction 7. Take this right, rejoining the Yellow Trail loop, and soon you will see the giant Whale Rock stretching out like a beached whale along the trail on your left.

Continue down Harwood Notch Trail, keeping watch for a trail that goes to the left beneath a sign that reads, "Lookout Point." (The lookout is a narrow view that can be reached after a four- or five-minute walk.) Continuing down Harwood Notch Trail, pass tiny Notch Pond on your right then cross the intersection with Quarry Trail. About 400 feet after this intersection, you can either take the path on the left along the north end of Echo Pond or continue straight to the footbridge. From either route, turn left onto Echo Pond Trail/Yellow Trail to return to the parking area.

Northern section (Cedar Hill–Hemlock Knoll and Whale Rock Loop): This pleasant walk passes several attractions, including Chickering Pond and a scenic vista at the summit of Cedar Hill. From the parking area, follow Red Trail along the entrance road for roughly 0.25 mile to the start of the loop at Chickering Pond. Bear right and continue along the eastern shore of the scenic, 5-acre pond. There is catch-and-release fishing here during the warmer months. Picnic tables and grills, some of which are ADA accessible, are scattered about the shoreline. Watch for great blue herons hunting along the shallow edges of the pond. You can also see kingfishers; it's thrilling to watch one dive from its perch and pluck a small fish from the water. Chickering Pond is a good spot to fish with kids, as sunfish are relatively easy to catch here with worms or other bait. You never know when a largemouth bass might be hungry, so bring some lures. All fish you catch must be released.

At junction 4, turn right onto Tower Trail and ascend moderately steep Cedar Hill via an old gravel road. After approximately 0.25 mile, you'll reach the partially exposed ridge. There is nothing quite so peaceful as gazing over the valleys and hills from the multiple viewpoints, with cool breezes whispering through the cedars.

Boulders, such as this erratic, dot the landscape of the appropriately named Rocky Woods Reservation.

After enjoying the views, retrace your steps downhill to junction 4. Bear right on Ridge Trail, which is marked with yellow blazes, then another right onto Hemlock Knoll Trail at the next (unnumbered) junction. One of the most interesting features is the minicanyon: a narrow, rocky passage that was formed during the time of the glaciers, when a stream passed through here.

At the end of Hemlock Knoll Loop, turn right, back onto Ridge Trail (marked with yellow blazes here), and continue to marker 7, where you'll take a left on Harwood Notch Trail. This takes you to the massive Whale Rock, where kids will enjoy climbing. From Whale Rock, follow the Harwood Notch Trail (also yellow-blazed) past a short side trail to a vista and Notch Pond. At junction 6, turn left onto Quarry Trail. On your way back to the parking area, you will pass the remains of a quarry. In the early 1900s, blocks of stone were cut here and hauled out by horses and oxen. Drill marks can still be seen in the rocks. At junction 5, turn right to rejoin the red-blazed Chickering Pond Trail and follow the path along the pond's western shore to complete the loop then return to the parking area. Witch hazel, sassafras, shagbark hickory, and dogwood trees can all be seen in the final quarter-mile.

DID YOU KNOW?

Rocky Woods' trails and ponds are artifacts of logging that began during the nineteenth century. The ponds were created as water sources for controlling forest fires, and the roads were established to transport timber and, later, granite from the quarry sites.

MORE INFORMATION

The reservation is open year-round, sunrise to sunset. Parking is free for members of The Trustees of Reservations; for others, the $5 fee is payable at a self-serve station. Restrooms, picnic tables, and a universally accessible fishing platform are available. Follow posted leash rules for dogs. For more information, contact The Trustees of Reservations at 781-784-0567 or visit thetrustees.org.

NEARBY

Medfield buildings on the National Register of Historic Places include the Peak House at 347 Main Street, which was burned during King Philip's War in 1676 (see essay on page 177) and rebuilt. It is now owned by the Medfield Historical Society and is open for tours. The Dwight-Derby House at 7 Friary Street, built in 1651, is one of the ten oldest homes in the United States. Restaurants are located on and off Main Street (MA 109) and North Street.

41

NOON HILL RESERVATION

Secluded and heavily wooded, Noon Hill is a hidden gem that provides habitat for a diversity of wildlife. The abutting Henry L. Shattuck Reservation adds another 225 acres of conservation land along the Charles River.

DIRECTIONS

From I-95, take Exit 16B onto MA 109 west. Follow it 7.5 miles, passing through Medfield Center. Turn left onto Causeway Street (approximately 200 feet after crossing MA 27) and continue 1.6 miles. Turn left onto Noon Hill Road. Drive 0.2 mile to a small parking area on the right. *GPS coordinates:* 42° 09.894′ N, 71° 19.110′ W.

TRAIL DESCRIPTION

Noon Hill, which is owned and managed by The Trustees of Reservations, is part of a scenic area of protected land in Medfield's Charles River Valley. The hike detailed here combines portions of the long-distance Bay Circuit Trail, which is well marked with white blazes, and the reservation's Yellow and Red trails. A short portion of the return loop crosses Medfield town conservation land.

From the parking area, follow the Bay Circuit and Yellow trails, marked with white and yellow blazes, southeast past side trails at junctions 1 and 2. You will pass through a low-lying area, with Yellow Trail turning right at junction 3 to make a 2.5-mile loop around Noon Hill. This is not the way to Noon Hill's summit, but it's worth a side trip, as it leads you to a tiny mountain stream, Holt Brook, that tumbles over granite boulders en route to Holt Pond. The path crosses the stream via a wooden bridge.

From junction 3, continue to follow the Bay Circuit Trail, which now coincides with Red Trail, straight through junction 5. After a half-mile, you will be at the

LOCATION
Medfield, MA

RATING
Moderate

DISTANCE
2 miles

ELEVATION GAIN
280 feet

ESTIMATED TIME
1 hour

MAPS
USGS Medfield; online: thetrustees.org/assets/documents/places-to-visit/trailmaps/NH_Web_TMap_Jan2010.pdf

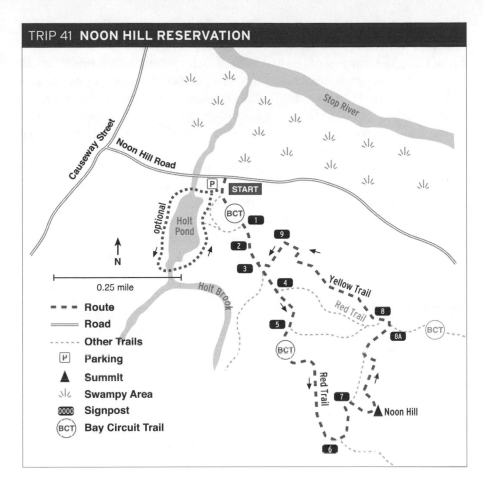

Causeway Street

Noon Hill Road

Stop River

P

START

BCT

optional

Holt Pond

N

0.25 mile

Holt Brook

1

9

2

3

4

5

Yellow Trail

Red Trail

8

8A

BCT

BCT

Red Trail

7

Noon Hill

6

- - - Route
===== Road
····· Other Trails
P   Parking
▲   Summit
⅄   Swampy Area
0000   Signpost
BCT   Bay Circuit Trail

base of Noon Hill. Beech trees and exposed boulders hug the slopes to your left. Watch for the ruffed grouse (called partridges by old New Englanders) that live here year-round; they may give you a start if you accidentally flush them. Thoreau wrote, "Whichever side you walk in the woods the partridge bursts away on whirring wings," adding, "this brave bird is not to be scared by winter." Other prominent birds seen here include turkey vultures, owls, and kingfishers.

The Bay Circuit and Red trails briefly follow the base of the hill then turn left at junction 6, climbing gently to the summit ridge. After about 500 feet, bear right at junction 7 and continue on to the partially exposed rocky overlook for fine views across the countryside. The views from the crest look southeast, where you can see across the forested hills of Medfield and Walpole to Gillette Stadium.

To descend Noon Hill, you can either retrace your path to the parking area or continue a slightly more rugged circuit by following the combined Bay Circuit and Red trails north along the ridge. For the latter, follow the trail north about 750 feet then make a quick descent to junction 8A on the north side of the hilltop. Turn left here to leave the Bay Circuit Trail, which continues to the right. At nearby junction 8, continue straight on Yellow Trail. (Red Trail branches left here; either route will eventually return you to the trailhead.) From this point, the rest of the hike follows Yellow Trail, which briefly leaves Noon Hill Reservation, descending through Medfield town conservation land before reentering Trustees land. You'll continue over rolling terrain to marker 9. Turn left in front of a stone wall and follow the narrow path, which winds through tall pines and closes the loop as it rejoins the Bay Circuit and Yellow trails at marker 2. Turn right to reach your car.

At the start or finish of your hike, you can walk the easy 0.4-mile Orange Loop that circles Holt Pond (an artificial pond built circa 1765 to power a saw-mill), adjacent to the parking area. This circuit, which includes a portion of the Bay Circuit Trail, can be completed in as little as fifteen minutes. There are nice views across the water from the shore and from the two wooden bridges that cross the pond's inlet and outlet streams. Look for kingfishers perched on branches above the water.

DID YOU KNOW?

Noon Hill got its name from early settlers, who noted that the sun rose above the hill around noontime.

Noon Hill Reservation is part of a network of conservation land along the Charles River in Medfield. Photo by Marc Chalufour.

MORE INFORMATION

The reservation is open year-round, sunrise to sunset. There is no fee; there are no restrooms; dogs are allowed (follow posted rules). For more information, contact The Trustees of Reservations at 508-785-0339 or visit thetrustees.org.

NEARBY

The nearby Medfield Rhododendrons, managed by The Trustees of Reservations, is a 196-acre preserve that protects an uncommon stand of rosebay rhododendrons. The easy Rhododendron Yellow Trail (0.9 mile) explores this area. To reach it from the junction of MA 27 and MA 109, follow MA 27 south for 0.5 mile then turn right onto Woodridge Street.

The adjacent Shattuck Reservation, also owned by The Trustees of Reservations, lies across the street from Noon Hill Reservation. Trails include the 1.5-mile Shattuck Red Loop and the Bay Circuit Trail leading to the banks of the Charles River. Restaurants are located in the center of Medfield on Main Street (MA 109) and North Street.

SOUTH OF BOSTON/ CAPE COD

The southeast region of Massachusetts stretches from Boston's southern suburbs west and south to the Rhode Island border and Narragansett Bay, and south and east to Buzzard's Bay and Cape Cod. Like other areas of eastern Massachusetts, it is home to a wide diversity of natural features, although the topography is somewhat more level, with only scattered low hills, such as Moose Hill in Sharon and the distinctive Granite Hills of Borderland State Park in North Easton.

While the terrain may be gentle, the impoverished, sandy soils that characterize much of the region are anything but. As a result, there is much less forest variety here than in other areas of Massachusetts. The dominant species—such as pitch pine and scrub oak (also known as bear oak)—are well adapted to marginal growing conditions. The oak-hickory woodlands, with their more diverse layers of shrubs and wildflowers, grow in richer, more hospitable soils.

There's no lack of wetland variety, including tidal rivers, streams, and creeks; salt and freshwater marshes; bogs; and an extensive network of swamps. There are hundreds of kettle ponds, which were formed by melting blocks of ice as glaciers retreated from the landscape more than 10,000 years ago. The major rivers drop just a matter of feet from headwaters to mouth due to the level topography.

The best-known feature of the southeast region is Cape Cod, a long, sandy peninsula that was also formed by moving glaciers. In response to ever increasing development throughout the twentieth century, the 40,000-acre Cape Cod National Seashore was established during the 1960s. Although most people come for the sandy ocean beaches that stretch from Chatham to the tip of the Cape in Provincetown (an area commonly known as the Outer Cape), the seashore's other features include Atlantic white cedar and red maple swamps; marshes and tidal flats; coastal pitch pine, scrub oak, and beech groves; cranberry bogs; dunes; and historical sites. Most of the park's land lies on the ocean side, but one exception is the Great Island peninsula, which juts into Wellfleet Bay.

Facing page: Arguably one of the best hikes on Cape Cod, Great Island offers an array of diverse marine life from whales to Atlantic horseshoe crabs to quahogs.

Across the bay from Great Island are the tidal flats, creeks, and heathlands of the Wellfleet Bay Wildlife Sanctuary, home to wildlife ranging from crabs and shorebirds to songbirds and turtles. One of the best destinations for exploring the Cape's interior habitats is Nickerson State Park in Brewster, where extensive woodlands surround a series of kettle ponds. There are roughly 300 of these glacial ponds, which are replenished by rainfall and groundwater alone, throughout Cape Cod.

The wider Upper Cape, the area closest to the mainland, is home to a number of natural areas, including Sandy Neck Beach, a 6-mile-long barrier beach bordered by a 3,500-acre salt marsh on Cape Cod Bay in Barnstable. The nearby Lowell Holly Reservation in Mashpee encompasses a small peninsula between two scenic freshwater ponds.

Along the mainland coast, the 14,000-acre Myles Standish State Forest protects one of New England's largest pitch pine and scrub oak forests, as well as a series of small kettle ponds. Nearby Ellisville Harbor State Park protects a rocky beach that is home to a large colony of harbor seals during the winter months. Farther north, Great Esker Park in Weymouth is home to a prominent glacial ridge that rises above Weymouth Back River and its marshes.

42

MOOSE HILL WILDLIFE SANCTUARY

Moose Hill Wildlife Sanctuary protects nearly 2,000 acres, featuring trails, forests, fields, a red maple swamp, and a secluded hilltop with long views.

DIRECTIONS

From I-95, take Exit 9 for US 1 north. Turn right onto MA 27, follow it 0.5 mile, and turn right onto Moose Hill Street. In 1.3 miles, turn left onto Moose Hill Parkway. The parking lot will be immediately on your left. *GPS coordinates*: 42° 07.409' N, 71° 12.434' W.

By public transportation, take the Providence/Stoughton line of the MBTA Commuter Rail to Sharon Station in Sharon. Walk to Depot Street, follow it north for two blocks, and take a left onto Moose Hill Parkway. Walk about a mile and bear left at Upland Road to stay on Moose Hill Parkway. Continue to the top of the hill; the visitor center is on the right.

TRAIL DESCRIPTION

The Bluffs: The Moose Hill Wildlife Sanctuary features varied topography. As in many areas of New England, the forests here were cleared for agriculture in Colonial times but have grown back. The sanctuary offers 25 miles of walking trails, and one of the most popular leads to the Bluffs, offering one of the best views in eastern Massachusetts. Stunted cedar trees and sheer rock walls give the illusion that this is a hilltop in Maine, New Hampshire, or Vermont. And for a view this good, the trail to the top is surprisingly gentle.

From the sanctuary entrance, follow Moose Hill Parkway and cross Moose Hill Street, watching for light traffic. Look for the stone pillars that mark the entrance to Billings Loop Trail. The trail follows a wide gravel road

LOCATION
Sharon, MA

RATING
Moderate

DISTANCE
The Bluffs, 2.5 miles; Ovenbird/Kettle trails, 1.75 miles

ELEVATION GAIN
The Bluffs, 130 feet; Ovenbird/Kettle trails, 50 feet

ESTIMATED TIME
The Bluffs, 1.5 to 2 hours; Ovenbird/Kettle trails, 1 hour

MAPS
USGS Brockton, USGS Norwood; online: massaudubon.org/content/download/8080/145429/file/moosehill_trails.pdf

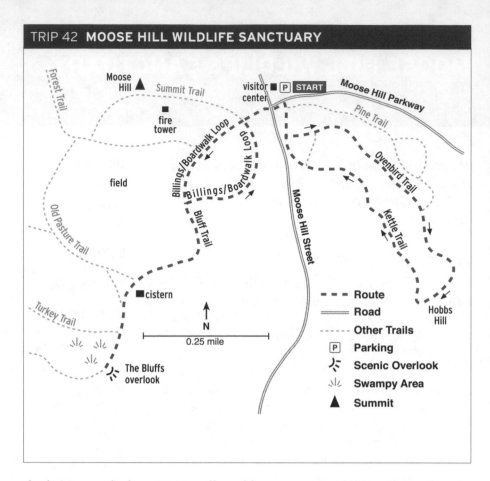

that's easy on the legs. Stone walls and large sugar maples line the trail, making it a visual treat. You will pass the old Billings barn on the right and two enormous maples on the left. A short way from the large maples is a circular opening in the woods, where an assortment of trees are labeled, providing the perfect classroom for a young naturalist interested in identifying white pine, Colorado blue spruce, white birch, hickory, red oak, red pine, sassafras, and northern white cedar. After studying the trees, continue down the trail. (Look over your shoulder to see the blue spruce framed against the sky.) Soon you will enter another open area of low-lying plants and bushes. More than 400 species of wildflowers grow here, as well as 27 species of ferns, and thanks to the high elevations in the sanctuary, yellow and white birches add to the feeling of being in the North Country. Spring is the time to see the woodland wildflowers bloom. Numerous nesting boxes in the fields provide homes for tree swallows, black-capped chickadees, and bluebirds.

At a marked junction in a field, bear right onto Bluff Trail and follow it into the woods. (Those looking for a shorter hike can continue to the left on Billings Loop Trail through a red maple swamp on a boardwalk.) The exposed roots seem to grab at your boots, but the grades are gentle. A maple, oak, and pine forest surrounds the trail. On the left, you will pass a huge, round cistern dug into the earth and lined with stones. Like the stone walls and old chimney remains scattered through these woods, it is an artifact of past land use. Cisterns are used to catch and store rainwater; they differ from wells in that they are lined with waterproof materials. The trail now becomes part of two thru-trails, Warner Trail and the Bay Circuit Trail. Just beyond the cistern is an impressive stand of beech trees on the left and a swampy area on the right. Stay straight (left) where the Old Pasture and Turkey trails branch to the right.

Look for red and gray squirrels scrambling on the branches overhead. Other animals in the sanctuary include skunks, opossums, foxes, raccoons, fishers, coyotes, and deer. All are nocturnal, so your best chance to catch a glimpse of them is at dawn or dusk. The birdlife is varied and easier to see. It includes warblers, nuthatches, scarlet tanagers, northern orioles, bluebirds, woodpeckers, and a wide assortment of hawks, such as kestrels, red-tailed hawks, and broad-winged hawks.

Here the trail starts its gradual climb to the Bluffs. The designers of the trail knew what they were doing when they picked this route to the summit: It never gets steep and is a relatively easy walk to the top. Just as you begin your final steps to the summit, you'll see the gnarled and windswept branches of the eastern red cedars that dot the hilltop. These trees can be distinguished from the white cedars by their needlelike leaves with bluish-green berries. These hard fruits are eaten by birds.

The granite ledge at the 491-foot overlook offers sweeping views to the south and west. Gillette Stadium, home of the New England Patriots, is visible a few miles off. This is one of the nicest hilltops in eastern Massachusetts; it's the perfect place to sit, gaze off into the distance, and let your mind wander. You'll hear no traffic sounds, only the breeze as it whispers through the trees. There are a number of outcrops along this hilltop ridge offering vista changes. Use caution along the edge, as the dropoff is steep. During autumn, you might be able to see a hawk riding a thermal—a column of warm, rising air—on its migration.

When you are ready to head home, retrace your steps to the parking lot. More ambitious hikers can try Forest Trail, which makes a long loop at the northern end of the property (see map).

Ovenbird/Kettle Trails: On another trip, you may want to try the less-traveled eastern end of the property. Coyotes have been seen here, and it may be only a matter of time before more are spotted, as this is a secluded area of the sanctuary. These trails are reached via the white-blazed Bay Circuit Trail and Warner Trail, which enters the woods across the road from the parking area. This trail soon turns left to follow Ovenbird Trail, which descends gradually through an oak–pine woodland, passing several junctions with Pine Trail. After about a 10-minute walk, the path follows a bubbling brook. Swamp maples

Moose Hill is the oldest of Mass Audubon's sanctuaries. Its boardwalk through a red-maple swamp provides an opportunity to view wildlife up close. Photo by Kelsey Quartuccio.

soon mix in with the other trees as the trail veers to the southeast. Woodland wildflowers abound here: pink lady's slipper, jack-in-the-pulpit, and maple leaf viburnum, to name just a few. It's impressive to see plants with such dazzling displays of color in a natural setting.

You'll reach a "T" junction where Ovenbird Trail meets Kettle Trail. For a longer hike, take the path on the left that leads to Hobbs Hill Loop, which makes a circuit around 342-foot Hobbs Hill near the sanctuary boundary, or continue to the right on Kettle Trail. This trail got its name from the many kettle holes formed by huge blocks of ice left by the glaciers roughly 10,000 years ago. It is rugged in spots, hugging the ridges, called eskers. The eskers formed when streams, flowing beneath the glacial ice sheets, deposited sediments along the streambed that now makes up the thin ridgeline. The basin along Kettle Trail was once home to beautiful groves of rhododendrons and mountain laurel, but these were largely eaten by deer. Kettle Trail loops through the forest back toward the Bay Circuit and Warner trails and the trailhead, passing through a stand of hemlocks and then past a lush green field on the left. Backtrack across Moose Hill Parkway to the visitor center.

DID YOU KNOW?

The hill that the sanctuary now stewards was named long ago, and there are several theories behind the name. "Moose" is an Algonquin word, so the name may predate Colonial settlement. It is also said that the hill is shaped like a moose's hump. This would have been more easily visualized after settlers had cleared the forests for agricultural use. Historical records of early Sharon tell of a man having a startling encounter with a moose.

MORE INFORMATION

The sanctuary is open weekdays from 9 A.M. to 5 P.M. and weekends from 10 A.M. to 4 P.M. Admission is free for Mass Audubon members and Sharon residents; otherwise, it's $4 for adults, $3 for children and seniors. The sanctuary offers programs for children, families, adults, and groups, as well as events including a Maple Sugaring Festival in March and a Halloween Prowl in October. The sanctuary's Vernal Pool Trail is a great place to look for frogs and other wetland creatures. The sanctuary offers a Quest Pack for the Vernal Pool Trail (similar to a geocache) that is available at the visitor center and on its website. For more information, call 781-784-5691 or visit massaudubon.org/moosehill.

NEARBY

Sharon's historical district is located on both sides of North Main Street, from Post Office Square to School Street. Among the old homes remaining in town are the houses of patriots Job Swift and Deborah Sampson Gannett. There are several restaurants on North and South Main streets, a short distance from the sanctuary. The sanctuary is a short drive from Borderland State Park and Lake Massapoag (see Trip 43).

43

BORDERLAND STATE PARK

The level walking trails at Borderland State Park lead to close-up views of ponds, fields, and forests.

DIRECTIONS

From I-95, take Exit 8 and follow South Main Street 3.3 miles to Sharon Center. Turn right onto Billings Street at the traffic signal then immediately right again onto Pond Street. Stay south on Pond Street for 0.9 mile to a small rotary and continue on Massapoag Avenue. Drive 3.6 miles on Massapoag Avenue, and the park entrance will be on the left. *GPS coordinates:* 42° 03.641′ N, 71° 10.023′ W.

TRAIL DESCRIPTION

Borderland was opened as a state park in 1971. Prior to that, it served as the country estate of the Ames family, who named it Borderland because it is on the border of Sharon and Easton. The family constructed the stone mansion in 1910, and the house is open for regularly scheduled guided tours in spring, summer, and fall.

Hiking alongside water always makes an outing special, and Borderland State Park has no fewer than six ponds to explore. Add to that the flat hayfields and the option to test your legs on hilly, rocky terrain, and Borderland has something for everyone. Borderland can be a popular place, but with 1,773 acres it's easy to find the quiet and solitude that make hiking special. Small, rocky hills cover the northern acres, while flatter land lies to the south.

You can make either a 3-mile circle via Leach Pond Loop (marked on the map as the Pond Walk) or a 3.5-mile walk by continuing around Upper Leach Pond. From the parking lot off Massapoag Avenue, follow the gravel path through the fields. (The mansion will be off to your right.) At the "T" intersection in the trail, there is an excellent

LOCATION
North Easton, MA

RATING
Moderate

DISTANCE
3.5 miles

ELEVATION GAIN
50 feet

ESTIMATED TIME
1.75 hours

MAPS
USGS Brockton; online: mass.gov/eea/docs/dcr/parks/trails/borderland.pdf

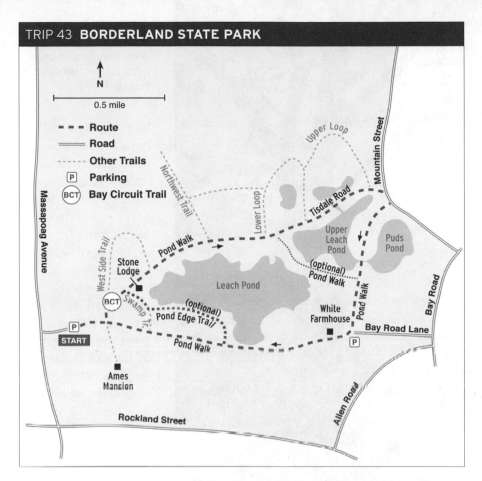

map posted. Go left here to start your walk on the north side of the ponds, following a portion of the white-blazed Bay Circuit Trail. (Follow the sign to Leach Pond.) The trail leads down to the water's edge, where a stone building called the lodge is located. The pond-side trails are wide, flat, and well maintained—excellent for cross-country skiing. This is also a good spot for viewing waterfowl.

Continue to follow the main trail straight at a junction with West Side Trail, where the Bay Circuit Trail leaves to the left. (The route is unmarked from this point but easy to follow.) At various intervals, you will pass benches that offer scenic views of the islands near the pond's center. Near the junction of Northwest Trail, you will see a wetland and fields to the right that deer are said to frequent. Farther up the trail on the left is a little stone cave that was probably a farmer's root cellar but could make a good home for the Virginia opossums sighted in the park in recent years.

Separating Leach Pond from Upper Leach Pond is Long Dam, built by the Ames family to create Leach Pond in 1939. If you wish to limit your walk to 3 miles, turn right here, cross the stream on the wooden footbridge, follow this path to its end, and go right to reach the parking lot. To complete the 3.5-mile

A day-hiker takes a break at Borderland State Park, which offers hikes for all ability levels, families, and dogs. Photo by Ryan Smith.

loop, continue following the pond-side trail (now Tisdale Road) to the northeast. You may wish to detour to the left on one of the Granite Hills trails, which explore open fields and lead to views of two secluded ponds. The main trail takes you around Upper Leach Pond and eventually to the old Tisdale cellar hole, near Mountain Street, where there is a beautiful view of Upper Leach Pond. The trail intersects with Mountain Street, and you must follow this paved town road for a short distance to the right before the footpath leads back into the woods at a gate on the right. This pathway soon takes you through a field to a bridge spanning the outflow stream from Puds Pond.

Some of Borderland's ponds are covered with waterlilies and blue-flowered pickerelweed in summer. All of the ponds are shallow, with significant amounts of vegetation growing. As the vegetation dies and fills the bottom of the ponds, swamp shrubs begin to encroach along the shorelines, and the ponds will slowly turn to marsh.

Follow this trail through a large, restored agricultural field all the way to the white farmhouse and bear right. The fields and wooden fence here are especially scenic. Keep an eye out for red-tailed hawks, which have adapted fairly well to human presence. They often can be seen along our highways, perched in trees and keeping a sharp eye out for any movement in the grassy strips along the roadways. They are one of the few birds that winter here, and Thoreau acknowl-edged their hardiness when he wrote of "the hawk with warrior-like firmness abiding the blasts of winter."

The wide, level trail next passes a large cove of Leach Pond, a good spot to launch a canoe after parking in the small lot nearby. There are a few rare Atlantic white cedars growing adjacent to the cove, and Pond Edge Trail will be on your right. You can take Pond Edge Trail, Swamp Trail, or the main trail back toward the parking lot and the Ames mansion. Pond Edge Trail is recommended, as it is a pleasant walk off the main path with nice views of the pond.

DID YOU KNOW?

Prior to the Ames family ownership, the ponds and streams powered a num-ber of mills at various times during the eighteenth and early nineteenth cen-turies, including a sawmill, a nail factory, a cotton mill, and an ironworks. The nearby land was cleared for farming, and stone walls can still be seen crisscrossing the woodlands.

MORE INFORMATION

The park offers organized hikes and birding. Challenging mountain biking trails are very popular in the park as well, mostly on the northern side. A $5 fee is charged at the main entrance parking lots. For more information, call 508-238-6566 or visit mass.gov/dcr.

NEARBY

On the way to Borderland, you'll pass 353-acre Lake Massapoag. The lake is the headwaters of the Canoe River and is a summer resort area that includes a large town beach. It is also popular with sailors and sailboarders. Restau-rants in Sharon are located on North and South Main streets. For day-trippers, Borderland can be combined with a visit to the nearby Moose Hill Wildlife Sanctuary (Trip 42).

44

AMES NOWELL STATE PARK

This hike offers a variety of wildlife and terrain, from woods to water.

DIRECTIONS

From MA 3 south, take Exit 16B for MA 18 south. (If traveling north on MA 3, take Exit 16 for MA 18 south.) Follow MA 18 for 6.2 miles until you reach the center of Abington and the intersection with MA 123. Turn right and take the next right onto Rockland Street. After 0.7 mile, bear left to remain on Rockland Street. When you reach the end, turn right onto Linwood Street and take it to the end. *GPS coordinates*: 42° 06.895′ N, 70° 58.570′ W.

TRAIL DESCRIPTION

This scenic property features an 88-acre pond, a waterfall, brooks, boardwalks, and approximately 7 miles of hiking trails. Due to its proximity to Brockton and other densely populated towns, you might want to arrive early in the morning so you can have the trails to yourself and improve your chances of seeing wildlife.

Go to the front of the information kiosk after you park. (Rangers are often on duty here and are a wealth of knowledge about flora and fauna.) Standing in front of the information kiosk, locate the road about 50 feet ahead of you and take it downhill toward the pond. Follow this road about 200 feet and bear left toward the water, ignoring paths on your right.

You will soon reach the dam at the southern end of Cleveland Pond, also known as Ames Pond. The artificially constructed pond was formed in 1920 when Beaver Brook was dammed. At the time, the Holmes family owned the land. On a concrete marker near where the water flows over the dam, look for an etching that reads, "1920," and the words, "Semloh Pond"—Holmes spelled backward.

LOCATION
Abington, MA

RATING
Easy

DISTANCE
2 miles

ELEVATION GAIN
Minimal

ESTIMATED TIME
1 hour

MAPS
USGS Abington; online: mass.gov/eea/docs/dcr/parks/trails/amesnowell.pdf

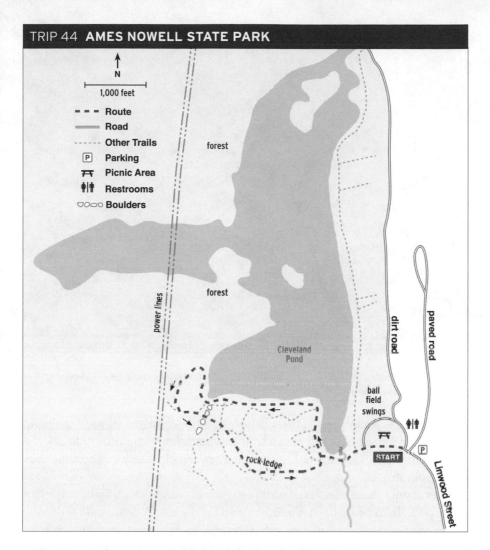

No matter the name, it's a scenic body of water that supports a range of warm-water fish, such as largemouth bass, pickerel, crappie, and sunfish. (The boat launch is open June through September for canoes and boats with motors of 10 horsepower or less.) White and yellow waterlilies and purple pickerelweed grace the pond with color in the warm-weather months. The elegant flowers of the pickerelweed are funnel-shaped and bloom from June until autumn. Its leaves are heart-shaped and taper to a point. Along the edge of the pond you will find blueberries, huckleberries, raspberries, and sweet pepperbush, with its pleasant summertime scent. In winter, ice skating is allowed.

A footbridge spans the brook that tumbles in a waterfall from the pond. There is a nice picnic area on the other side, along the banks of the stream. Cross the footbridge, continue across the earthen dam to its end, and stay to the right to follow a narrow path that hugs the shoreline of the pond and enters

Dragonflies are among the wildlife—frogs, snakes, raccoons, butterflies, birds, deer, turkey—you might spot at Ames Nowell.

the woods. The rocky path features little hills and occasional views of the pond through the foliage. You will pass a trail on your left but continue to follow the pond. Most of the trees are oak, although a few small American chestnut trees grow from stumps.

After about fifteen minutes of walking you will pass through an opening in a stone wall. Then you will pass another trail on the left. A boardwalk will soon be on your right; follow it over the wetlands. In autumn the swamp maples here are ablaze with color. Also called red maples, they thrive in wet soil and are among the first trees to turn color in New England, sometimes as early as the end of August. Be sure to look beneath the boardwalk for frogs and snakes hidden in the grass. Raccoons also prowl both the swamp and the shoreline looking for freshwater mussels, crayfish, frogs, salamanders, fish, snakes, and a wide range of plants. They use their extremely dexterous front feet to probe every nook and cranny.

On the other side of the boardwalk the trail splits. Before continuing the walk along the pond's edge, take time to go left on the trail for a few feet. After you reach the power-line clearing, walk to the right a few more feet to climb a rock overlooking a portion of the park. The clearing beneath the power lines is a good place to see butterflies and birds, such as the kestrel, which hunts insects and small rodents. If you are here early you might also see a white-tailed deer, a red fox, or a wild turkey.

The park's supervisor, David Green, says that raccoon, pheasant, and quail live in the park, and muskrat live along the banks of the pond. He also reports sightings of nesting marsh hawks, and several other species of hawks, including red-tailed and sharp-shinned, near the picnic area by the pond. A fully mature sharp-shinned hawk is about 10 inches long with a wingspan of 21 inches, and it is fairly common along the edges of the woods. It has a brown and tan pattern on its underside with a long, narrow tail. Sharp-shinned hawks often fly above the treetops in the early morning and soar higher at midday. Small birds are its preferred prey.

Retrace your steps to the pond and continue northward. Soon you will pass a nice clearing with a large rock by the edge of the pond, which makes a good rest stop. Scan the water for wading birds, such as great blue herons or the belted kingfisher, which does not wade but scouts from branches along the water's edge. Both birds feed primarily on small fish. Osprey are also seen here during brief periods in spring and fall, when they're migrating. The pond-side path continues north for another quarter-mile before ending at the water's edge.

To return to the parking area, retrace your steps to the boardwalk. Once you cross the boardwalk, you can take a different trail back. Follow the unnamed trail to the right and make a quick left onto another unnamed trail that leads eastward. This trail is fairly level, passing small oaks and gray birch. Ignore the side trails on your left that connect back with the pond-side trail.

About five minutes down the path there is a rock ledge on your right that makes a good resting spot in the sun. From here it's only another five minutes back to the dam and parking area.

DID YOU KNOW

Abington factories that were powered by water, such as those that were located on this property, supplied almost half of the Union army's shoes during the Civil War.

MORE INFORMATION

The park is open sunrise to sunset. There is no admission fee. Restrooms are open seasonally. Dogs are allowed on-leash. For information, visit mass.gov/dcr or call 781-857-1336.

NEARBY

Fuller Craft Museum, off Oak Street in Brockton, is an interesting oasis of modern handcrafts, about 4 miles from Ames Nowell State Park. Children's classes are offered, as well as entertainment and an array of demonstrations. See fullercraft.org for more information.

Many restaurants and businesses are located nearby in the center of Abington, near the intersections of MA 18 and MA 123.

45

GREAT ESKER PARK

Easy trails exploring a glacial esker lead to views of the Weymouth Back River and a salt marsh.

LOCATION
Weymouth, MA

RATING
Easy

DISTANCE
1.5 miles

ELEVATION GAIN
285 feet

ESTIMATED TIME
1 hour

MAPS
USGS Weymouth

DIRECTIONS

From MA 3 south, take Exit 16B for MA 18 south. (If traveling north on MA 3, take Exit 16 for MA 18 south.) At the first traffic light, turn left onto Middle Street. At the end of Middle Street, in 2.9 miles, bear left onto Commercial Street and proceed 0.4 mile to the first traffic light. Turn right onto Green Street and go 0.6 mile to the triangular divider. Bear right onto Elva Road and go uphill 0.2 mile to the road's end and park in the large lot adjacent to a playground. *GPS coordinates:* 42° 14.178′ N, 70° 55.905′ W.

By public transportation, take the MBTA Red Line to Quincy Center and transfer to the #220 bus. Take it to Riverway Plaza on Bridge Street (MA 3A). From there it's a short walk west along Bridge Street to Great Esker Park.

TRAIL DESCRIPTION

With a little imagination, a walk on top of the glacial esker at Great Esker Park is like walking on the back of a giant snake. Formed by glacial deposits during the last ice age, some 12,000 years ago, the 1.25-mile-long esker rises above the woodlands and the marsh, reaching a height of 90 feet. Eskers were shaped when rivers within retreating glaciers filled with debris as the ice melted. Two walks are described here, both of which lead to fine views of Weymouth Back River (also called Back River) and its associated salt marshes.

For the Reversing Falls loop, follow the paved road (closed to vehicles) that begins to the right of the maintenance buildings in the parking area. Within five minutes you'll reach the top, at an intersection with another paved

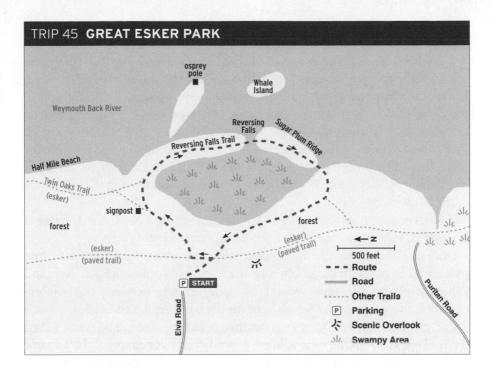

path (unnamed) that follows the contours of the esker. Turn left here and walk along the top of the esker in a northerly direction, passing beneath oaks (red oaks have bristle-tipped lobes; white oaks have rounded lobes) and maples. In the understory are gray birch and staghorn sumac. The staghorn sumac gets its name from the velvet covering its stems that looks like the velvet on a stag's antlers. It is nonpoisonous and especially colorful in autumn, when the leaves are a dark crimson.

In roughly 200 feet, when you come to a sign for Reversing Falls, turn right (Twin Oaks Trail is to the left) and follow the unnamed dirt path downslope toward a salt marsh in the basin below. At the next intersection, bear right and continue toward Reversing Falls, keeping the marsh on your right. The path follows the edge of the marsh; here you can look through the trees to spot birds feeding in the grass. Watch for wood ducks, snowy egrets, great egrets, and even an occasional little blue heron in the marsh. In winter, look for bald eagles, which are fairly new to the area, in the tops of trees.

The trail climbs a smaller esker and turns right at the top of the ridge. There are good views of the marsh from both sides of the trail, and if you look to your left near Reversing Falls, you will see a pole that the magnificent osprey use as a nesting platform. Osprey have successfully bred here since 1992. They enjoy an abundance of fish in Back River and at nearby Whitman's Pond, and they generally return to the area at the time of the herring run each spring.

After a quarter-mile, the trail reaches Reversing Falls, where there are scenic views across Weymouth Back River and the adjacent salt marsh. These "falls" are not a waterfall but instead a narrow passageway between two sections of the marsh, where water rushes in at high tide and exits at low tide.

The salt marsh and estuary at Great Esker is quite large. More than 30 species of fish can be found here, including flounder, bluefish, striped bass, eel, herring, and smelt. Many young fish and invertebrates grow up here, finding shelter in the dense grasses. Beneath the water's surface, a variety of creatures, such as soft-shell clams, shrimp, and worms, live and feed on top of or beneath the mud. Crabs use the tides to their advantage, burrowing in the mud at low tide for protection and scavenging along the bottom at high tide. Each spring, there is a herring run up Weymouth Back River to Whitman's Pond, where the fish spawn in the freshwater.

A series of steppingstones crosses the passage, making it possible to traverse at low tide. At high tide, remove your shoes and carefully wade across.

Once on the other side of the passage, follow the unnamed narrow trail that passes over Sugar Plum Ridge, offering nice views of Weymouth Back River and Whale Island. Look for mute swans floating out on the water. Lowbush blueberries are scattered about the woods beneath the oaks. At the end of Sugar Plum Ridge, cross another low-lying area (remove your shoes at high tide) and follow the trail straight into the woods, bypassing a side trail on your left. In a couple of minutes, bear to the right, passing beneath a power line. At the next fork, stay to the right. (If you go straight, it leads directly to the paved trail on top of the

The salt marsh and estuary of the Weymouth Back River offer habitat for fish and other intertidal marine life.

esker.) The path leads through a grove of beech trees with smooth gray trunks then crosses the power lines again with the esker on your left.

After about three-quarters of a mile, the trail swings left and climbs to the top of the esker, where it intersects the paved road. From here, you can return to your car.

DID YOU KNOW?

Weymouth was once a hub for shipbuilding. In 1884 one of the largest schooners ever built was launched from Keen's Shipyard into the Fore River in Weymouth. Historical accounts say there were 1,000 people aboard the four-masted, 209-foot-long *Haroldine* when she was launched.

MORE INFORMATION

The park is open sunrise to sunset, year-round, seven days a week, and there is no fee. There are no restrooms; dogs are allowed on-leash. In season, the town offers kayaking and other outdoor recreation classes and opportunities. Contact Weymouth Recreation Department, 1393 Pleasant Street in East Weymouth, at 781-682-6124 or visit weymouth.ma.us/recreation.

NEARBY

Webb Memorial State Park on River Street offers walking, picnicking, fishing, and views of Boston from a peninsula that juts into Hingham Bay. Boats to the Boston Harbor Islands depart from neighboring Hewitt's Cove. Nearby Wompatuck State Park, which is located off Free Street in Hingham, offers more than 260 campsites, 12 miles of paved bicycling trails, and hiking trails. Restaurants are located along and off Washington Street in Weymouth.

CLIMATE CHANGE IN NEW ENGLAND

When we stroll along a riverside path or climb a mountain in New England, we imagine we're seeing the same landscape enjoyed by Longfellow, Thoreau, and Metacomet. Due to climate change, we're not. The forests and their inhabitants are changing rapidly under our gaze in ways our forefathers never could have foreseen.

Flowers in New England bloom 2.3 days earlier for each 1-degree Fahrenheit increase in temperature, and migration patterns are changing. Most visibly, maple trees, hemlocks, and spruces are likely to die off as a result of higher temperatures and invasive pests. In the future, pockets of these trees may survive on colder, north-facing folds of northern mountains, but unless fossil fuel emissions are significantly reduced, future generations of hikers and nature lovers in central and southern New England won't know the landscapes we enjoy today.

In the next 75 years, scientists predict New England's currently diverse flora could closely resemble North Carolina's pine and oak forests, with fewer evergreens, less boreal forest, and disappearing wildlife—consequences of modern civilization that were unforeseen just a few decades ago. Changes are predicted to hit New England especially hard, affecting weather patterns and animal habitat from the ocean to the mountains.

Scientists have documented steady increases in temperatures across the Northeast—an average of 2 degrees Fahrenheit since 1970—and predict as much as a 10-degree increase in the next 85 years. These increases have allowed invasive species of plants and insects to flourish and kill native flora. Changes in temperature can weaken native species and make them more susceptible to disease and invasive pests.

Animals have been affected as well. The moose population has plummeted as the tick population has increased and weakened the animals, killing them before they are old enough to reproduce. Scientists have documented so many blood-draining ticks on moose that the animals become anemic and weak. Shorter winters are taking a toll, too, forcing cold-weather animals to adapt to warmer temperatures, and leading moose to rest on hot days instead of foraging for food.

Watchful and concerned scientists from local observatories, universities, and conservation groups are studying and quantifying the creeping effects of climate change in New England and are putting in place plans to slow these repercussions. Their efforts have included the Regional Greenhouse Gas Initiative, which caps the amount of carbon dioxide a power plan can emit. The Appalachian Mountain Club's Mountain Watch program encourages citizen scientists to monitor alpine flowers, tracking climate change's impact. Learn more at outdoors.org/mountainwatch and outdoors.org/can.

46
WORLD'S END RESERVATION

Tremendous views, rolling fields leading to the ocean's edge, and an impressive assortment of flora and fauna make for a beautiful walk.

DIRECTIONS

From MA 3, take Exit 14 to MA 228 north. Go 6.5 miles to MA 3A and turn left. Proceed on 3A for 1.2 miles, then take a right onto Summer Street and proceed 0.5 mile. Turn left onto Martin's Lane at the light and proceed 0.7 mile to the entrance and parking area. *GPS coordinates: 42° 15.490' N, 70° 52.412' W.*

By public transportation, from the MBTA Quincy Center Red Line station, take the #220 bus (Hingham Depot) and exit at the intersection of North Street and Otis Street. From here, it is a 1-mile walk to the World's End Reservation (start walking northeasterly; Otis Street joins with Summer Street).

TRAIL DESCRIPTION

World's End, a peninsula jutting out from the mainland that separates Hingham Harbor from the mouth of the Weir River, provides magnificent views in every direction. The rolling, open terrain will make you feel like you're on the landscaped grounds of an English estate. World's End has escaped development a number of times, as the property has been considered for projects ranging from a nuclear generator to public housing—even a possible site for the United Nations. In 1967, local residents raised the money for The Trustees of Reservations to purchase the property.

Every season is a good one at World's End. In summer there are cool ocean breezes; in fall the foliage is alive with color; and in winter the cross-country skiing is superb when there's enough snow to cover the gentle

LOCATION
Hingham, MA

RATING
Moderate

DISTANCE
4.5 miles

ELEVATION GAIN
300 feet

ESTIMATED TIME
3 hours

MAPS
USGS Hull; online:
thetrustees.org/assets/
documents/places to visit/
trailmaps/World-s-End-
Trail-Map.pdf

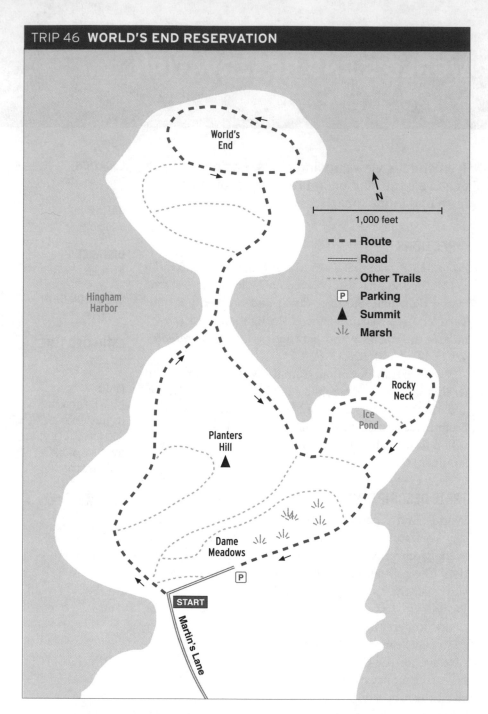

World's
End

Hingham
Harbor

1,000 feet

- - - Route
═══ Road
- - - Other Trails
P Parking
▲ Summit
� Marsh

N

Rocky
Neck

Ice
Pond

Planters
Hill
▲

Dame
Meadows

P

START

Martin's Lane

slopes. And if it's springtime, flowering trees, such as the sweet-smelling apple tree, will be in bloom. World's End is also a prime spot for viewing migratory birds, including wintering sea ducks.

After entering the reservation, take the Planters Hill Loop to the left, which leads to the reservation's two smooth hills. The trails here include roughly 4 miles of carriage roads that were designed by Frederick Law Olmsted during the 1890s as part of a proposed subdivision that was never built. Just a short way up the path is an area with a sweeping view of Boston Harbor, with the city's skyline rising in the distance. The path then climbs Planters Hill, which, at 120 feet, is the highest point on the reservation. Along the way, there are benches placed at some of the more strategic points for capturing the views.

From Planters Hill, the trail descends to the sandbar that links the Planters Hill drumlin to the main World's End drumlin. Early settlers built this causeway, known as the "bar," to allow travel between the two islands during high tide. Crossing the causeway allows you easy access to the rocky beach. It's a perfect spot for children to explore. As you climb the outer hill, look back toward Planters Hill and admire the topography. The outer island has two connecting roads that loop around this island's two highest mounds.

Small clumps of woodlands, primarily composed of eastern red cedar and tall hardwoods, such as maple and oak, provide habitat for a variety of small animals hunted by hawks. Lichen-covered stone walls are visible in some spots, reminding you of the area's former agricultural days. Also visible along the woods and in the meadows is poison ivy. Learn to recognize the plant's three-leaf stems and give it a wide berth.

Walking in World's End Reservation feels like stepping back in time; the rolling hills and landscaped grounds are reminiscent of an English estate. Photo by Liz West, Creative Commons on Flickr.

Familiar small mammals of New England are present here, including the red fox, an extremely human-shy animal that relies on its strong sense of smell to avoid interaction. They have learned to live in close proximity to us by making nocturnal forays to hunt for mice, moles, and other small rodents. The cotton-tail rabbit, a significant prey species for foxes and coyotes, also thrives in this combination of fields, shrubs, and small patches of woods. This rabbit was once much more common in New England, when farmlands, rather than forests and development, dominated the region.

After exploring this area, cross the sandy causeway again then bear left onto an unnamed road that leads to Rocky Neck. Through the trees on the left, you can see the jagged cliffs of Rocky Neck standing in contrast to the smooth hills you have just explored. Bear left at the next fork in the trail then take the first left after that. As you enter Rocky Neck, the open landscape transitions to a more intimate woods, where the trail is often shaded. You will soon come to the edge of a cliff that rises 50 feet above the water.

Ice Pond, built by farmers in 1909 as a wintertime source of ice, adds to the enchanting character of Rocky Neck. Today this little pond attracts wildlife. Mallards, wide-ranging ducks that often form flocks with shyer black ducks, are common. They are surface feeders that eat aquatic vegetation and an occasional insect or mollusk. The males have green heads with white neck bands and rusty breasts. Females are a mottled brown, and both sexes have a distinctive blue rectangle at the hind area of their wings. When you surprise a mallard, it may let out a loud quack and take off nearly vertically.

After following the perimeter of Rocky Neck, the trail soon intersects with another trail. Turn left here onto the unnamed trail and follow it past the north-eastern end of a marshy area. Just as you reach an area of hemlock trees on a knoll, about a quarter-mile down the path, there is a trail through a field on the right. This leads to the boardwalk that passes through tall cattails and marsh grass. You can hear the birds in the reeds, but it's often impossible to see them. Just up ahead is a rock ledge that offers a sweeping view of the marsh. The ledge can easily be climbed from the rear, and it's a great place to sit and watch a few minutes of marsh life unfold.

From here, it's only a short walk to the parking lot by continuing on this foot trail or by returning to the cart path near the hemlocks and going right.

DID YOU KNOW?

In pre-Colonial times, World's End was an island when tides were high, before colonists dammed the adjacent salt marsh for the purpose of growing hay.

MORE INFORMATION

World's End is open year-round, 8 A.M. to sunset on weekdays and 7 A.M. to sunset on weekends. Admission is free for Trustees members; for others, there is a $5 fee. It's advisable to arrive early, as the parking area fills quickly in good weather. Dogs are allowed on-leash; picnicking and swimming are prohibited; and horseback riding is by permit only. Portable restrooms are available. For more information, contact The Trustees of Reservations at 781-740-6665 or visit thetrustees.org.

NEARBY

Restaurants are located along and off North Street near the center of Hingham. Wompatuck State Park, off Free Street, offers 260 campsites (140 of which have electricity), paved bicycling trails, and hiking trails. Whitney and Thayer Woods (see Trip 47) are a short drive from World's End.

47

WHITNEY AND THAYER WOODS

Depending on the season, these peaceful, well-maintained woodland trails offer easy hiking, cross-country skiing, or views of colorful rhododendrons.

DIRECTIONS

From MA 3, take Exit 14 to MA 228 north. Follow MA 228 north for 6.5 miles then turn right (southeast) onto MA 3A. Follow MA 3A for 2 miles and turn right onto Howes Lane. Follow Howes Lane to the parking area at its end. *GPS coordinates:* 42° 14.046′ N, 70° 49.443′ W.

TRAIL DESCRIPTION

Quiet woodland trails, and plenty of them, are the primary feature of this large reservation that straddles the towns of Cohasset and Hingham, adjoining other Trustees of Reservations properties. A large stand of giant rhododendrons and azaleas located on the southern border of the property provides an attractive contrast to the thickly forested hills and glacial boulders that characterize the bulk of the preserve. This ramble makes a loop of the eastern portion of the property, including a stroll through the tunnel of rhododendrons and azaleas.

Before starting the walk, take a moment to scan the small open area adjacent to the parking area for birds and insects, such as red-spotted purple and monarch butterflies. The wide gravel trail begins to the left of the information sign, where maps are available. Follow this path through pines and hardwoods for about five minutes then turn right onto the first trail you come to, at a green gate. This is the appropriately named Boulder Lane, as it passes many large erratics that were deposited by retreating glaciers.

This is also a good section of trail for viewing the American holly tree's shiny green foliage in the understory of the

LOCATION
Hingham and Cohasset, MA

RATING
Easy

DISTANCE
3 miles

ELEVATION GAIN
200 feet

ESTIMATED TIME
1.75 hours

MAPS
USGS Cohasset; online: thetrustees.org/assets/documents/places-to-visit/trailmaps/Whitney-and-Thayer-Woods-Weir-River-Farm-Trail-Map.pdf

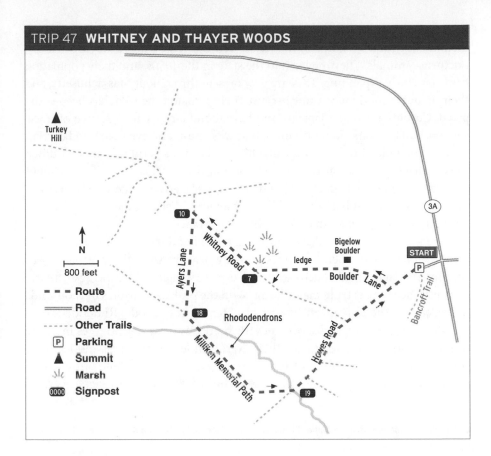

larger oaks, pines, and maples. The native holly found here might be the north-ernmost stand in the United States. The hollies are easiest to see during winter, because their prickly evergreen leaves are still on the tree. The distinctive red fruit is also on the tree in winter if it hasn't been consumed by wildlife, such as migratory songbirds, wild turkeys, and bobwhite quail.

About three-quarters of a mile into your walk, you will pass Bigelow Boulder, which weighs an estimated 200 tons, on your right. Another couple of minutes down the trail is a pair of balanced boulders, with nooks and crannies in the jumble of rocks around them.

Boulder Lane passes beech trees that brighten the forest with their light gray trunks. Even in winter they add a touch of color because the lower limbs' papery, golden-brown leaves often stay on the trees until new growth pushes them off in spring. Large outcroppings of rock line Boulder Lane on the right and left before the trail crosses through a small swamp and arrives at the intersection with Whitney Road at marker 7, about 1.25 miles into your walk. Stay to the right at the intersection and continue walking for another 0.5 mile to a junction at marker 10, where you should turn left onto Ayers Lane.

Along the trail, you may see coyote scat, especially at or near junctions along their hunting routes. It is uncommon to see a coyote in the wild, as they are stealthy, nocturnal animals. They moved into the state in the 1950s, and their population has been slowly expanding. They are now present throughout Massachusetts, and their numbers continue to grow because their predator, the wolf, has been extirpated. Coyotes are very adaptable and have found a ready food source of mice, carrion, birds, rabbits, domestic animals (ducks, geese, and even cats), and berries.

We often look straight ahead while hiking, but it's a good idea to look down to see what's growing on the forest floor. On this section of trail, you might spot sarsaparilla, partridgeberry, and club mosses. Ayers Lane winds south to junction 18; bear left here onto Milliken Memorial Path, named by the former resident Arthur Milliken in honor of his wife, Mabel.

Rhododendrons and azaleas, which were planted during the 1920s, line this trail, with hollies and hemlock trees growing nearby. All of this greenery gives the area a mysterious and enchanting feel, even in winter. In late spring and early summer, the scene is truly magnificent, with the pinks and whites of thousands of azalea and rhododendron flowers brightening the woods. Rhododendrons grow up to 30 feet fall, and sometimes the branches from several trees interlace to form an impenetrable jungle. Their evergreen leaves are large and leathery, sometimes reaching a length of 10 inches. Flowers are often white or pink, and grow in showy clusters. The bark is reddish brown, and the new twigs are green.

Bright pink rhododendron grow along Milliken Memorial Path, a dazzling sight in spring and summer.

While rhododendrons flourish in southern New England, they are rare in the northern states.

Old stone walls crisscross these woods, indicating that the area was once used for pasture or farming—hard to believe, given the large white pines and other trees towering overhead. Settlers called their annual harvest of stones "New England potatoes" because the frost pushed up stones at such a great rate. If you look closely at stone walls, they yield clues. Walls with lots of little stones mixed with the bigger ones indicate the adjacent land was probably cultivated, but if there are only large rocks in the walls, the land was probably used for grazing livestock or mowed for hay.

Milliken Memorial Path narrows in some spots, and the rhododendrons along the trail's edge give it the appearance of a tunnel. During wet periods, areas near swamps and streams may be flooded or muddy. After walking about a mile down the trail, you come to junction 19; bear left here onto Howes Road, which crosses a stream via a bridge. Follow it straight past a solar panel on a pole and several junctions with other trails. You'll eventually come to a chain barrier near a private residence. Walk around it and follow Howes Road along the edge of the wetland opposite the house (please respect the private property) then reenter the woods on the other side of the clearing. The trail, which turns into a gravel road, will lead you back to the parking lot in 0.5 mile.

If you are interested in a longer walk on your next visit, explore Turkey Hill at the northwest end of the property (see map). There is a nice view of Cohasset Harbor from the summit. Adjacent to Turkey Hill is another Trustees property, Weir River Farm, which encompasses 75 acres of hayfields and woodlands. Both Turkey Hill and Weir River Farm can be reached from Turkey Hill Lane.

DID YOU KNOW?

The reservation is named in honor of Henry Whitney, who designed the property's original horse trails in the early 1900s, and Mrs. Ezra Ripley Thayer, who donated a significant parcel of land in 1943. A portion of the property was once part of the Bancroft Bird Sanctuary.

MORE INFORMATION

The woods are open year-round, dawn to dusk. There is no fee, but donations are accepted. There are no restrooms; dogs are allowed on-leash. For more information, call 781-740-7233 or visit thetrustees.org.

NEARBY

Wompatuck State Park, off Free Street, offers more than 260 campsites, paved bicycling trails, and hiking trails. World's End Reservation (Trip 46) is a short drive from Whitney and Thayer Woods. Restaurants are located along and off North Street in Hingham.

48

WHEATON FARM CONSERVATION AREA

Wheaton Farm offers an easy ramble through level terrain, with highlights including a white pine and oak forest, shallow ponds, and open fields.

DIRECTIONS

From I-495, take Exit 9 and follow Bay Road north for 3.2 miles to the sign for Wheaton Farm, near a brown barn. The entrance road to the conservation area is on the left, immediately after a beautiful, old, Federal-style house set behind evergreens. *GPS coordinates:* 42° 00.334′ N, 71° 07.234′ W.

TRAIL DESCRIPTION

Wheaton Farm is the largest conservation area in Easton and is a great place for walking with children or cross-country skiing in winter. Some of the property is still actively farmed, but the majority of the preserve now protects the source of Easton's public water supply.

To begin your walk from the parking area, take the white-blazed Bay Circuit Trail. (The trail runs alongside a wooden fence and passes behind the pumping station.) There is a gentle descent as you enter the woods then cross an earthen dike between Ward Pond and Fuller-Hammond Reservoir. You may meet a local angler here, as the pond offers good fishing for bass and other species.

The dike is an ideal spot to look for wood ducks, muskrats, great blue herons, and other wildlife. The shallow waters provide hunting grounds for herons, which stalk the pond for fish and frogs to snatch with their long bills. Once the prey is caught, the heron tips its head and swallows its food whole. With a wingspan of 44 inches, black-crowned night herons are smaller than great blue herons. The black-crowned night heron has short, gray wings and

LOCATION
Easton, MA

RATING
Easy

DISTANCE
2.75 miles

ELEVATION GAIN
Minimal

ESTIMATED TIME
1.5 hours

MAPS
USGS Easton; online: easton.ma.us

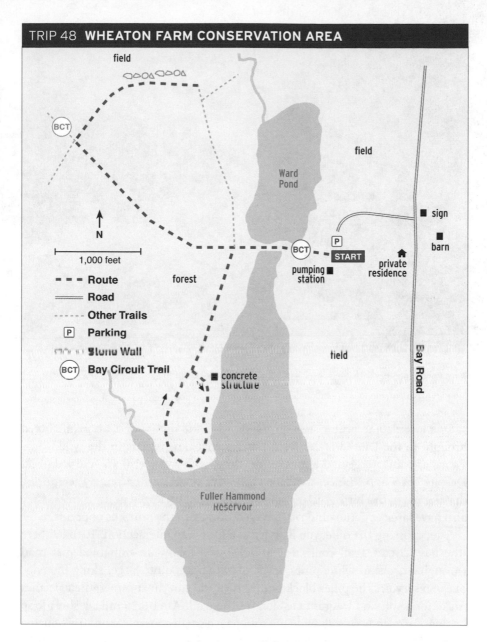

white underparts, and as its name implies, it is mostly nocturnal, roosting in trees during the day. Populations have been gradually dropping over the past 40 years due to pesticides and loss of habitat. Yellow-crowned night herons also migrate as far north as Massachusetts; adults are slate gray with a black head and white cheeks. The yellow-crowned night heron is not seen as often as its black-crowned cousin; most sightings occur in the eastern part of the state during late summer.

Ward Pond is popular with anglers for its bass and other species of fish.

One unwelcome visitor seen on the pond is the mute swan, an exotic breed brought to the United States from Europe that now breeds in the wild. Mute swans are quite large and almost pure white, with a graceful, "S"-curved neck. Despite their appearance, they are aggressive birds and extremely territorial, driving out native birds, such as wood ducks, from preferred nesting areas. They also have large appetites and rip up vegetation from the bottoms of ponds.

After crossing the dike, you'll arrive at a four-way intersection. Turn left here (the Bay Circuit Trail continues straight) and follow an unnamed dirt road through a grove of white pines, some of which are quite large, along the edge of the reservoir. The pines block out most of the sun. In summer, their needles make for a soft and fragrant cushion on the trail. After 0.25 mile, a short loop begins. Turn left here, following the trail past a small concrete structure housing a well. The dead trees you see at the water's edge benefit a variety of wildlife. Hawks often use them as perches because they offer unobstructed views of the forest floor. Woodpeckers peck at the rotting wood for insects, and raccoons and other animals will use the hollow areas for shelter.

The trail loops around to the right, heading back the way you came. From here, it's an easy 0.5-mile walk back to the junction with the Bay Circuit Trail by the dike. Here you have several options. A right turn will return you to the parking area. The unnamed trail that continues straight (north) at the intersection passes an overgrown field, a meadow, and a stone wall, then rejoins the Bay Circuit Trail north of the dike junction.

This trip's chosen hike continues left on the Bay Circuit Trail, a pleasant and easy one-way walk through the mixed forests in the northern portion of the property. Bear right at a directional marker and follow the white-blazed Bay Circuit Trail along an old cart road.

Here a few pitch pines mix in with the white pines that dominate the woods of Wheaton Farm. Notice how the pitch pine's bark is more furrowed than the white pine's. The pitch pine's needles are also more rigid, its cones more rounded, and it is smaller overall than the white pine.

A familiar resident of these woods is the eastern chipmunk, which likes to burrow in stone walls beneath the rocks. Often you will see them running along the top of the wall before disappearing into one of their holes. You may want to scan the trees for signs of opossums, often seen here.

Follow the Bay Circuit Trail straight at a junction with unmarked paths. In the woods on the left is a small kettle pond similar to those found on Cape Cod. About a mile north of the causeway junction, the trail bends to the right and reaches the edge of a large field. This marks the endpoint for this walk. (The Bay Circuit Trail continues past the field to Mulberry Brook and a parking area off Bay Road.) Retrace your steps south along the cart path to the four-way junction then cross the dike to return to the parking area. Before leaving, be sure to take a brief walk along the fields, which are home to bluebirds and tree swallows.

DID YOU KNOW?

Wheaton Farm was threatened in the 1960s, when a developer posing as a conservation buyer acquired the land. Thanks to the efforts of concerned citizens, adequate funds were raised to purchase the land in 1967.

MORE INFORMATION

The conservation area is open year-round, dawn to dusk. There is no fee; there are no restrooms; and dogs are allowed on-leash. Contact the town of Easton at easton.ma.us or 508-230-0500 for more information.

NEARBY

The Xfinity Center, originally the Great Woods Center for the Performing Arts, is located near the junction of MA 140 and Interstate 495 in Mansfield. Since 1986, it has hosted concerts by well-known musical artists. The facility includes nearly 20,000 covered, pavilion, and lawn seats. Restaurants are located along MA 123 and MA 106 just north of Wheaton Farm, and on MA 138 in South Easton.

49

MASSASOIT STATE PARK

This forested hike features glacial topography, waterfowl, and historical sites.

DIRECTIONS

From I-495, take Exit 5 for MA 18 south, following it for 0.6 mile, then turn right onto Taunton Street. The entrance for Massasoit State Park will be on your left in 2.2 miles. *GPS coordinates: 41° 53.062′ N, 70° 59.700′ W.*

TRAIL DESCRIPTION

This 1,500-acre state park serves the residents of many nearby towns who come to walk, bike, paddle, and ride horses, but it's large enough to make you feel like you're on an adventure of your own. Use this hike to familiarize yourself with the park then branch out to explore a variety of trails, waterfront vistas, historical sites, and glacial potholes deep in the park. Be aware, though, that as of this writing, the park's condition is in flux. The campground has been closed for nearly a decade and the trails have been lightly maintained due to state budget restrictions. As a result, unauthorized trails emerged and are being evaluated for removal as the state revisits and reinvests in management of the park. Fortunately, intense neighborhood advocacy for proper funding and management of the property has led to a renewed interest in its restoration. Although reopening the campground is not yet on the horizon, it is a long-term goal, according to a DCR park manager.

Park in the lot off Middleboro Avenue, where bright crimson cranberry bogs open the treeline to the left, curving out of sight. On the right, a ridge parallels the parking lot and paved road, with Lake Rico beyond it (near the park's headquarters). Following the paved road into the park from the ranger station, look for an unnamed path on the right side, at the first gate. Take the path, which is

LOCATION
Taunton, MA

RATING
Moderate

DISTANCE
4 miles

ELEVATION GAIN
Minimal

ESTIMATED TIME
2.5 hours

MAPS
USGS Taunton; online: mass
.gov/eea/docs/dcr/parks/trails/
massasoit.pdf

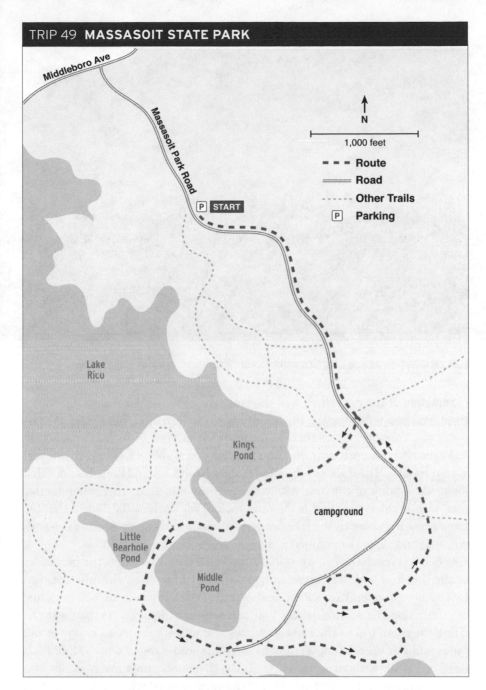

brief, and continue straight at the first intersection. Turn right at the second intersection onto an unnamed path, which will take you toward the shore of the lake and some picturesque overlooks. You'll find opportunities to scan the waterfront for birdlife, from migrating geese to kingfishers, streaking along the shoreline in search of small fish and frogs in shallow water.

Look carefully: The mist on Lake Rico might obscure kingfishers. Photo by Lori Bradley.

Stay right at the next three trail intersections, walking parallel to the waterfront, and you will soon see the buildings of the former campground. At this point you are near the southern portion of Kings Pond, which is attached to Lake Rico. In this area, near the campground, you will find a couple of unusual glacial erratics. These rocks are called puddingstone, a standalone boulder that looks like a hunk of concrete with fist-size rocks mixed in. This conglomerate rock forms underwater and is the state rock of Massachusetts. Notice that the trees along the shore of the lake are generally pines, while those near the park entrance and along the cranberry bog are oaks and other hardwoods.

When you reach the campground, stay on the path that skirts the perimeter of the sites and look for the unnamed path that follows an isthmus between two bodies of water, Kings Pond and Middle Pond. If you're sure-footed, just after crossing the section where you can see both ponds, you may want to climb the small hill to the right. It allows you to walk under a canopy of tall pines and out onto a long peninsula that juts into Kings Pond. While it's a dead-end walk without a formal trail, the diversion offers lovely views of a marshy section of the lake that hosts many varieties of ducks and birds flitting among the cat-o'-nine-tails.

Returning to the main route, which is unnamed, you'll now follow the contour of Middle Pond, on your left. Stay left when the horse trail branches off to the right, along Lake Rico. Middle Pond, Little Bearhole Pond, and Big Bearhole Pond are glacial potholes, created when the last glacier melted and left behind big puddles. On the far side of Middle Pond is a dam that separates it from Big Bearhole Pond, the site of the Dean Cotton Mill in the 1800s. The city of Taunton once had 2,000 residents employed in similar industries.

Turtles thrive in the environment of these ponds and their sandy banks. Scan the shoreline closely for telltale lumps on rocks and logs at the water's edge, where you may see the dark shells of sun-loving painted turtles. They have smooth shells, yellow stripes on their heads, and distinctive yellow spots behind each eye. Box and Blanding's varieties are also residents of this park and may be seen foraging in the water or walking through the woods. It is difficult to distinguish between these two types of turtles, as they are of similar size and have yellow markings on their necks. Snapping turtles, which grow to nearly 20 inches long, are also found here. Snappers and other turtles leave the ponds in early summer to bury nests of eggs in open, sandy areas. The eggs will stay there, at the mercy of raccoons and opossums looking for an easy meal, until they hatch in late summer.

A little farther on, the path crosses the dam between the two ponds and turns left, following the paved road briefly. A short dirt bypass road where anglers park their cars intersects here; watch for the unnamed path in the trees on the right that departs from the paved road and follows the shore of Big Bearhole Pond. Follow it through the woods, keeping your eyes open for the pale yellow leaves of beech trees growing under the pines. The contrast of the beech's heart-shaped, paper-thin leaves against the dark green needles of pines is dramatic, particularly when the ground is covered with an orange layer of pine needles.

Near the campground's former dumping station, the path parallels the paved road. You may rejoin the road for the walk back to the parking lot or explore cart paths in the woods between the road and the adjacent golf course.

DID YOU KNOW

The hills of the park and the cranberry bog area were formed by the excavation and dumping of earth when iron was extracted and smelted here in the eighteenth century.

MORE INFORMATION

The park is open year-round, dawn to dusk. There are portable toilets near the parking lot. Dogs are allowed on-leash. For more information, contact the Department of Conservation and Recreation ranger station at 508-828-4231 or visit mass.gov/dcr.

NEARBY

About 7 miles away in Middleboro is the Massachusetts Archaeological Society's Robbins Museum, with information on local history and artifacts, such as Native American arrowheads. Hours are Wednesdays and Saturdays, 10 A.M. to 4 P.M. Check the website or call first: massarchaeology.org or 508-947-9005.

50

BURRAGE POND

This hike combines wide-open views of a cranberry bog with numerous freshwater ponds, forests, and a white cedar swamp.

DIRECTIONS

From I-93, take MA 24 south to exit 16A. Take Route 106 east toward East Bridgewater. Stay left at the fork (Spring Street) where Route 106 turns south. In the center of East Bridgewater, cross Route 18 to follow Central Street, a slight right. When Central meets Cedar Street, turn right onto Cedar. This road becomes Franklin Street then intersects with MA 27. Take a right onto MA 27 then the first right onto Elm Street. Watch for a small parking area on the left, before the intersection with Hudson Street (approximate address 443 Elm Street, Hanson). There may not be a formal sign for Burrage Pond access; look for a simple metal gate across the access road. *GPS Coordinates*: 42° 01.766' N, 70° 53.370' W.

TRAIL DESCRIPTION

The Burrage Pond Wildlife Management Area, a 1,680-acre property straddling the Hanson–Halifax town line, includes cranberry bogs, woods, and ponds. The state Division of Wildlife & Fisheries acquired it in 2002, and it is on the Bay Circuit Trail. About 100 acres are still actively farmed for cranberries.

Hikers, casual mountain bikers, snowshoers, anglers, and bird-watchers find Burrage Pond a treasure. Located in the coastal plain area of southeastern Massachusetts, it is a flat property crisscrossed by multiple cart paths and causeways, creating many opportunities for access and long-distance views. The wildlife management area provides habitat to bird and wildlife species by linking parcels of open space throughout the area, which is near the

LOCATION
Hanson and Halifax, MA

RATING
Easy

DISTANCE
3 miles

ELEVATION GAIN
90 feet

ESTIMATED TIME
2 hours

MAPS
USGS Hanover, USGS Whitman; online: town.halifax.ma.us

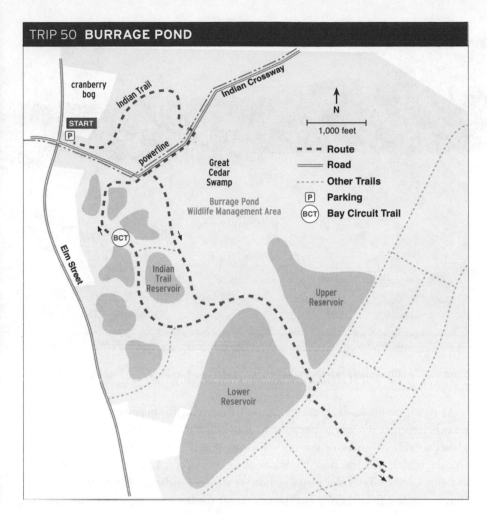

cranberry bog

Indian Trail

Indian Crossway

START

P

powerline

N

1,000 feet

Great Cedar Swamp

Burrage Pond Wildlife Management Area

- - - **Route**

===== **Road**

····· **Other Trails**

P **Parking**

BCT **Bay Circuit Trail**

BCT

Indian Trail Reservoir

Elm Street

Upper Reservoir

Lower Reservoir

Taunton River. State wildlife officials have released rehabilitated species here as part of their repopulation efforts.

This approximately 3-mile walk features broad vistas with short passages through wooded paths. It's easy to follow, but trails are unmarked. There are no facilities on-site, nor does the Elm Street entrance include an information kiosk or map board. (An alternative entrance with parking and a map is located behind the state environmental police building, on Pleasant Street.) Follow these directions and you will see it's easy to navigate by line of sight, but downloading and printing a map from the town's website is recommended.

Starting at the Elm Street entrance, where there is parking for about six vehicles, proceed 800 feet through the gate and onto the property. To your left are cranberry bogs, and to your right is a series of small ponds connected by unpaved causeways. Turning left, follow the outer edge of the cranberry bog area, watching for great blue herons feeding in the irrigation canals and red-tailed hawks perched in trees at the perimeter.

State wildlife officials have released rehabilitated species on Burrage Pond. Photo by Lisa Day.

At dawn or dusk, deer, raccoons, or other wildlife may venture out of the woods here, so it's advisable to stop and scan the edge of the woods. After about fifteen minutes of casual walking, you'll enter a path through some woods, which will reach a "T" intersection at a power line. This is a portion of the Bay Circuit Trail (labeled "Indian Trail" or "Indian Crossway" on maps) that turns to the left, crosses through Great Cedar Swamp, and heads toward the back of the Hanson Police Station and Crooker Place Road.

Turn right at the power line and follow the trail to a "T" intersection with a cart path. Take a left at the intersection and continue on a wooded path not far from the edge of a series of irrigation ponds. Take your first left to head directly toward the reservoirs.

On the left you may have a view of the remnants of Great Cedar Swamp, a large area of white cedars that abuts the larger Upper Reservoir between Elm and Main streets. All of the ponds here are shallow—anglers say they're less than 10 feet deep—but still hold perch, largemouth bass, crappies, turtles, and water snakes. Fishing is generally catch-and-release.

The path enters a road-width causeway between the two reservoirs, with Lower Reservoir on the right and Upper Reservoir on the left. Straight ahead is a series of telephone poles, one of which is topped by an osprey nest. Depending on the time of year you visit, you may witness a mature bird returning to the nest with a fish in her talons to feed her young. Ospreys are hawklike birds of prey with brown wings and white undersides. Their call is a piercing screech. If you're truly lucky, you may have an opportunity to see an osprey fishing. It begins by circling high above the water, slows and practically hovers, then dives straight in for its prey, usually emerging with a fish in its grasp.

Burrage Pond is a wonderland for those interested in bird-watching, and its inhabitants vary from season to season. In spring, red-winged blackbirds swarm the marshes, one of the first signs of warmer weather to come. Summertime may be dominated by hundreds of fast-flying swallows that zip along, inches above the water. If you're lucky enough to watch one until it lands on a branch, you'll enjoy the glossy teal color of its plumage, which is not quite visible when the bird is flying at top speeds. Other summer birds may include cedar waxwings, which have dark markings, similar to blue jays, around their eyes but a distinctive line of yellow feather at the bottom of their tails; blue kingbirds skirting the edges of ponds, fishing for frogs; and gray catbirds, whose song often sounds like a cat's meow. In late fall, many varieties of ducks will stop here on their long migrations, and you may spot mergansers and buffleheads by the distinctive white swoop of plumage on the sides of their heads. (On buffleheads, the white goes all the way around the back of the head.) Mallards and glossy wood ducks can also be spotted.

Follow the causeway to the right, crossing between Lower Reservoir on your right and the cranberry bogs on your left. At the end of the reservoir, continue straight across the causeway to the cranberry bogs and Stump Brook beyond, at the perimeter of the park property. Stump Brook runs between West Lake and Robbins Pond, which flow into the Taunton River.

Retrace your steps to the causeway, past the osprey nest and between the reservoirs. Just beyond the end of the lower reservoir on your left, take a left and walk toward the small irrigation ponds. As the ponds come into view, take the causeway that splits the two bodies of water. Notice which tree species are retaking the edges of the water; you'll want to return in the fall with a camera to capture the russet oaks and yellow maples reflecting off the water.

Whether you visit during summer and enjoy the shade of the young trees that have sprung up on the edges of the ponds, or in winter, when snow creates a glittering tunnel of bowed limbs, this stretch has a magical feel. You'll pass two larger ponds on your right, and you may find endangered box turtles sunning themselves on a rock or, in winter, observe various animal tracks as they cross the path in search of open water. A real treat is seeing evidence of otters: smooth snow or mudslides that end near the water's edge, clear proof that a small animal has shimmied along.

After passing the end of the second pond on your right, you'll come out at the main entrance road, near the cranberry bogs where you started. If you turn left, your car should be visible in the small lot off Elm Street.

DID YOU KNOW?

Great Cedar Swamp was not valued for its wildlife habitat or healthy watershed contributions until recently. Prior to cranberry businesses taking possession, there was a long history of local residents harvesting cedar for shingles, using the swamp for munitions development (including lobbing mines across the property), filling in the ponds for cattle grazing, and dumping manure. But by 2003, a survey showed 81 species of birds using the area.

MORE INFORMATION

Burrage Pond is maintained by the state Division of Fisheries & Wildlife, which allows hunting on the property at certain times of year. For more information, see mass.gov/masswildlife or call the Southeast District office at 508-759-3406.

NEARBY

Bordering the preserve to the north is Main Street (Route 27) in Hanson with a variety of cafes and services. Across Elm Street from the Elm Street parking area is the Smith-Nawazelski Conservation Area, worth a short hike.

51

NORTH HILL MARSH WILDLIFE SANCTUARY

Well-marked trails offer views of a wildlife-rich freshwater pond, its surrounding forests, and a small cranberry bog.

DIRECTIONS

From MA 3, take Exit 11 (Congress Street) and head east toward Duxbury. About 100 feet from the exit, take the first right onto Lincoln Street. Follow Lincoln Street for 0.8 mile and bear left onto Mayflower Street. Follow Mayflower Street for 0.3 mile and bear left where the road forks to stay on Mayflower. The parking lot is about 0.5 mile down Mayflower Street, on the left. From MA 3A in Duxbury, drive south past the town hall, turn west onto Mayflower Street, and continue 1.3 miles to the parking lot on the right. *GPS coordinates: 42° 02.143′ N, 70° 42.733′ W.*

TRAIL DESCRIPTION

North Hill Marsh, jointly owned and managed by Mass Audubon and the town of Duxbury, is an 823-acre tract of wetlands and forests within the town's Eastern Greenbelt. The preserve, which is centered on a 90-acre freshwater pond, includes several miles of nature trails that are split between the east and west sides of the pond. The main routes are color-blazed, while other paths are unmarked and potentially confusing for first-time visitors. A detailed trail map and brochure are available at the entrance.

This walk, a 3.3-mile excursion along the south and east sides of the pond, follows a series of blazed trails that make a wide loop of the area. The first part of the outing hugs the pond's shoreline, and the return portion passes through a pine-oak forest and then goes on to a scenic cranberry bog. The walking is mostly easy, with a few ups and downs over rolling terrain. If you have young

LOCATION
Duxbury, MA

RATING
Moderate

DISTANCE
3.3 miles

ELEVATION GAIN
110 feet

ESTIMATED TIME
2 hours

MAPS
USGS Duxbury; online: massaudubon.org/content/download/8090/145521/file/northhill_trails.pdf

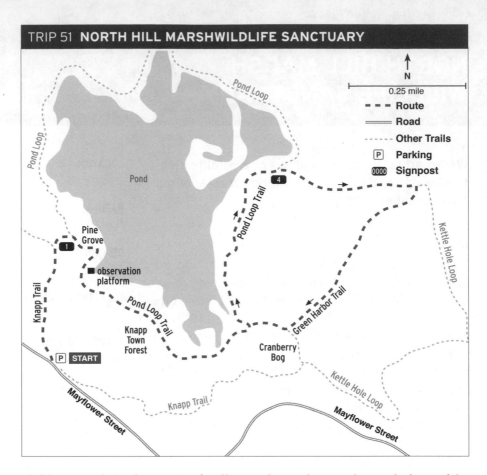

children, you have the option of walking a shorter loop to the south shore of the pond before doubling back.

Start your walk from the signboard at the parking lot and follow the yellow-blazed Knapp Trail north to marker 1, where you should bear right on a short path that soon joins the blue-blazed Pond Loop Trail. Turn right onto Pond Loop Trail, which quickly leads to a pine grove with nice views across the water. A short distance farther along is an observation platform that overlooks a small cove. From the platform, continue to follow the blue-blazed Pond Loop Trail along the south shore, passing several other trails that branch to the left and right.

The pond and its surrounding wetlands and forests are a magnet for a variety of birdlife. Species to watch for include ring-necked and black ducks, mute swans, buffleheads, hooded mergansers, herons, kingfishers, and egrets. Wood ducks find this a good place to nest due to the dead timber standing in the pond and the many nesting boxes that have been erected. The deadwood offers nesting birds a bit of protection from predators, such as raccoons. The nesting boxes with the small holes are for tree swallows, while those with larger holes are for wood ducks. The timber is also excellent cover for warm-water fish species, such as pickerel and largemouth bass. There have been a number of recent sightings of osprey near the pond, and a platform has been erected to induce these birds of prey, which have recovered nicely from mid-twentieth-century losses caused by DDT, to nest here. Several species of turtles also inhabit these waters. Snapping and painted turtles are fairly common, while spotted and box turtles are rare.

Near the pond's southeast corner, Pond Loop Trail turns sharply left (north) at a junction where a red-blazed trail, which is part of this hike's return leg, continues straight. Pond Loop Trail curves downhill then leads north along the pond's eastern shore. After snaking to the right to bypass a closed section of trail, the path zigzags up a small hill.

As you follow the trail through the woods, keep an eye out for great horned owls. They do their hunting at night, but people have spotted them perched on limbs of the tall white pines. They swoop into their nests, bringing mice, squirrels, rabbits, and skunks to their young.

After you have walked 45 minutes or so from the parking area (about 1.75 miles), the trail passes between two posts, the second of which is marker 4. Here you should bear right (straight) off Pond Loop and follow the unnamed red-blazed connector trail, which leads due east through the woods, crossing a four-way junction. After a little more than a quarter mile on this trail, turn right on the white-blazed trail, which leads south through both mature and sapling pines, with glimpses of the pond valley through the trees on the right. This

This cranberry bog is part of the diverse habitats of North Hill Marsh Wildlife Sanctuary.

portion of the trail was once part of the 1623 Green Harbor Trail, a historical route that linked Marshfield and Plymouth.

After a half-mile of easy walking, the white-blazed trail descends to a sign marking Duxbury town conservation land then soon reaches the cranberry bog. Bear right here off the white-blazed trail and follow the red-blazed trail along the edge of the bog.

To conclude the walk from the bog, follow the red-blazed trail for a short distance to a junction where it rejoins the blue-blazed Pond Loop Trail. Turn left onto Pond Loop Trail and retrace your steps along the south shore of the pond, making sure to keep the water on your right. You can save a few minutes of walking by bearing left onto the red-blazed trail near the observation platform and following it back to the yellow-blazed Knapp Trail, or you can continue to the pine grove viewing area and the connecting path near junction 1. Either way, turn left onto Knapp Trail and make the short, easy walk back to the parking area on Mayflower Street.

DID YOU KNOW?

The sanctuary land on the west side of the pond is home to 140-foot Waiting Hill, the second highest point in Duxbury. It is so named because the wives of fishermen and merchants would stand on the hill and scan the ocean for returning ships. Today the woods obstruct the views.

MORE INFORMATION

The sanctuary is open daily, dawn to dusk. Boating, hunting, and trapping are prohibited, and dogs must be under control at all times. (They are not allowed in the pond.) There are no restrooms. For more information, contact Mass Audubon at 781-837-9400 or massaudubon.org, or the Duxbury Conservation Commission at 781-934-1100 ext. 5471 or town.duxbury.ma.us.

NEARBY

The Myles Standish Burial Ground, located at the intersection of Chestnut Street and Pilgrim Byway, is the burial site of several prominent Pilgrims from the 1620 voyage, including Captain Myles Standish, and is the oldest maintained cemetery in the United States. Several restaurants are located in South Duxbury near the meeting of Bay, Chestnut, Washington, and Depot streets.

52

MYLES STANDISH STATE FOREST

At more than 14,000 acres, Myles Standish State Forest is one of the largest reservations in the state system and offers many recreational opportunities.

DIRECTIONS

To reach the forest from MA 3, take Exit 3 for Clark Road. Turn right (west) onto Long Pond Road and travel about 3 miles to the park entrance on the left, which is Alden Road. Park headquarters is located on Cranberry Road at the opposite end of the park. To reach the headquarters from Alden Road, follow Alden Road south to a four-way intersection and take a left onto Upper College Pond Road. Follow Upper College Pond Road to its intersection with Halfway Pond Road and go right onto Halfway Pond Road. When Halfway Pond Road curves sharply left then forks, take the left fork to follow Lower College Pond Road. This will intersect with Cranberry Road at the state park headquarters, where the hike begins.

From I-495, take Exit 2 (South Carver) to MA 58 north. Continue on Tremont Street and after about 2.5 miles, where MA 58 bears left, stay on Tremont Street and proceed a little less than a mile to Cranberry Road on the right. Follow Cranberry Road through the park gates to the ranger station, where the hike begins. *GPS coordinates: 41° 50.343′ N, 70° 41.453′ W.*

TRAIL DESCRIPTION

Myles Standish State Forest is home to one of the largest pitch-pine and scrub-oak forests in New England. The forest is also well known for its numerous kettle ponds, which were created as huge chunks of glacial ice became partially embedded in the ground and then melted when the last ice age ended. There are many fragile natural ar-

LOCATION
Plymouth and Carver, MA

RATING
Moderate to Strenuous

DISTANCE
3 miles, 4.5 miles, or 7.5 miles

ELEVATION GAIN
50 feet

ESTIMATED TIME
2 to 4 hours

MAPS
USGS Wareham; online:
mass.gov/eea/docs/dcr/parks/
trails/mssf.pdf

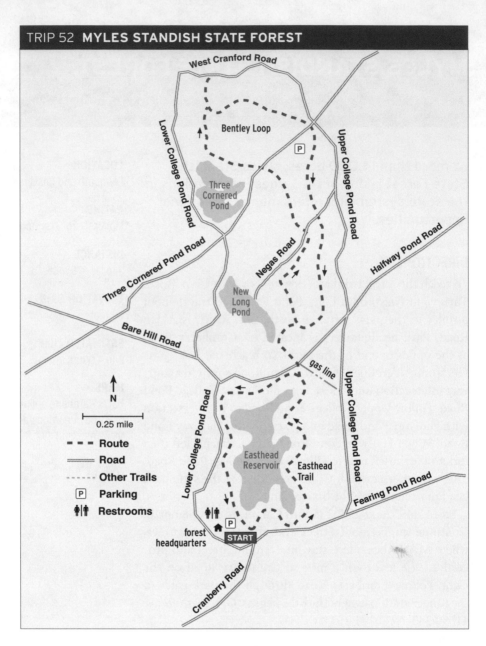

eas in the forest, including the shores of the kettle ponds, and these are marked with signs. Please stay on the trail in these areas.

This hike encompasses two of the forest's hiking loop trails, both of which are well blazed and maintained. Easthead Trail is an easy, level, 3-mile circuit that is well suited for families. The 4.5-mile Bentley Loop, which begins at the northern end of Easthead Trail, is a somewhat more rugged route that winds through forests, meadows, and ponds. The two routes may be walked individually or combined as a 7.5-mile outing.

From the forest headquarters and parking lot at the end of Cranberry Road, walk to the right (east) and cross a small bridge on Fearing Pond Road. Easthead Trail enters the woods on the left and follows Easthead Reservoir's southeastern shores. At marker 1, there's a nice view from the waterside. The narrow path curves to follow a promontory with more good views then turns north to follow the eastern side of the reservoir. Pitch pines rise high above the trail, while shadbush, withered viburnum, inkberry, red maple, and scrub oak are among the shrubs and saplings that grow along its margins. In summer, eastern pondhawk and blue dasher dragonflies are common.

After about 1.4 miles, the trail reaches the northern tip of the reservoir and turns left onto a well-used bridle path that follows a gas pipeline. Here you may turn left to follow Easthead Trail on its return to the starting point via the western side of the reservoir. Or you can extend the hike by walking to the start of Bentley Loop.

To reach Bentley Loop from the junction, continue straight past a metal gate then turn right onto a paved road. Walk along the road, watching for light traffic, then turn left onto the first dirt road on the left (junction B-2, with a metal gate numbered 75). The trail continues along this dirt road then turns right onto a woods road. At the end of this road, just before a meadow, is a trail junction where Bentley Loop begins.

Fall colors at Myles Standish State Forest set the landscape ablaze. Photo by Steve Nikola.

This hike continues to the left, making a clockwise circuit. Bentley Loop is well marked with blue blazes, but hikers should use caution, as there are many other unmarked paths that cross the trail in this section. If you don't see a trail marker after a short distance, retrace your steps to the last intersection. Bentley Loop leads north through the forests on the eastern shores of New Long Pond, bears to the right above another small pond, and then briefly follows Negas Road, a grassy unpaved road. It then bears left (north) off the road and crosses Three Cornered Pond Road. (You can detour left here for a short walk to the edge of Three Cornered Pond.)

After passing views of the pond, Bentley Loop traverses a series of meadows. This mix of fields, forest, and water is ideal wildlife habitat, and you should watch for a variety of species, including coyotes, deer, foxes, butterflies, dragonflies, frogs, and turtles. The path proceeds across the first meadow then turns left just before a second meadow, heading north toward College Pond. In summer, common mullein wildflowers, which are part of the snapdragon family and can grow as tall as 7 feet, rise high above the grasses.

Bentley Loop turns left at another meadow and continues some distance along its left edge. The path turns left into the woods at yet another marker and quickly reaches its northernmost point at a junction. The path you see heading north leads to the College Pond parking area, while Bentley Loop turns right and proceeds south.

After about 50 yards, Bentley Loop turns left and descends the hill, turns right sharply, and comes to a meadow (the first since turning south). Traverse the meadow and exit left at the far end. Soon, College Pond Road is visible on the left. The trail enters and briefly follows the edge of a parking lot, then turns right into the woods at the kiosk. After crossing another meadow, enter the woods before proceeding straight across another large field at the bottom of a hill. From here, Bentley Loop follows a winding course to arrive back at its starting point; watch for the blue blazes at junctions.

After completing Bentley Loop, backtrack to Easthead Trail by walking down the woods road then turning left on the dirt road and continuing to gate 75. Turn right onto the paved road and walk back to the junction with Easthead Trail. Bear right to follow Easthead Trail, which continues another 1.5 miles along the reservoir's western shores as it returns to the headquarters and trailhead. After crossing two boardwalks, you'll reach a vista across the northern portion of the reservoir. The path jogs right and briefly follows Lower College Pond Road then reenters the woods and continues along the southwest shores, with more views across the water. Easthead Trail returns you to the parking area behind the forest headquarters.

DID YOU KNOW?

With about 14,000 acres, Myles Standish State Forest is the largest state-owned recreation area in southeastern Massachusetts.

MORE INFORMATION

The forest offers universally accessible restrooms, five camping areas, and sixteen ponds. A portion of Charge Pond is set aside for equestrian camping. There are 15 miles of paved and single-track cycling paths, 35 miles of equestrian trails, and 13 miles of hiking paths that venture deep into the woods. For more information, visit mass.gov/dcr.

NEARBY

Restaurants are located on Main Street (Route 58) in Carver, west of the state forest.

53

ELLISVILLE HARBOR STATE PARK

This compact reservation's diverse habitats include large, open meadows and a rocky ocean beach where seals gather in winter.

DIRECTIONS

From MA 3, take Exit 2 and follow signs to MA 3A north. Take MA 3A north for about 2.4 miles and turn into the large parking area on the right at the state park sign. *GPS coordinates:* 41° 50.717′ N, 70° 32.474′ W.

TRAIL DESCRIPTION

Ellisville Harbor State Park is one of the lesser-known parks in Massachusetts, but if you love beachcombing and watching seals and other wildlife, it will soon become one of your favorites. Located at the southern end of the town of Plymouth, the park spans 101 acres of meadow, woodlands, salt marsh, and rocky shoreline. This combination of terrain attracts seals, a variety of birds, and other wildlife, so be sure to bring your binoculars.

You don't have to go far for the first view, as an overlook at the parking area offers a vista across a tidal marsh and mudflats. Scan the flats carefully for sandpipers and other shorebirds, especially during the height of migration in August and September.

The trail begins next to the information sign and follows the edge of the large fields adjacent to the entrance. The woods here include groves of scrub pine and oak, while staghorn sumac grows among the cedars and other evergreens in the meadows. Both the cedars and sumac are opportunistic trees, among the first species to colonize abandoned fields. The field is a good spot to look for kestrels, which hunt in open areas for insects and small rodents. Sometimes they can be seen perched at the tops of cedar trees. Other animals that visit the

LOCATION
Plymouth, MA

RATING
Easy

DISTANCE
3 miles

ELEVATION GAIN
40 feet

ESTIMATED TIME
1.5 hours

MAPS
USGS Sagamore; online: mass.gov/dcr

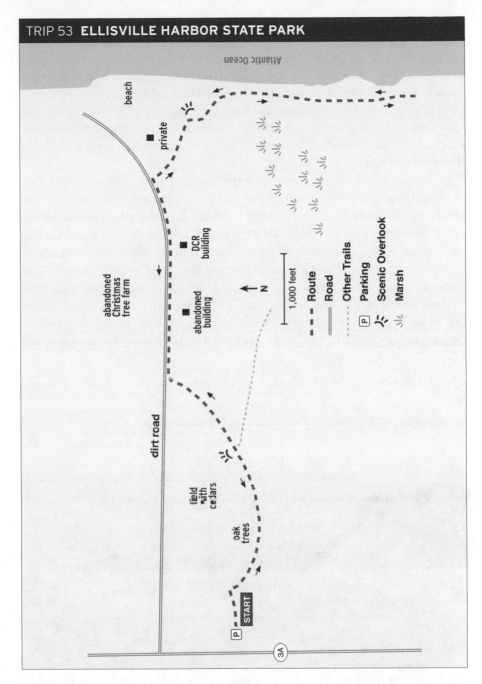

fields include white-tailed deer, red foxes, and cottontail rabbits. Another familiar resident is the woodchuck (also known as the groundhog), which will make a beeline for its burrows when in danger. Here you can take a few moments to detour off the main trail and walk the perimeter of the fields, looking for wildlife and wildflowers.

Continue down the gravel path, and within a few minutes you will pass a picnic table at an overlook with scenic views across the marsh below to the ocean, followed by a Department of Conservation and Recreation building on the right. Soon you will come to a sign announcing that the rest of the road leads to private homes on Grace's Way (one of which is directly ahead). A short walk leads to a wooden platform on a high bluff over the beach with sweeping views. During spring and fall, with the aid of binoculars you may be able to spot whales from the platform. The coast to the left is considerably rocky, while the shoreline is sandier.

Using those binoculars, scan all of the exposed rocks for seals. The best viewing time is low tide, when more rocks are exposed. You may also see loons, double-crested cormorants, and buffleheads bobbing beyond the breakers. It wasn't too long ago that seals were unwelcome in the Bay State. During the late nineteenth and much of the twentieth century, there was a bounty on seals, and fishermen would kill them, fearing they were eating too many fish. Instead it was humans who were depleting the fish stocks, while seals were feeding primarily on sand lance, a small fish that has virtually no commercial value but is an important prey species for seals and many other marine creatures. The legal killing of seals was halted in 1972 with the passage of the Marine Mammal Protection Act.

Ellisville Beach is a great spot for watching seals and other aquatic wildlife.

Both gray and harbor seals are often seen at Ellisville Harbor. Harbor seals, which migrate each winter, head down from Canada and Maine to Massachusetts. They arrive in October and leave in early spring. During low tide, they sun themselves on the rocks, where they are safe from humans on the beach. Known as dog-faced seals due to their pug noses and canine looks, they can grow to 5 or 6 feet in length and weigh as much as 250 pounds. If you're fortunate enough to see a baby seal alone on the beach, do not approach it. People may think an immature seal alone has been abandoned, but it is a normal part of the maturation process.

In winter, common loons are sometimes seen here. These birds' underwater feats are legendary, but their flight is equally impressive, as loons are surprisingly fast for such large, heavy birds. Their distinctive summertime black-and-white coloring is replaced in winter by brownish-gray feathers.

Take the path down to the beach (which can be steep and sandy) and walk to the right about 400 feet. You will be able to see the salt marsh on your right, where great blue herons and other wading birds may be stalking the shallows. In October, the autumnal tints of the marsh include soft hues of gold, rust, yellow, and brown. Be sure to soak up the sounds and smells of the ocean, as well as its sights.

Walk the beach for 0.75 mile to arrive at the mouth of the creek that drains and fills the marsh. During low tide, the creek carries small fish out to the ocean, and both birds and seals often station themselves just off the creek's mouth. To the south, the cliffs along the beach are of visual interest. Scan the water for cormorants diving beneath the surface as they hunt for fish. To return to the parking lot, simply retrace your steps to the junction at the private home then backtrack along the gravel path to the parking area.

DID YOU KNOW?

A Christmas tree farm once operated on these grounds, and today you may see Colorado blue spruce mixed in with the uniformly green balsam fir.

MORE INFORMATION

The park is open year-round, dawn to dusk, and there is no fee. There are no restrooms. Dogs are allowed on-leash. For more information, contact Ellisville Harbor State Park at 508-866-2580 or visit mass.gov/dcr.

NEARBY

The nearby Scusset Beach State Reservation includes 1.5 miles of frontage along the historic Cape Cod Canal, where visitors can watch for loons, seals, and other wildlife and enjoy a popular paved recreational trail along the canal. There are restaurants along and off MA 3A both north and south of the park and along the Cape Cod Canal.

54

LOWELL HOLLY RESERVATION

A pleasant woodland trail winds through groves of beech and American holly and over a peninsula between two scenic ponds.

DIRECTIONS

Take US 6 to Exit 2 and follow MA 130 south for 1.6 miles. Turn left onto Cotuit Road and after 3.4 miles, turn right onto South Sandwich Road and continue 0.6 mile to the year-round parking area on the right. (The road to the seasonal entrance is just beyond the lot.) *GPS coordinates:* 41° 39.668′ N, 70° 28.468′ W.

TRAIL DESCRIPTION

Abbott Lawrence Lowell, a former president of Harvard College, donated Lowell Holly to The Trustees of Reservations in 1934. With the exception of the cart paths that Lowell constructed, the reservation has been left primarily in its wild state for the past 200 years. It's a special place where cool breezes coming off Wakeby and Mashpee ponds pass over the large stand of massive beech trees that shade this peninsula. Small pockets of white beaches, more than 300 native American holly trees, and several varieties of colorful rhododendrons are just a few of the reservation's numerous natural attractions.

This hike begins at the reservation's year-round parking area off South Sandwich Road and follows a pleasant woodland path to Wakeby and Mashpee ponds then follows a series of trails that explore the peninsula between the ponds. It is an easy walk along mildly rolling terrain with scenic views of the trees, shrubs, and ponds, and access to beaches. The trail names correspond with color blazes.

From the entrance, follow Red Trail northwest through a mixed forest of oak, beech, and pine toward the ponds.

LOCATION
Mashpee and Sandwich, MA

RATING
Moderate

DISTANCE
2.7 miles

ELEVATION GAIN
100 feet

ESTIMATED TIME
1.5 hours

MAPS
USGS Cotuit, USGS Sandwich-Cotuit; online: thetrustees.org/assets/documents/places-to-visit/trailmaps/Lowell-Holly-Trail-Map.pdf

The winding path curves right at a junction then rises easily through a beech grove. Holly trees, which are near the northern limit of their range on Cape Cod, are scattered about the understory and thrive quite well in the shade of the beech trees. In addition to the numerous native trees, 50 more were planted by Wilfrid Wheeler, who was the first chairman of the reservation. In spring, the pink and white flowers of rhododendrons and mountain laurel are especially handsome.

The large beech trees are quite different from the typical oaks and pines that cover so much of Cape Cod. Their smooth, gray trunks stand out like sentinels guarding the peninsula. In winter, the lower branches of the beech often retain their dried yellow-brown leaves, making a beautiful contrast with the snow. Other tree species here include pitch and white pines (the former is distinguished by its ball-shaped needle bundles), black birch, and red maple, which adds a splash of bright color in autumn. Any walk through the woods is made more pleasant when you can see deep blue water—in this case, Wakeby Pond—through the green foliage.

After fifteen to twenty minutes of easy walking, you'll reach the narrow neck between Wakeby and Mashpee ponds. Red Trail bears to the left to cross the neck at the narrow swimming beach, where the resident flock of mallards may greet you. Here a picnic table at the water's edge makes an ideal stop for a break and a snack. The path then passes behind the seasonal parking area and continues

Mallards bob in the surf at Mashpee Pond.

a short distance to the end of the neck and the edge of the peninsula, where the White Trail loop begins.

Turn right here onto White Trail, which leads north over the gently rolling terrain along the eastern shores of the peninsula. A bench offers a rest stop with views across Wakeby Pond. After quickly climbing a small hill, the path continues to a three-way junction. Here you can detour to the right on the Blue Trail, a 0.3-mile, out-and-back trail that leads through a dark tunnel of trees and shrubs to the tip of Conaumet Point, a narrow sliver of land that extends into Wakeby Pond. There are limited views through the vegetation of Wakeby Pond. The pond's three small islands lie just beyond the point.

After exploring the point, backtrack to the junction and bear right onto White Trail, which continues for a short distance to another fork. Bear right here again onto Orange Trail, a 0.6-mile, one-way path that leads southwest toward the southern end of the peninsula. (To shorten this hike, you can bypass this section and continue to follow White Trail.) It seems few of the reservation's many visitors walk to the end of the peninsula, so chances are you will have these woods to yourself.

From the junction, Orange Trail follows gently rolling terrain as it negotiates a series of low hills then forks into a short loop that winds around the peninsula's southwest corner. You can go either way here. From atop the 60-foot-high knolls, there are fine views through the trees to the south across Mashpee Pond.

Both Mashpee and Wakeby ponds are well known for their excellent fishing. Trout are stocked in both spring and fall. Warm-water species are present, including largemouth bass, smallmouth bass, pickerel, and bluegill. The ponds also attract a variety of birdlife, including great blue herons, ducks, and Canada geese. Some lucky hikers have spotted osprey. Frequent visitors have told us they occasionally see raccoons and foxes stalking the edges of the wetlands.

After completing the loop, backtrack to the junction with White Trail and go right. There are some very large holly trees on this side of the peninsula. A short side trail on the right leads to a small, sandy beach on the north shores of Mashpee Pond where there's another nice view across the water. White Trail turns to the left and then to the right as it follows the base of another low hill. It then returns you to the start of the loop at the western edge of the neck. From here, simply retrace your steps across the neck, along Red Trail and through the forest, back to the trailhead.

DID YOU KNOW?

The reservation was once known as Conaumet, which was derived from "Ku-wunut," a Wampanoag term for beach.

MORE INFORMATION

The seasonal lot (twenty cars), which offers direct access to the beaches on the neck between Mashpee and Wakeby ponds, is open Memorial Day to Labor Day. The main lot (six cars) is open year-round. For more information, call 508-636-4693 or visit thetrustees.org.

NEARBY

With no freeways or railroad lines, Mashpee has retained a rural character. Other nearby reservations include Quashnet Woods State Reservation on MA 28, Mashpee River Woodlands just east of the junction of MA 151 and MA 28, and South Cape Beach State Park at the end of Great Oak Road. Restaurants are located south of the reservation at the junction of MA 151 and MA 28.

These trails offer excellent views of a long barrier beach's diverse habitats.

DIRECTIONS

From US 6 in Barnstable, take Exit 5 and follow MA 149 north to the junction with MA 6A. Turn left and follow MA 6A west for 2.5 miles then turn right onto the well-marked Sandy Neck Road and continue to the gatehouse. Limited free parking is available for hikers adjacent to the gatehouse; a seasonal fee ($20 weekends, $15 weekdays) is charged at the main beach parking lot. *GPS coordinates:* 41° 44.121′ N, 70° 23.100′ W.

TRAIL DESCRIPTION

Sandy Neck is a 6-mile-long barrier beach with associated marshes that borders Cape Cod Bay. Due to its unique and varied natural communities, the area has been designated an Area of Critical Environmental Concern by Massachusetts, and it is also recognized as a Cultural Historic District for its dune cottages and lighthouse.

Marsh Trail, several numbered connecting trails, and the beach itself offer options ranging from a 1.6-mile nature walk to a hike of more than 13 miles along the protected marsh and 100-foot-tall dunes to the open waters of Cape Cod Bay. Detailed here is the 4.7-mile option that uses dune crossover number 2. During exceptionally high tides, low-lying areas on Sandy Neck's marsh side, such as the start of Marsh Trail, may be flooded. Hikers are not allowed to enter private property or areas designated for erosion control, and they must stay off the dunes, crossing over only on designated trails.

Begin this circuit on Marsh Trail; the trailhead is located at the entrance to the parking area adjacent to the gatehouse. The trail initially passes through an area of red pine

LOCATION
Barnstable, MA

RATING
Moderate

DISTANCE
1.6 miles, 4.7 miles, 9 miles, or 13 miles

ELEVATION GAIN
Minimal

ESTIMATED TIME
2 to 3 hours for the 4.7-mile loop

MAPS
USGS Hyannis; online: town.barnstable.ma.us/ sandyneckpark

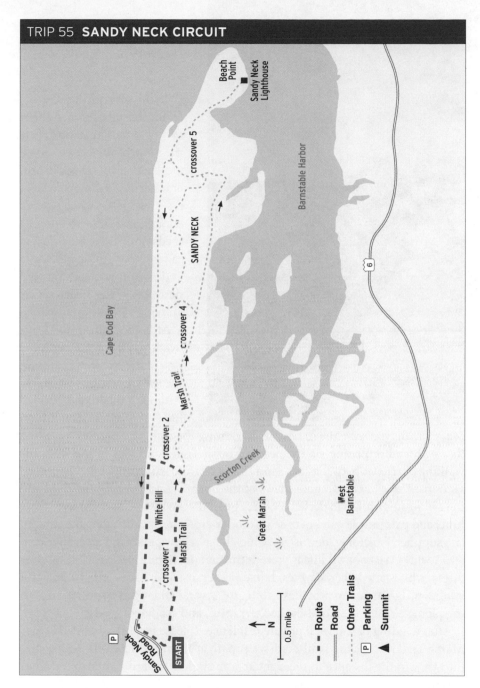

and scrub oak and then follows the edge of Great Marsh, an expansive 3,500-acre marsh that borders Scorton Creek and its vast maze of short tributaries. Large, blue boxes line the marsh. These are traps to control greenhead flies, which are most active during hot, sunny periods toward the end of July. Greenheads have a nasty bite, and insect repellents are ineffective at keeping them away.

To the left is an entirely different coastal habitat, a chain of tall dunes that obstructs the view of the ocean. Some are capped by trees, shrubs, cranberries, and wildflowers that grow when there's enough leaf litter to support seeds and roots. Stay on the sandy trail to avoid ticks and poison ivy, and to avoid destroying the beach grass and other fragile dune plants.

At 0.5 mile from the trailhead, you'll reach Trail 1, the first of the crossover paths on the left, opposite a rest bench. Although the hike described here continues straight on Marsh Trail, you have the option of shortening the walk to 1.6 miles by taking this path and returning via the beach. Marsh Trail continues to the west; the walking alternates between soft, sandy stretches and easier, more firmly packed sections. There are continuous views of the open Great Marsh on the right and the rolling high dunes to the left. Poverty grass displays its yellow blooms in early June, and pale purple patches of sea lavender grow prolifically along the trail. In late summer, look for golden asters, which have yellow petals and an orange center. A wide variety of wildlife is present throughout Sandy Neck, including river otters, white-tailed deer, coyotes, horseshoe crabs, and flocks of barn and tree swallows. The area also provides habitat for several endangered species, including piping plovers, diamond-backed terrapins, and spadefoot toads.

After winding past several private residences (please respect all posted areas), Marsh Trail reaches the Trail 2 crossover path at 1.5 miles. Scorton Creek comes into view in the distance to the right as it meanders toward Barnstable Harbor and the bay.

This hike continues to the left on Trail 2, following the 4.7-mile loop. Those looking for a longer expedition can continue straight on Marsh Trail to Trail 4 (there is no Trail 3), a 9-mile round-trip via the beach. The historical cottages on Beach Point and the Sandy Neck Lighthouse come into view en route to Trail 4. Trail 5 is 1.5 miles beyond Trail 4 and offers a hardy, 13-mile hike; an optional detour east along the beach, past private land to the lighthouse and the tip of Beach Point, adds an extra 2 miles. Another option is Horse Trail, which runs east–west between Trails 4 and 5—a great way to explore the neck's dunes and maritime forests.

Trail 2 winds to the north across the dunes and soon reaches the edge of Sandy Neck Beach, a 1,390-acre barrier beach that extends 6 miles along the southern tip of Cape Cod Bay. At this point, you are roughly 2 miles from the entrance (to the left) and 4.25 miles from Beach Point to the east. Visible across the bay to the left is the coastline near Plymouth, while the Lower Cape's shoreline is on your right. Unlike other areas of Cape Cod, where substantial land has been lost to erosion, Sandy Neck Beach gains size annually from sands deposited from areas to the north, including Plymouth. In late autumn, migrating sea turtles often wash up on Sandy Neck and other bay beaches after becoming hypothermic in the cold ocean waters. Stranded turtles are taken to rehabilitation centers and transported to southern wintering grounds.

Turn left and walk due west along the beach for 2 miles. This is one of the most popular Lower Cape beaches, and during summer, there may be a long line of recreational vehicles parked along the sands. The middle portion of the beach is rather rocky, but the shoreline offers easy walking along the tidal flats. As you near the entrance, you'll pass the Trail 1 crossover path on the left and then reach wooden stairs that lead to the parking area. From the parking lot, follow the entrance road back to the hiker parking area.

DID YOU KNOW?

During World War II, the U.S. Army used Sandy Neck beach and dunes as a training ground for troops bound for the Sahara Desert.

MORE INFORMATION

The beach is open daily from 8 A.M. to 8 P.M. The gatehouse is open seasonally or by appointment. Four-wheel-drive vehicles are allowed in certain areas by permit, and hunting is permitted during designated seasons; visitors in late autumn should wear blaze-orange clothing. A primitive tent area is available on Trail 4. Contact the Barnstable Marine and Environmental Affairs Department at 508-790-6272, the gatehouse at 508-362-8300, or visit town.barnstable.ma.us.

NEARBY

Scenic Barnstable Harbor is the departure point for whale-watching cruises to Stellwagen Bank, near Provincetown. The nearby Coast Guard Heritage Museum at 3353 Main Street (Route 6A) is dedicated to the history of the Coast Guard. There are restaurants on and off Main Street in Barnstable, and there are many more restaurants in the nearby village of Hyannis.

56

NICKERSON STATE PARK

A scenic loop trail circles Cliff Pond, one of Cape Cod's largest kettle ponds.

DIRECTIONS

From US 6, take Exit 12 and follow MA 6A west toward Brewster for 1.5 miles to the well-marked park entrance on the south side of the highway. Follow the park entrance road for 0.4 mile, turn left onto Flax Pond Road, and continue 1.2 miles to the parking area at the road's end. *GPS coordinates:* 41° 45.618′ N, 70° 01.110′ W.

TRAIL DESCRIPTION

Situated on the elbow of Cape Cod, Nickerson State Park protects nearly 2,000 acres of inland coastal habitats, including eight kettle ponds and an extensive scrub-oak and pitch-pine forest. Recreational opportunities abound here, as the park is home to hiking trails, boat launches, a 420-site campground, and an 8-mile paved bicycle trail that connects to the Cape Cod Rail Trail. The park was created in 1934 through the donation of a 1,700-acre private estate and was subsequently upgraded through the efforts of the Civilian Conservation Corps.

This hike makes a long, clockwise loop around Cliff Pond, which, at roughly 200 acres, is the largest of the park's numerous kettle ponds. Although the route is easy to follow, it is narrow in places and sporadically marked, and there are a number of unmarked junctions with other side trails. Along the way, you'll pass several sand beaches and boat launches that offer scenic views, swimming, or just places to rest and enjoy the sun. These areas may be crowded during summer, although the rest of the route offers plenty of solitude.

From the parking area, walk past the sign reading, "No Vehicles Beyond This Point," to the narrow neck

LOCATION
Brewster, MA

RATING
Easy to Moderate

DISTANCE
3.25 miles

ELEVATION GAIN
50 feet

ESTIMATED TIME
1.75 hours

MAPS
USGS Harwich, USGS Orleans; online: mass.gov/eea/docs/dcr/parks/trails/nickerson.pdf

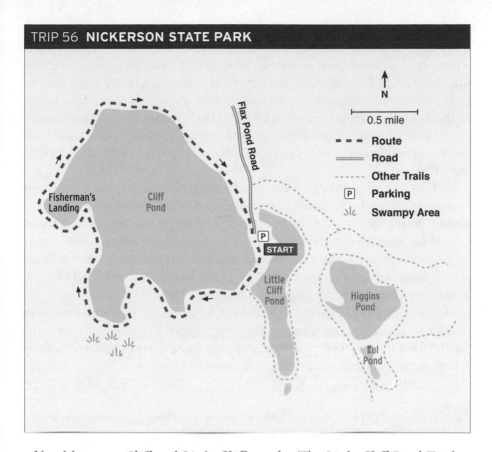

of land between Cliff and Little Cliff ponds. (The Little Cliff Pond Trail, a short loop around Little Cliff Pond that rejoins the Cliff Pond Trail south of the boat launch, begins at a trailhead on the east side of the parking lot.) The popular Cliff Pond swimming beach will be on your right, with the boat launch at Little Cliff Pond to the left. Follow the Cliff Pond Trail away from the beach, along the water's edge, and beneath a steep hillside on the left. After a few minutes, reach another beach. Here, the privately operated Jack's Boat Rentals offers canoes, kayaks, sailboats, and paddleboats from mid-June to Labor Day. Continue straight past the southern junction with Little Cliff Pond Trail on the left.

Cliff Pond and the park's other kettle ponds, which include Flax, Little Cliff, and Higgins ponds, are among the roughly 300 kettle ponds of various sizes that dot Cape Cod. These ponds, which formed some 10,000 years ago as glaciers retreated, are not fed by any streams or brooks. They are dependent on precipitation and groundwater, which means water levels can vary annually.

Continue to another beach on the pond's southeast corner. Walk across the beach and follow the trail back into the woods, keeping the water close to your right. Another hill rises out of the shoreline to the left, and the slopes are forested with pitch pine. Note the almost complete lack of vegetation in the grassy understory. The park's extensive forests provide food and cover for all of the familiar mammals of southeastern Massachusetts, including eastern coyotes, white-tailed deer, red foxes, raccoons, and striped skunks. All of these creatures are highly adaptable and thrive in a variety of habitats, including areas close to humans. Like the other animals, skunks are most often encountered early or late in the day, when they make feeding forays as the light changes. As those unfortunate enough to be sprayed by skunks can attest, the critters often make their dens under buildings or near campgrounds, such as those found at Nickerson State Park.

Birds of prey that inhabit these woodlands include great horned, eastern screech, and barred owls; woodland warblers and other migratory songbirds are present during spring and summer. During spring and fall, the ponds serve as crucial rest stops for large flocks of waterfowl, such as ring-necked ducks, common goldeneyes, and common and red-breasted mergansers, as they migrate to and from northern summer breeding grounds. Also watch for bald eagles, which frequented the pond during the summer of 2015.

The Cliff Pond Trail then curves to the left, following the first of several coves that jut out of the pond's southern and western shores. In another quarter-mile, you'll arrive at the second cove; here, the path turns sharply right and follows a narrow beach that separates the pond's southern tip from a shallow wetland

Canoe on a beach at Cliff Pond. Nickerson State Park's many recreational opportunities include paddling, horseback riding, fishing, and biking the Cape Cod Rail Trail.

known as Grassy Nook. Scan this marshy area for great blue and green herons and other wading birds. At the next fork, bear right and continue to follow the pond edge. The trail rises gently as it traverses the mildly rolling terrain along the southwest corner and follows bluffs above the water. The swimming beach at the trailhead will be visible through the trees, across the water to the northeast.

The path turns abruptly left again to follow the last of the coves at the pond's west side. Here you'll get a good perspective of how large the pond is. A short distance farther along are the boat launch and beach off the park's Joe Long Road, an area known as Fisherman's Landing. Another small, shallow pond will be on your left, just beyond the boat launch. Bear right here to follow Cliff Pond Trail along Cliff Pond's northwestern shores. (Note: Other trails lead up the slope toward camping Area 4; if you wind up at this campground, follow the paved road to a sign marking sites 21–ABCD then turn right and follow a path back to the pond edge.) Continue past a series of small beaches below the campground, a large boulder, and another small pond on the left.

From the last shallow pond, it's a relatively easy walk of roughly half a mile back to the parking area. The trail leads through pitch-pine groves along Cliff Pond's northeastern shores, passing a private path that leads up the slopes on the left. (Please respect all posted areas.) After making a quick climb to follow the bluffs above the water, the trail curves to the left and returns you to the parking area, opposite the trailhead for the Little Cliff Pond Trail.

DID YOU KNOW?

The Massachusetts Department of Conservation and Recreation owns and manages more than 450,000 acres of land statewide.

MORE INFORMATION

Nickerson State Park is open to day-use visitors from 8 A.M. to 8 P.M. year-round. From Memorial Day to Labor Day, Massachusetts residents pay $8 to park ($10 for out-of-state visitors). More than 400 campsites are available. There are 8 miles of paved bike trails in the park, and the park staff offers numerous interpretive trails and recreational activities in season. Contact the park at 508-896-3491 or visit mass.gov/dcr for further information.

NEARBY

Nickerson State Park offers direct access to the popular Cape Cod Rail Trail, a paved 22-mile bike trail that runs from South Dennis to Wellfleet. The Cape Cod Museum of Natural History, which includes walking trails to Wing's Island and Cape Cod Bay, is located on US 6 near the Brewster–Dennis town line. There are restaurants on MA 6A west of the park in Brewster and along MA 6A and MA 28 east of the park in Orleans.

57

FORT HILL

This varied hike offers scenic views from open meadows and explores the heart of a large red maple swamp.

DIRECTIONS

From the rotary junction of US 6, MA 6A, and MA 28 at the Orleans–Eastham town line, drive north on US 6 for 1.3 miles. Following signs for the Fort Hill area, turn right onto Governor Prence Road, and after about a quarter-mile bear right onto Fort Hill Road. Continue past the lower parking lot on the left to the upper parking area at the road's end. *GPS coordinates: 41° 49.097′ N, 69° 57.723′ W.*

By public transportation, the Cape Cod Regional Transit Authority's Flex bus offers stops between Harwich and Provincetown. Riders may board at scheduled stops or make arrangements for other stops. The Flex bus also connects with other lines, including the Plymouth & Brockton service. A bike shuttle is offered to the National Seashore from several Outer Cape towns in summer. Visit capecodtransit.org for information.

TRAIL DESCRIPTION

The Fort Hill area encompasses low hills, meadows, and a coastal red maple swamp that borders Nauset Marsh and a long barrier beach. It is located in the southern portion of the 44,000-acre, 40-mile-long Cape Cod National Seashore, which stretches from Chatham all the way to the tip of the Cape in Provincetown.

Treat yourself to a sunrise from the top of Fort Hill, a small hill with a great panoramic view. Top it off with a walk through the hillside fields along Nauset Marsh and return to the hill via a long boardwalk that winds through the red maple swamp. You can extend your hike by

LOCATION
Eastham, MA

RATING
Easy

DISTANCE
2 miles

ELEVATION GAIN
50 feet

ESTIMATED TIME
1 hour

MAPS
USGS Orleans; online: nps.gov/caco/planyourvisit/upload/CACOmapweb.pdf

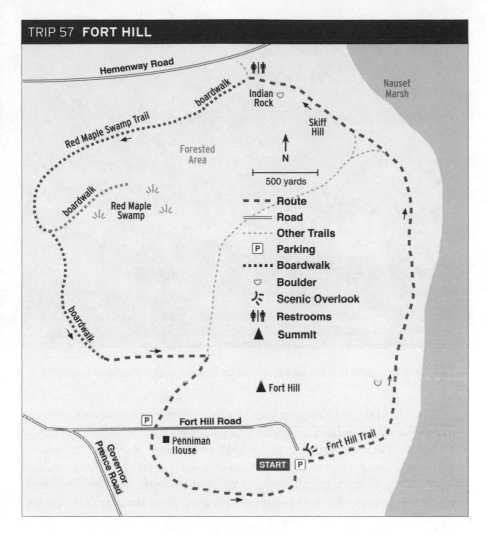

viewing the historical Penniman House, once owned by a whale-ship captain, and continue back to the parking lot on the trail that runs behind the house. The combination of water, boardwalk, and expansive views makes this hike a favorite of children. Sections of the boardwalk were closed as of 2016, although much of the boardwalk and the rest of the trail remain open. Contact the seashore headquarters for updates.

This walk begins at the upper parking lot at the top of Fort Hill. You might spot a snow bunting, a small bird that looks a bit like a large sparrow until it reveals a belly that is almost pure white. This ground bird is about 6 inches long and is seen on tundra, amid dunes, and in open fields. Monarch butterflies are common in late summer, while eastern cottontail rabbits can be seen year-round. Familiar summer flowers include Queen Anne's lace, goldenrod, common evening primrose, chicory, and sweet pea—an escaped garden perennial distinguished by its pink and white petals.

Fort Hill offers some of the best and most accessible scenic views at Cape Cod National Seashore.

Follow Fort Hill Trail along the edge of the meadows as it descends gently to the marsh and a huge boulder, which is a glacial erratic, deposited during the last ice age. Watch for northern harrier hawks hovering above the salt marsh; wading birds, such as great blue and green herons; and shorebirds, such as greater yellowlegs and semipalmated plovers, feeding in the mudflats. Bayberry, black cherry, honeysuckle, and salt-spray rose grow along the edge of the marsh. Autumnal tints here are subtle but pleasing to the eye, with golden marsh grass ringed by russet vegetation.

From the boulder, bear left in a northerly direction for about a half-mile until you reach the woods, composed primarily of cedar trees. Bear right into the woods, and in a couple of minutes you will arrive at a pavilion atop Skiff Hill, from which there's another fine view. Inside the pavilion is Indian Rock, a boulder used by the Nauset to sharpen fishhooks and tools. The abrasive qualities of this fine-grained metamorphic rock were perfect for grinding and polishing implements. Let children run their fingers over the grooves in the rock and explain how American Indians sharpened their tools in those same grooves. This glacial boulder was originally farther out in the marsh but was moved here for viewing.

From the pavilion, leave Fort Hill Trail and continue for roughly 300 yards to the start of Red Maple Swamp Trail, opposite the restrooms near the Hemenway Road entrance. Portions of the boardwalk may be closed for repairs. If the northern section at the Hemenway entrance is inaccessible, from the Skiff Hill shelter follow the lower portion of Fort Hill Trail west along the field edge, then turn right at the junction with Red Maple Swamp Trail. Follow the boardwalk to the closed area then retrace your steps to the field. The path descends into the swamp, where a long boardwalk will keep your feet dry and will delight children. The contrast between this dark, shaded wetland and the sunny fields at the hike's start makes this walk special. Interpretive signs along the trail identify highbush blueberry, netted chain fern, and fox grapes. There is also winterberry, a low plant with bright red berries that are a favorite food for birds, and sweet pepperbush, which gives off a fragrant aroma from its flowers in August.

The standing water here is freshwater (not saltwater), and the swamp maple (also known as red maple) can tolerate wet roots. Extremely adaptable, it is one of the Northeast's most common tree species. You'll pass a grove of tall, twisting specimens and cross under a giant fallen tree that overhangs the trail.

At a junction, a short, one-way segment of the boardwalk offers a five-minute detour to the heart of the swamp. From the boardwalk's end, follow the dirt-and-gravel path on a gentle climb to rejoin the fields of Fort Hill. Look for meadowlarks and bluebirds here.

Turn right and follow Fort Hill Trail to the lower parking lot (the upper lot where you parked is visible up the hill to the left) then cross Fort Hill Road and walk a short distance to the Penniman House on the left. You can't miss this historical home: At the front of the yard is an enormous archway formed by the jawbones of a whale. Captain Edward Penniman first took to the sea in 1842 at age 11 and eventually circled the world seven times. His home became a local landmark. From the back of the house, Fort Hill Trail continues in an easterly direction through low-lying woods for about a third of a mile back to Fort Hill. Make an easy ascent to the parking area to complete the loop.

DID YOU KNOW?

The scenery and wildlife here inspired Henry Beston's classic book *The Outermost House,* which he wrote while living in a cottage on Nauset Beach during the 1920s.

MORE INFORMATION

The Fort Hill area is open year-round, dawn to dusk, and there is no fee. Dogs are prohibited. Red Maple Swamp Trail is universally accessible. Contact Cape Cod National Seashore Headquarters at 508-771-2144 or visit nps.gov/caco.

NEARBY

Nauset Beach is home to the historical Nauset Lighthouse, which was moved to the area from Chatham in 1923 and then moved farther inland in 1993, after the bluffs it once stood atop had eroded substantially. There are many restaurants on US 6, MA 6A, and MA 28.

GREAT WHITE SHARKS RETURN TO MASSACHUSETTS

The 1975 movie *Jaws*, about a fictional great white shark that terrorized a New England seaside community, drew record-breaking audiences. Forty years later, the real-life return of great whites to the coastal waters of Massachusetts has also attracted worldwide attention.

As one of the ocean's apex predators, great white sharks are at the top of the marine food chain. They can weigh as much as 5,000 pounds each and live more than 70 years. Relatively little is known about their historical presence in New England, which is at the northern limit of their Atlantic range. Prior to 2012, there were only four known attacks on humans by great white sharks in Massachusetts. The shark's western North Atlantic population declined late in the twentieth century, and sightings were sporadic in Massachusetts. In recent years, however, this trend has reversed, and great white sharks rapidly have become a well-established presence around Cape Cod and the adjacent mainland coast. They arrive during summer, when the ocean warms, and head south when the water temperature drops in autumn.

The return of great white sharks is largely due to the recovery of gray seals, one of their primary prey species. An adult seal can weigh as much as 700 pounds and can sustain an individual shark for a month or longer. After hunting led to significant declines, state and federal officials placed the gray seal on protected lists. With the seals shielded from hunters, their population in Massachusetts has grown from a low of 15 estimated individuals in the mid-twentieth century to more than 15,000.

With the surging shark population has come inevitable conflicts with humans. Many beaches have been temporarily closed to swimming after shark sightings, and one person was attacked and seriously injured while wading at Truro's Ballston Beach in 2012. Several paddlers have been pursued and even displaced from their boats. An increasing number of shark attacks on seals have been witnessed close to beaches. Beach visitors should be alert for advisories and should avoid swimming, wading, or paddling near seals, since sharks are drawn to them.

Great white sharks are an indicator of a healthy marine ecosystem, as topline predators are essential to keeping the food web in balance and maintaining healthy populations of prey species. An increasing number of people have come to appreciate their role in nature, and shark- and seal-related tourism is now thriving on Cape Cod. While great white shark sightings are unpredictable, gray seals are common at Cape Cod's outer beaches, from Chatham to Provincetown, and along the mainland coast, near Ellisville Harbor State Park and Plymouth.

58

WELLFLEET BAY WILDLIFE SANCTUARY

Enjoy the excellent birding, diverse plant life, and scenic views along Silver Spring Brook, Goose Pond, and the marshes and mudflats near Try Island.

DIRECTIONS

Follow US 6 for 0.3 mile north from the Eastham–Wellfleet town line to signs marking the sanctuary on the left (west) side of the highway. Turn left and follow the sanctuary entrance road 0.4 mile to the visitor center. *GPS coordinates: 41° 52.937' N, 69° 59.638' W.*

TRAIL DESCRIPTION

Wellfleet Bay Wildlife Sanctuary is one of Cape Cod's most popular outdoor destinations due to its extensive bayside trail system and its salt marsh. All of the trails are worth exploring, but this hike follows the Goose Pond and Try Island trails, both home to great vistas and diverse coastal flora and fauna.

Access to the trails is through the nature center during operating hours; follow the signs at other times. Be sure to check out the natural history exhibits, aquariums, and butterfly garden, where you may see butterflies and hummingbirds. Following signs for Goose Pond Trail, take the path to a "T" junction at the edge of the expansive salt marsh. Go left here (Bay View Trail branches to the right) and follow the trail for a short distance to a pond formed by a dam at the end of Silver Spring Brook. The shoreline of the pond on your left is surrounded by marsh fern, white poplar trees, swamp milkweed, and purple loosestrife—a nonindigenous plant that crowds out native vegetation. Sanctuary staff periodically pull up the latter for this reason. The plant is easily identified by its bright

LOCATION
South Wellfleet, MA

RATING
Easy

DISTANCE
2 miles

ELEVATION GAIN
50 feet

ESTIMATED TIME
1.5 hours

MAPS
USGS Wellfleet; online: massaudubon.org/content/download/7939/144410/file/wellfleet_trails.pdf

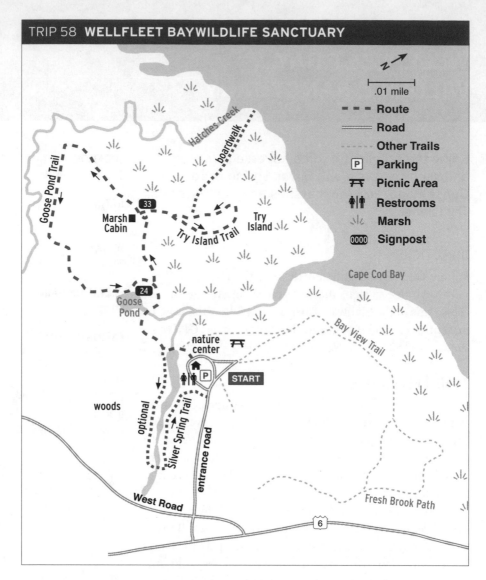

purple flowers that bloom in summer. Scan the lilies for basking painted turtles and frogs during warm months.

If you want to explore Silver Spring Brook, you can walk a 0.6-mile loop trail that follows the west bank, crosses the brook on a wooden bridge, and loops back along the east bank to rejoin Goose Pond Trail. This is an especially good route for viewing migratory songbirds in spring and summer.

After you cross the dam over Silver Spring Brook on Goose Pond Trail, you will emerge into an area of pines, including white, pitch, red, and Scotch varieties. All were planted here to stabilize the sandy soil. It's interesting to note that when the Pilgrims landed at Cape Cod, the peninsula was covered with trees, but by the time Thoreau made his four explorations of the Cape, he lamented that the land was literally blowing away because almost every tree had been cut down.

Follow Goose Pond Trail through the pine woods for two or three minutes, to a junction at Goose Pond. A short side trail leads to an observation blind, where you can watch for green herons, snowy egrets, kingfishers, and migratory shorebirds. Goose Pond Trail bends to the right and follows a short boardwalk with a good view of Goose Pond on your left and the marsh on your right. Red-winged blackbirds are present here from March to October; the male is identifiable by its red shoulder patch, while females are dark brown. These birds nest in the wetlands, in grass-and-weed nests usually set in low bushes, and they feed on insects and marsh plants. Warblers also visit the thickets here during migratory periods. Other pond dwellers include the snapping turtle, which has a ridged green-black shell, and the painted turtle, identifiable by its smooth black shell and its head streaked with yellow markings.

Continue westward past the pond and into the forest that borders the edge of the marsh. Red cedars are scattered throughout the woods, and a small observation deck on the right offers views across the marsh. About 0.25 mile from Goose Pond, you'll reach a major junction at marker 33 near Marsh Cabin, a small cabin that once hosted visitors to the sanctuary but is now empty.

Sunset over Cape Cod Bay from the tidal flats at Wellfleet Bay Wildlife Sanctuary.

Turn right here on Try Island Trail, which leads west through the heart of the marsh. Northern harriers and red-tailed hawks can be seen in this area.

You will soon come to a fork in the trail. Bear right toward Try Island, a small oasis of forest rising out of the marsh. The trail winds to an overlook on a bluff with an excellent view of the bay and the salt marsh then quickly descends to an intersection with the boardwalk. Turn right onto the boardwalk to head toward the beach. (During some high tides, the boardwalk may be temporarily flooded; check tide times at the nature center.) It's about a quarter-mile walk to the shore through the fine-bladed, high tidal grass that Colonial farmers used for cattle feed. The well-adapted beach grass has a narrow profile that reduces the amount of evaporation caused by the constant coastal winds. It also has an extensive root system that helps hold the sand on the dunes and beach. Hatches Creek empties into the bay on the left. If you venture to the water's edge at the end of the flats, keep an eye on the tides.

After exploring the beach, retrace your steps over the boardwalk then bear right past Try Island. Once you cross the marsh, you will be back at the intersection by Marsh Cabin. Turn right to continue the loop on the outer portion of Goose Pond Trail. The path is wide and sandy, with fields and woods to your left and the salt marsh to your right. Look for Virginia rose and salt-spray rose with curved thorns and pale pink blossoms in early summer. Sea lavender, also called marsh rosemary, grows at the upper edge of the marsh, staying close to the ground to conserve moisture. It has tiny white flowers that remain on the plant into fall.

About a quarter-mile down this path is an arrow pointing you left at a fork. Bear left, heading into the fields. Beach plums, which have pink and white flowers in May before the leaves are fully out, grow in sheltered spots. In September they yield deep-purple fruit that is eaten by red foxes, raccoons, and birds. Other plants seen here include black locust, pokeweed, goldenrod, spindle tree, and golden aster. If you look closely, you might be able to see the tall, green, fernlike leaves of asparagus, the wild descendants of farming that took place here more than 60 years ago. One of the dominant trees, the oak, will carry its rusty leaves well into November, when many other trees have lost their foliage.

Bear left off the dirt road at a trail sign and complete the loop at marker 24, near Goose Pond. Turn right and retrace your steps along Goose Pond Trail to the parking lot.

DID YOU KNOW?

Before Mass Audubon acquired the Wellfleet Bay sanctuary, it was the site of an asparagus farm and a bird-banding station.

MORE INFORMATION

The trails are open every day, 8 A.M. to dusk. Admission is free for Mass Audubon members; for others, there is a fee. Dogs are prohibited. The nature center, which includes restrooms and natural history exhibits, is open daily from Memorial Day to Columbus Day, from 8:30 A.M. to 5 P.M. From Columbus Day to Memorial Day, it is open Tuesday through Sunday, 8:30 A.M. to 5 P.M. For more information, call 508-349-2615, email wellfleet@massaudubon.org, or visit massaudubon.org.

NEARBY

The Wellfleet Drive-In Theatre, on US 6 just south of the sanctuary, is open from late May to early September. There are many restaurants along US 6 north and south of the sanctuary.

A HAVEN FOR COASTAL WILDLIFE

Wellfleet Bay Wildlife Sanctuary is one of the finest places on Cape Cod for viewing wildlife, as a full range of both coastal and inland species inhabits the grounds, including more than 250 recorded species of birds. Children will enjoy the easily accessible views of fiddler crab colonies, basking painted turtles, frogs, and cottontail rabbits along the sandy paths.

The sanctuary's diverse terrain makes it a magnet for wildlife. It is home to a wide range of both coastal and upland salt- and freshwater habitats. Coastal habitats include the ocean, tidal flats, and marshes, while upland habitats include forests, ponds, brooks, and meadows.

In marshy areas and along mudflats, watch for the greater yellowlegs, a 14-inch-long wading bird with long yellow legs and grayish underparts. The best times for shorebird viewing are spring and late summer, when many species migrate to and from their Arctic breeding grounds. During this long flight, they use Wellfleet Bay and other preserves along the Atlantic coast as resting areas.

Muddy areas along and near the Try Island boardwalk offer close-up views of fiddler crab colonies. Enjoy watching these small crabs as they scamper in and out of the thousands of narrow holes that serve as their homes.

The upland meadows host an entirely different suite of creatures. Tree swallows—with their glistening, blue-black coats and white bellies—can be seen swooping through the air, catching insects above the marsh in midflight. They prefer nesting boxes in open areas, such as the large fields adjacent to the nature center, and often compete with bluebirds for choice spots. Box turtles, distinguished by their high-domed shells with yellow, orange, and black markings, are present but uncommon, as human development has led to a loss of suitable habitat. Another uncommon reptile you may encounter is the black racer, a rather large, extremely quick, and nonpoisonous snake. It can grow to more than 5 feet in length and can be seen basking in the sun or hunting for small rodents.

Study the tall trees in the forests along Silver Spring Brook and Bay View Trail for migratory songbirds. One warbler that favors the pitch-pine groves is the pine warbler, whose trilling call somewhat resembles those of juncos and chipping sparrows. White-tailed deer and eastern coyotes are among the large mammals present in these woodlands.

59

GREAT ISLAND

The combination of quiet pine woodlands, towering dunes, and scenic coastal views makes Great Island a special place to explore.

DIRECTIONS

From US 6, take the Wellfleet Town Center exit. After 0.2 mile, turn left onto East Commercial Street and continue 0.8 mile to the town pier. Turn right onto Kendrick Road and follow it about 1 mile to its end. Turn left onto Chequesset Neck Road and continue 1.7 miles to the Great Island parking lot on the left. *GPS coordinates:* 41° 56.008′ N, 70° 04.157′ W.

By public transportation, the Cape Cod Regional Transit Authority's Flex bus offers stops between Harwich and Provincetown. Riders may board at scheduled stops or make arrangements for other stops. The Flex bus also connects with other lines, including the Plymouth & Brockton service. A bike shuttle is also offered to the National Seashore from several Outer Cape towns in summer. Visit capecodtransit.org for information.

TRAIL DESCRIPTION

The Great Island peninsula is a knob of glacial debris connected to the mainland by a narrow hill of sand. Winds and tides have continually reshaped this area, which was an island until a storm linked it to the mainland during the early nineteenth century. In the late 1600s and early 1700s, a tavern served mariners on Great Island, and the walk detailed here goes to this historical site.

Because the island is large and visitors often bypass areas away from the beach, you can enjoy Great Island in relative solitude. The only sounds you will hear are the lapping waves and bird calls. Be sure to bring drinking

LOCATION
Wellfleet, MA

RATING
Moderate

DISTANCE
4 miles

ELEVATION GAIN
120 feet

ESTIMATED TIME
2.5 hours

MAPS
USGS Wellfleet; online: nps.gov/caco/plan yourvisit/upload/ GreatIslandseparationsfinal .pdf

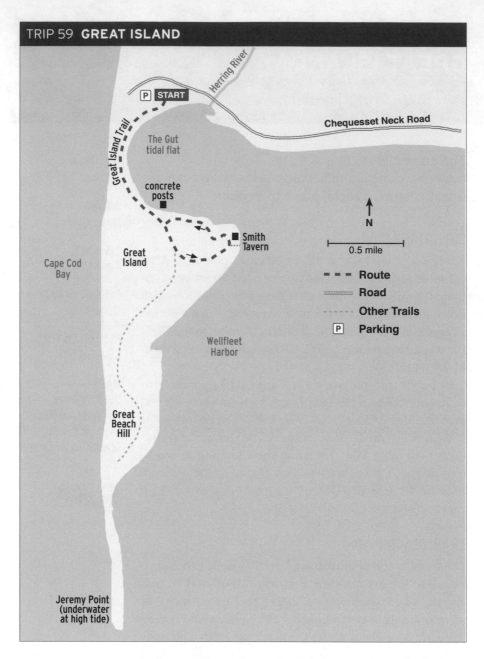

water, sunscreen, and a hat, as the walk is relatively long and much of it is in the open.

From the information sign at the parking lot, follow Great Island Trail downhill through a stand of pitch-pine trees that was replanted here at the end of the nineteenth century. Early settlers cut down most of the timber that once covered Cape Cod, and without diverse tree cover, the Cape was literally blowing away before planting efforts began to stabilize the soil.

In less than five minutes, you will arrive at the water's edge on the Wellfleet Harbor side of the peninsula. Turn right here and follow the shore in a southerly direction. A sign reports the mileage of the island's various walks. The estuarine tidal flats formed by the Herring River drainage are rich habitat for marine life, such as fiddler crabs, oysters, and quahogs. The latter (pronounced "KO-hog" and also known locally as a hard-shell clam) is a clam that can live as long as 20 to 25 years. The salt hay growing along the shore was used by early settlers as cattle feed. On a winter walk here, you might get lucky and see a harbor seal swimming in the bay or sunning on the shore.

As you walk the shore, look for oyster shells. Oysters were important to the diet of the American Indians who lived here and later to the settlers who commercially harvested them for food and used their shells to make lime. Overharvesting, and perhaps other unknown factors, led to the disappearance of the Wellfleet oyster. In an attempt to reestablish oysters in the bay, oyster stock from the southern United States has been introduced.

During high tide, this shoreline walk can be a bit muddy, so wear boots during cold-weather months. About fifteen minutes into the walk, reach the junction with a short crossover path on the right that leads over the dunes to the Cape Cod Bay side of Great Island; you can visit the beach now or at the end of your walk.

The molted skins of Atlantic horseshoe crabs are a familiar sight along the estuarine tidal flats, which also offer rich habitat for marine life such as fiddler crabs, oysters, and quahogs.

Great Island Trail continues along the tidal flat known as the Gut. Follow the path as it curves to the left in front of a tall dune. (Please respect all posted signs, as dune access is restricted to prevent erosion.) You might see fiddler crabs burrowing into the sand. The males have a large single claw they use in battle during mating season.

Continue along the contour of the shore for about a half-mile to a marked junction just beyond the concrete posts. Turn right, away from the shore, onto the trail that leads to the island's interior, following the sign for Great Beach Hill. On hot days, the pitch pines in the woods provide welcome shade. You will find you make better time on this woodland path because you are walking on firm ground rather than sand.

Continue for about a quarter-mile to another marked junction (1.4 miles from the trailhead). This hike continues left here on the narrow path that leads across the peninsula to the tavern site. (The trail straight ahead continues to Great Beach Hill and Jeremy Point.) Cross over a low hill and continue to a short unmarked side trail on the right that leads to fine views from atop a small bluff; it is a nice resting spot. After about a half-mile of walking from the junction with the trail to Great Beach Hill, you will arrive at a sign for Smith Tavern, which once served as a meeting place for weary mariners, including ship and shore whalers. A recent excavation of the site revealed more than 24,000 artifacts, from wine glass stems, to clay pipes—even a lady's fan.

Bear left at the trail signs and continue to the tavern interpretive sign and an overlook with an impressive view across the sparkling blue water of Wellfleet Bay. In pre-Colonial times, the American Indians were on the lookout here for shore-stranded whales to eat. When the Pilgrims landed on the Cape prior to settling in Plymouth, they came upon American Indians butchering a whale on a beach near Great Island. During one of his four mid-nineteenth-century visits to Cape Cod, Henry David Thoreau witnessed 30 blackfish (small whales) stranded on the beach: "They were a smooth shining black, like India-rubber, and had remarkably simple and humplike forms for animated creatures, with blunt round snout or head, whale-like, and simple, stiff looking flippers."

Indeed, whales were once so plentiful in the bay and its surrounding waters that lookouts were posted on the high ground at Great Beach Hill. These spotters would alert the waterborne whalers, who in turn pursued the great mammals in small boats equipped with harpoons and lances. Shore whalers stayed close to land, often driving the whales up on the sand, where the animals could be killed and butchered. Whale houses (in which gear was stored) and try-works (used to boil the whale oil from the blubber) were built around the perimeter of the island. The height of whaling activity in New England came in the 1840s, when there were more than 700 American whaling vessels at sea. After the discovery of petroleum oil in Pennsylvania, the demand for whale oil dropped. Today, whale-watching tours are a popular attraction for many visitors to Cape Cod. Conservation groups continue efforts to protect whales worldwide, as the animals are still killed by commercial whalers overseas.

Retrace your steps from the bluff to the tavern sign and bear right to complete the loop through the woods above the shore back to the Gut. (You also have the option of walking along the shore, reachable via a side path on the right.) In about five more minutes, you will be back at the shore, at the junction by the concrete posts. Turn left and retrace your earlier steps along the marsh to the parking lot.

If you enjoyed this 4-mile walk, you may want to return and try a more ambitious stroll farther out on Great Island, to the rise of land known as Great Beach Hill. Many hikers continue to the end of the peninsula and return via the beach: a 6- to 7.5-mile round-trip walk, depending on how far you venture toward Jeremy Point, the southernmost end of Great Island that may be flooded at high tide. Be sure to bring plenty of water, be prepared for sun exposure and soft sand, and watch the tides carefully around Jeremy Point.

DID YOU KNOW?

There once was a community south of Jeremy Point, called Billingsgate that was home to 30 families and a lighthouse. By 1935, it was lost to the rising tides.

MORE INFORMATION

Great Island is open year-round, 6 A.M. to midnight, and there is no fee. There is no visitor center on-site. Portable restrooms are available seasonally. Dogs are prohibited. For more information, contact Cape Cod National Seashore Headquarters at 508-349-3785 or visit nps.gov/caco.

NEARBY

The nearby center of Wellfleet is home to a number of art galleries along and off Main and Commercial streets. The road to Great Island passes scenic Wellfleet Harbor. There are restaurants on Main and Commercial streets and along US 6.

60

CAPE COD NATIONAL SEASHORE: PILGRIM HEIGHTS

Attractions here include a former farm in a kettle hole, panoramic overlooks, and the Pilgrim Spring historic site.

DIRECTIONS

From US 6 on the Truro–Wellfleet line, drive north for 7.5 miles. At the well-marked exit for Pilgrim Heights, bear right and follow the entrance road through the large parking area 0.5 mile to the trailhead at a small interpretive shelter. *GPS coordinates:* 42° 03.317′ N, 70° 06.388′ W.

By public transportation, the Cape Cod Regional Transit Authority's Flex bus offers stops between Harwich and Provincetown. Riders may board at scheduled stops or make arrangements for other stops. The Flex bus connects with other lines, including the Plymouth & Brockton service. A bike shuttle is also offered to the National Seashore from several Outer Cape towns in summer. Visit capecodtransit.org for information.

TRAIL DESCRIPTION

Situated at the narrowest part of Cape Cod, between Highland Cliffs to the south and Pilgrim Lake and the Province Lands dunes to the north, the Pilgrim Heights area of Cape Cod National Seashore is a locale rich in both history and scenery. Artifacts indicate American Indians were present at least 7,000 years ago. This was one of the first sites visited by the Pilgrims when they landed in the area in 1620, and during the late nineteenth and early twentieth centuries, a large farm operated in the base of a sheltered kettle hole.

This walk combines the Small's Swamp and Pilgrim Spring trails to form a 1.3-mile outing that visits the historical sites and three scenic overlooks with outstanding

LOCATION
Truro, MA

RATING
Easy

DISTANCE
1.3 miles

ELEVATION GAIN
115 feet

ESTIMATED TIME
1 hour

MAPS
USGS North Truro; online: nps.gov/caco/planyourvisit/upload/CACOmapweb.pdf

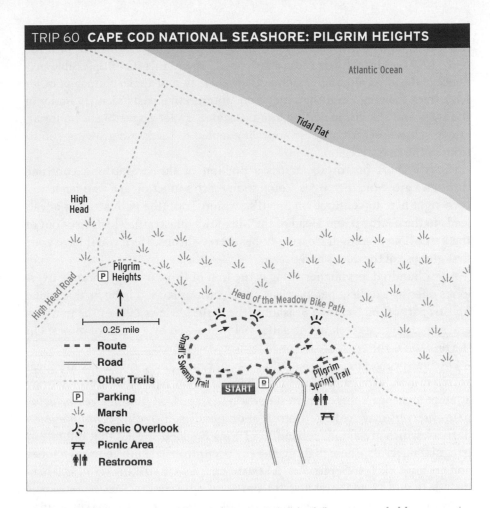

panoramic coastal views. The route, which is ideal for young children, can be completed in an hour or so, although you'll want to allow extra time to enjoy the views. It is an easy walk, with several short climbs and descents over gently rolling terrain.

Begin at the shelter at the edge of the parking area, where an interpretive sign details the routes followed by the Pilgrims when they arrived at the Outer Cape in 1620. A vista to the left overlooks the kettle hole and swamp that you're about to explore. From here follow Small's Swamp Trail, which descends into the woods to a fork where a 0.6-mile loop begins. To make a clockwise circuit, follow the left branch of the loop, which leads downhill through a grove of black oaks. The trail soon levels off at the base of the kettle, a large depression that formed more than 10,000 years ago, when a giant piece of ice that was left behind by a retreating glacier melted. Other similar depressions that filled with water are called kettle ponds and are common throughout eastern Massachusetts.

In more recent times, the kettle hole was the site of Small Farm, for which the trail is named. The Small family cultivated the land from 1860 until the early 1920s, when the farm was abandoned. Today there is little visible evidence of the farm, although careful observers may spot apple, plum, and other fruit trees growing amid the vegetation. Interpretive posts identify many of the trees and shrubs, including swamp azalea, sweet pepperbush, bullbriar, and Virginia rose. All of these are well adapted to the harsh growing conditions of the coastal region.

Cross a short boardwalk across a portion of the swamp and continue through a grove of aspen trees. You'll soon reach a junction at a wooden fence; turn right here to continue on Small's Swamp Trail (the path straight ahead leads to the nearby paved Head of the Meadows bike trail), which rises out of the kettle hole to a small clearing of bearberry shrubs. Here you'll have your first glimpse of the dunes and ocean.

A few hundred feet farther along is the first of three open panoramic overlooks offering excellent perspectives of the various coastal habitats that make up this part of the National Seashore. The easterly views take in the marshes and a meandering creek in the valley below, backed by a chain of dunes. On the horizon is the open ocean.

During spring, late summer, and early autumn, these overlooks are ideal places to watch for migrating birds. Raptors often pass close above as they attempt to navigate this narrowest portion of Cape Cod. In some years, fortunate observers may see large swarms of dragonflies, including common green darners, which are among a handful of New England species that migrate at irregular intervals. These flights generally occur from late July to mid-October and are most likely in September. A swarm makes for a striking sight, as it may include thousands of individual dragonflies.

Continue to the nearby second overlook, where the creek makes a wide "U"-shaped turn in front of the dunes. Watch for ducks and wading birds along the marsh edge here. A portion of the bike path is visible well below you, on the far right. From the vista, make a short descent through the woods to the start of the loop. Bear left and retrace your steps to the shelter.

The Pilgrim Spring loop begins adjacent to the shelter and leads through a grove of pitch pines. (A trail sign indicates 0.3 mile, but the full loop is 0.7 mile.) After about five minutes of easy walking, you'll pass through an open, shrubby area and reach the third and final overlook, which offers a similar perspective to those on Small's Swamp loop. Watch for white-capped waves on the horizon after passing storms.

From the vista, Pilgrim Spring loop descends through thickets of winterberry. A familiar resident of these shrubby areas during the warm months is the gray catbird, named for its catlike me-ow call. It is one of the most visible songbirds, and if you wait a few minutes, you'll likely get a good look at one as it hops about the shrubs and thickets that make up its preferred habitat.

Within a few minutes, you'll arrive at the base of the hill, at the site of a spring where the Pilgrims reputedly drank fresh water after landing in the area. The Head of the Meadows bike trail is adjacent to the spring; watch for eastern cottontail rabbits feeding along its edge early and late in the day.

Pilgrim Spring loop continues to the right of the spring, climbing back up the hill through another pitch-pine grove. In midsummer, watch for fruiting blueberries along the path's edge. After leveling off, the trail passes restrooms as it returns to the edge of the large parking area. To return to the shelter at the trailhead, follow the path across the lot and back into the woods at a posted National Seashore map; from here, it's an easy five-minute walk to your car.

If you have the time and energy for another walk, the nearby Beech Forest Trail at the Province Lands—a ten- to fifteen-minute drive away—is an excellent option. This 1-mile loop explores a shallow pond and a rare grove of mature coastal beech trees. To reach the trailhead, return to Route 6 and follow it north into Provincetown. Turn right at a well-marked sign for Province Lands and continue to the parking area on the left.

DID YOU KNOW?

The treacherous ocean waters off Pilgrim Heights caused many shipwrecks. The steamer *Portland* was lost in 1898 with 192 fatalities.

Vista on Small Swamp Trail at Pilgrim Heights, looking across marshes and dunes to the Atlantic Ocean.

MORE INFORMATION

There is no fee, and restrooms are available at the parking area. The closest National Seashore visitor center is at Province Lands, on Race Point Road off US 6 in Provincetown. Call 508-349-3785 or visit nps.gov/caco.

NEARBY

The historical Highland Lighthouse in Truro, located at the junction of Highland and South Highland roads, is one of Cape Cod's best-known landmarks. It includes a gift shop and a short walking path to an overlook with ocean views. There are several popular ocean beaches nearby, including Head of the Meadow and Coast Guard beaches. There are numerous restaurants along US 6 in Truro and many more in the center of Provincetown.

THE BIRTH OF CAPE COD NATIONAL SEASHORE

When sitting in heavy weekend traffic or navigating beaches crowded with sunbathers and umbrellas, it's hard to imagine that not long ago, the sandy, arm-shaped peninsula known as Cape Cod was considered an unfashionable, barren, and desolate wasteland. Most of the region's trees had been cut down by the mid-nineteenth century. But in the early twentieth century, when rail lines and increasingly popular automobiles facilitated access from Boston and other southern New England communities, the Cape began its transformation into one of the country's best-known vacation and weekend resort destinations.

In response to the rapid developmental pressures of the mid-twentieth century, especially during the building boom that followed the end of World War II, then-senators John F. Kennedy and Leverett Saltonstall proposed the creation of the Cape Cod National Seashore in 1961. The ambitious plan called for the protection of more than 40,000 acres of ocean beaches and associated habitats, stretching 40 miles from Nauset Beach at the elbow of the Cape in Chatham to Race Point in Provincetown.

The timing of the proposal was crucial, occurring at the end of a period when real estate prices were still relatively low and housing plans had already been drawn up for many of the areas to be protected. Shortly after the seashore's designation, land prices skyrocketed to values that likely would have been unacceptable to Congress. As would be expected with a plan that involved so much land in several towns, there was strong and often emotional local opposition to the project. Longtime Cape Cod residents speak of friendships and business relationships that were abruptly and permanently severed during the debates.

Nevertheless, the proposal proved successful, as people recognized the value in protecting this fragile landscape. In May 1966, the late President Kennedy was remembered during the dedication of the national park area he had helped create.

Thanks to these efforts, an estimated 5 million to 6 million visitors now come to the National Seashore annually. Although the beaches inevitably draw the bulk of visitors, there are a wealth of other features to explore, including coastal beech forests, an Atlantic white cedar swamp, and salt marshes. There are also several historical sites, including Pilgrim Spring and the Highland Lighthouse in Truro, and the site of Guglielmo Marconi's wireless telegraph station in Wellfleet.

APPENDIX A
THE BAY CIRCUIT TRAIL

First envisioned nearly 100 years ago by the open-space pioneers Henry Channing, Charles W. Eliot II, and Benton MacKaye (the founder of the Appalachian Trail), the Bay Circuit Trail and Greenway is an outer "emerald necklace," akin to the original necklace that links Boston's marquee parks. This permanent recreational trail connects 37 towns, from Plum Island in Newburyport to Kingston Bay in Duxbury, arcing through Boston's outer suburbs between Route 128 and Interstate 495.

As of 2016, more than 230 miles of multiuse, passive recreational trails are now designated and open to the public. The greenway has been expanded by more than 4,000 acres since the 1980s. Highlights include the completion of several connecting and spur trails, such as the Charles River Link from Newton to Medfield, that branch off the main route and link more tracts of protected land and historical sites. These routes provide additional points to access the trail, extending its reach into more communities. Another keystone component was the connection across the Massachusetts Turnpike in Ashland. Other projects are ongoing: filling in the few remaining gaps, moving the trail off-road, and improving existing sections. Although the trail primarily winds through woods, wetlands, and fields, some sections follow scenic country roads, passing many points of historical interest; other sections follow sidewalks in villages.

The concept of walking in peaceful solitude through so large a portion of highly developed eastern Massachusetts is exciting. The Bay Circuit Trail not only provides urban and suburban dwellers with critical connections to green spaces, it also draws nature lovers into our nation's past, when American Indians followed footpaths from one tribal land to another, and from inland hunting grounds to the coast. As more people discover and explore the trail, it has the potential to galvanize the public around protecting more of our open spaces before it's too late.

While the vision for the Bay Circuit dates to 1929, it wasn't until the 1980s that the trail became a reality, when what is now called the Massachusetts Department of Conservation and Recreation funded trail planning and some very important greenspace acquisitions. In the 1990s, the Bay Circuit Alliance, an entirely volunteer organization, was formed. Initially spearheaded by Alan French, who retired in 2012 after twenty years of dedicated leadership, the alliance is a dynamic partnership of towns, organizations, and dedicated individuals. The Appalachian Mountain Club and The Trustees of Reservations, which owns and manages several reservations that are part of the Bay Circuit Trail and are included in this book, now partner with the Bay Circuit Alliance to ensure the completion and long-term care of the trail system and greenway. Beginning in 2017, AMC will take over sole leadership of the Bay Circuit Alliance. In 2015, AMC published the *Bay Circuit Trail Map and Guide* which offers an overview of the entire region and details the trails that make up the Bay Circuit Trail. Also included are more than 30 multiuse trip suggestions and information on safety tips, natural, and cultural history of the area. To learn more about this map, visit amcstore.outdoors.org/books-maps/bay-circuit-trail-map-and-guide.

Volunteers are an integral part of the Bay Circuit Trail. There are many ways to participate, including trail maintenance and improvement, leading walks, planning, and fundraising. Massachusetts has a well-established network of long-distance trails. The Appalachian Trail runs through the Berkshires; the New England National Scenic Trail travels through the Connecticut River Valley; and the Midstate Trail winds through central Massachusetts, among many other regional trails. Thanks to the development of the Bay Circuit Trail, millions of residents in eastern Massachusetts now enjoy similar recreational opportunities close to home. To learn more, visit baycircuit.org.

The following hikes in this book are part of the Bay Circuit Trail.

Trip 18: Ward Reservation

Trip 19: Bald Hill Reservation

Trip 21: Bradley Palmer State Park

Trip 22: Appleton Farms Grass Rides

Trip 32: Great Meadows National Wildlife Refuge

Trip 33: Minute Man National Historical Park

Trip 34: Walden Pond

Trip 35: Lincoln Conservation Land

Trip 36: Nobscot Hill and Tippling Rock

Trip 38: Rocky Narrows Reservation

Trip 41: Noon Hill Reservation

Trip 42: Moose Hill Wildlife Sanctuary

Trip 43: Borderland State Park

Trip 48: Wheaton Farm Conservation Area

Trip 50: Burrage Pond

APPENDIX B
CROSS-COUNTRY SKIING

There is nothing glamorous or high-tech about it: only a pair of skis and the rhythm of your own pace, under your own power. One of the nice things about cross-country skiing is that you don't have to travel far to find some great trails. In eastern Massachusetts, there are a number of lesser-known reservations and sanctuaries that have flat terrain conducive to cross-country skiing.

For groomed trails, one has to look a little harder, but the selection increases as you head west. Here are a few places to check out:

EASTERN MASSACHUSETTS

Great Brook Farm Ski Touring Center in Carlisle has 10 miles of trails for beginner, intermediate, and expert skiers. Night skiing, rentals, and lessons are available (greatbrookski.com).

Weston Ski Track on Park Road in Weston is located on the DCR Leo J. Martin Golf Course. There are 9 miles of trails for all levels of skiers. It offers night skiing, rentals, and lessons (skiboston.com/skitrack).

CENTRAL MASSACHUSETTS

Wachusett Mountain Ski Area in Princeton has groomed trails and limited rentals (wachusett.com).

Northfield Mountain Cross-Country Ski Area is in the upper Connecticut River Valley in Northfield, with excellent groomed trails and rentals (snocountry .com/cross-country-ski-resorts/ma/northfieldmtnxc).

Brookfield Orchards in North Brookfield allows skiing at its orchards, although groomed trails are no longer maintained. There is also a country store (brookfieldorchardsonline.com).

At Red Apple Farm in Phillipston, skiers can connect to several trails adjacent to the farm; a map is available. There are no groomed or marked ski trails (redapplefarm.com).

Forests and parks in the Department of Conservation and Recreation's central region that are popular with cross-country aficionados include Rutland State Park in Rutland; Wendell State Forest in Wendell; and Otter River State Forest and Lake Dennison Recreation Area in Baldwinville (near Templeton and Winchendon). These include wide woods roads and forest trails. Blackstone River and Canal Heritage State Park has some gentle trails that were once canal towpaths in Uxbridge and Upton. A good starting point is at the River Bend

Farm parking area on Oak Street in Uxbridge. Call ahead for conditions: 508-278-6486 (mass.gov/dcr).

There are acres of open meadow and miles of forest trails at North Common Meadow, Brooks Woodland Preserve, and the Swift River Reservation in Petersham, off Routes 32 and 122 near the center of town. Trails are not groomed, but for those who like to blaze their own trail, it's a wonderful area (thetrustees.org).

THE BERKSHIRES

The Berkshires are conducive to cross-country skiing because the region receives more snow than the rest of the state—and because the scenery is spectacular.

Canterbury Farm in Becket, at an elevation of 1,600 feet, offers groomed skiing through 200 acres of rolling hills. Rentals, lessons, and a bed-and-breakfast are available (canterbury-farms.com).

Butternut Basin in Great Barrington offers cross-country skiing on groomed trails adjacent to the alpine-skiing area (skibutternut.com).

Notchview Reservation in Windsor is a true wilderness area with about 16 miles of trails passing through spruce and hemlock (thetrustees.org).

Two Mass Audubon properties in the Berkshires allow cross-country skiing: Canoe Meadows Wildlife Sanctuary in Pittsfield and Lime Kiln Farm in Sheffield (massaudubon.org).

There are many state forests in western Massachusetts that are ideal for skiing, including Savoy Mountain State Forest in Savoy, October Mountain State Forest in Washington, and Beartown State Forest in Monterey (mass.gov/dcr).

APPENDIX C
WILDLIFE WATCHING

The reservations, sanctuaries, and conservation lands reviewed in this book are all rich in wildlife. Seeing that wildlife, however, depends on both luck and one's knowledge of the creatures themselves. We can't do much about luck, but there are a number of steps you can take to increase your odds of spotting the birds, animals, and reptiles that live in eastern Massachusetts.

Thoreau was an expert wildlife watcher, patient and full of curiosity. He would think nothing of sitting for an hour to watch a bird gather food. "True men of science will know nature better by his finer organizations; he will smell, taste, see, hear, feel, better than other men," he wrote. "His will be a deeper and finer experience." Try following Thoreau's example and let yourself become absorbed by the forests, fields, and water. Even if you don't see wildlife, the walks themselves are more rewarding and refreshing.

Two of the key components of wildlife watching are knowing where and when to look. The best time to see most wildlife is at dawn or dusk. Many creatures are nocturnal, and there's also some overlap at dawn and dusk with daytime birds and animals. Spring and fall are the two best seasons, especially for migratory birds. Animals that hibernate will be active during spring after a long winter, and in fall, they will be eating as much as possible in preparation for the cold months to come. Winter has the least activity, but it does offer some advantages, such as easier long-range viewing (no foliage), the potential to see some animals crossing the ice (such as coyotes), and the relative ease of spotting tracks in snow; also, animals are often easier to spot against a background of white.

Look everywhere: in the fields, on the forest floor, on the water or ice, along shorelines, in trees, and in the sky. One of the most productive spots for seeing wildlife is at the edge of a field. Hawks and owls often perch here, and many animals make their dens and burrows where the woods meet the meadows. Creatures feel safer around the edges; deer, for example, often stay close to these fringe areas before entering a field at nightfall. Red foxes and coyotes hunt the margins, and they can be seen trotting through tall grass on their rounds.

Another productive area is along riverbanks and shorelines. Minks, weasels, muskrats, and raccoons—to mention a few—are commonly observed foraging next to water. And, of course, shorebirds, wading birds, and ducks are also found here. Scanning a shoreline with a pair of binoculars can be extremely rewarding. Many of the wild areas in this book offer excellent paddling, and this, too, affords opportunities for nature study at close range.

Obviously, when walking through the woods, you must do so quietly if you hope to get near wildlife, but being quiet is not enough. Most creatures would prefer to hide than run, and they will sit tight and let you walk right past. You should give the surrounding areas more than a casual glance. When trying to spot deer, look for parts of the animal between the trees rather than for the entire body. Look for the horizontal lines of the deer's back contrasting with the vertical trees. Knowing the size of an animal also helps; when scanning for deer, most people will do so at eye level, but deer are only about 3 feet high at the shoulder.

Many animals blend in with their surroundings so well it's almost impossible to see them. The American bittern, for example, may freeze with its head in an upright position to match the tall reeds and vegetation around it. A snapping turtle in shallow water looks just like a rock, and ruffed grouse can be indistinguishable from the fallen leaves on the forest floor. Even great blue herons will stop feeding and wait, silent and unmoving, until perceived danger passes.

Another key factor to consider is wind direction, which can carry your scent to wildlife. If traveling down a trail and the wind is coming from the left, look more in that direction, since your scent is not being carried there. If you have a choice when beginning your hike, travel into the wind. The same holds true when approaching a known feeding area. Serious wildlife photographers even go so far as wearing rubber boots to stop the scent of their feet from escaping into the air!

It is important, by the way, that humans do not approach too closely, or birds—such as the heron—will take wing, expending valuable energy to avoid us. Many creatures will allow us to observe them so long as we do not walk directly at them or linger too long.

Some animals are almost never seen because they are nocturnal and secretive. But you don't have to see them to know they are present. They leave clues. You will find the tracks of otter, heron, raccoon, and deer along the soft margin of a river or lake. Hiking after a snowfall can be especially rewarding, as fresh tracks are easier to spot. Some astute trackers can also identify creatures by the droppings the animals leave behind. Burrows and dens reveal where some animals, such as the fox and groundhog, live. Owls disgorge pellets, which can indicate their presence and what they have been feeding on. Look for these pellets underneath large pine trees. Deer leave a number of signs, including trails between their feeding and resting grounds, and scrapes and scars caused by a buck rubbing its antlers on saplings. Peeled bark can mean deer, mice, rabbit, or other creatures, depending on the teeth marks and the shape and height of the markings.

The time and patience required to find and identify clues can be significant, but so are the rewards. It is satisfying to solve a wildlife puzzle, not only by identifying a species' presence but also by deducing its activities. Children especially enjoy this detective work.

Besides using your sense of sight, use your hearing to help in wildlife identification. Many of us have heard the hooting of an owl at night or the daytime drumming of a male ruffed grouse. More and more folks in the outer suburbs will soon be hearing the wild and eerie yapping and howling of coyotes. Some animal sounds are quite surprising. Creatures you wouldn't expect to make a peep can be quite vocal. Deer snort, porcupines scream, and woodchucks grunt and click their teeth.

Knowing the behavior of birds and animals can often explain their actions. For example, if a ruffed grouse pulls the "wounded wing act," you can be sure its chicks are near, and it is trying to draw you away. The mother grouse makes a commotion, dragging its wing in a way that will get your attention. After watching the mother's act, take a moment to scan the forest floor, and you just might see the chicks. (Look but don't touch, and be careful where you step.)

It's even more important to understand behavior that serves as a warning sign, meaning you're too close. A goshawk guarding its nest will give a warning of *kak, kak, kak*. Don't go any closer, as it may attack you. Never get too close to nesting birds, or chase or corner an animal. The best way to get a second look at an animal often is to remain perfectly still. The creature may return out of curiosity.

Nature study is all the more fascinating when you learn the habits of each wild animal: what it eats, where and when it feeds and rests, whether it is active in winter or hibernates. Birds can be studied in a similar way, and migration patterns are crucial to understanding when and how long certain birds remain in our region. Reptiles, being cold-blooded, are active only in the warm-weather months. Their temperatures vary with that of the surrounding atmosphere, so they cannot survive freezing weather. The relatively few reptiles that live in Massachusetts must hibernate in holes or burrows below the frost line during winter. The best time to see some of these reptiles is late spring; that's when the snapping turtle comes out of the water to lay its eggs on land.

For wildlife photography, you need a zoom lens and a tripod. High-quality shots are extremely difficult. It's hard enough just locating an animal or an uncommon bird, but finding a clear shot for a picture can be quite frustrating. Patience is key. That's why professional wildlife photographers often spend days in the woods working from a blind.

Finally, don't discount dumb luck. Much wildlife is seen by accident, but repeat visits to your favorite reservations will greatly increase your odds.

INDEX

ABOUT THE AUTHORS

Michael Tougias is an expert on the wild places of Massachusetts and has authored more than a dozen books about New England. He leads visually impaired people on nature walks and is involved in protecting open space in Massachusetts. Visit michaeltougias.com to find out more.

John Burk is an outdoor writer, photographer, and historian from central Massachusetts. He has authored or edited more than a dozen books and guides, including AMC's *Massachusetts Trail Guide.*

Alison O'Leary is a longtime journalist, public speaker, and the author of two books, including *Inns and Adventures: A History and Explorer's Guide to New Hampshire, Vermont and the Berkshires.* She resides in southeastern Massachusetts.

AMC BOOK UPDATES

AMC Books strives to keep our guidebooks as up-to-date as possible to help you plan safe and enjoyable adventures. If we learn after publishing a book that relevant trails have been relocated or route or contact information has changed, we will post the updated information online. Before you hit the trail, visit outdoors .org/books-maps and click the "Book Updates" tab.

While hiking, if you notice discrepancies with the trip descriptions or maps, or if you find any other errors in the book, please let us know by submitting them to amcbookupdates@outdoors.org or to Books Editor, c/o AMC, 10 City Square, Boston, MA 02129. We will verify all submissions and post key updates each month. AMC Books is dedicated to being a recognized leader in outdoor publishing. Thank you for your participation.

ABOUT AMC IN EASTERN MASSACHUSETTS

AMC's Boston Chapter is the organization's largest, with more than 20,000 members. It offers a variety of hiking, backpacking, paddling, bicycling, skiing, and climbing trips each year, as well as social, family, and young member programs and instructional workshops. Members also partake in trail maintenance, outdoor skill instruction, and trip leadership.

AMC's headquarters supports its outdoor recreation, conservation, and education efforts across its service area of Maine to Washington, D.C., as well as programs that benefit Boston area residents. AMC's Boston Chapter also offers a variety of free, close-to-home outdoor activities led by experienced volunteers.

AMC's Southeastern Massachusetts Chapter offers outdoor activities, conducts trail work, and addresses local conservation issues south of Boston and on Cape Cod and the islands. Programs range from hiking and cycling to skiing, paddling, and backpacking.

AMC's Worcester Chapter is dedicated to the outdoor resources of central Massachusetts and offers activities and trips for all levels. Chapter members partake in a wide range of social events and educational programs.

To view a list of AMC activities in Massachusetts and other parts of the Northeast, visit activities.outdoors.org.

BE OUTDOORS™

Since 1876, the Appalachian Mountain Club has channeled your enthusiasm for the outdoors into everything we do and everywhere we work to protect. We're inspired by people exploring the natural world and deepening their appreciation of it.

With AMC chapters from Maine to Washington, D.C., including groups in Boston, New York City, and Philadelphia, you can enjoy activities like hiking, paddling, cycling, and skiing, and learn new outdoor skills. We offer advice, guidebooks, maps, and unique eco-lodges and huts to inspire your next outing.

Your visits, purchases, and donations also support conservation advocacy and research, youth programming, and caring for more than 1,800 miles of trails.

Join us!
outdoors.org/join